D1014987

DATE DUE   JUL 0 6

GAYLORD   PRINTED IN U.S.A.

A Thousand Clowns
Thieves
The Goodbye People

A Thousand Clowns
❖❖❖
Thieves
❖❖❖
The Goodbye People

BY

HERB GARDNER

NELSON DOUBLEDAY, INC.
Garden City, New York

Toot, Toot, Tootsie! (Good-bye). Words and music by Gus Kahn, Ernie Erdman, Dan Russo, and Ted Fiorito. Copyright 1922, renewed 1949, Leo Feist Inc., New York, N.Y. Used by permission.

Is It True What They Say About Dixie? by Irving Caesar, Sammy Lerner, and Gerald Marks. Copyright 1936 Irving Caesar, Inc., renewed 1963. Reprinted by permission of the publishers, Irving Caesar, Samuel M. Lerner Publications and Marlong Music Corp.

Yaaka Hula Hickey Dula. Words by E. Ray Goetz and Joe Young; music by Pete Wendling. Copyright 1916 by Mills Music, Inc., renewed 1944. Used with permission. All rights reserved, including public performance.

Moonlight Becomes You. By Johny Burke and Jimmy Van Heusen. Copyright 1942 by Famous Music Corporation, renewed 1970 by Famous Music Corporation. Used by permission.

CONTENTS

For Barbara, who understands me
and other myths

Introduction

IN THIS DREAM I always have I am sitting on the stage of the
Morosco Theatre wearing a tuxedo, writing the third act of a
play. Unfortunately, it is the opening night of the play I'm writing, and the opening night audience is filing into the theatre.
They come down the aisles and take their seats; I hear the familiar and expectant buzz of well-wishers and killers. I scratch
away with dried-out felt-tipped pen on loose-leaf paper on a
trembling card table, around me the crisp opening night air of
Bar Mitzvah and execution. I wave to them. I offer a comforting
smile. I am cordial; they are restless. I keep writing. I hold my
free hand up from time to time as though to say "please wait, I'll
be ready soon." The stage is littered with props, parts of costumes and pieces of sets. I look around for clues: there is a
trampoline and a piece of a train, the outside motor of a forties
icebox is strangely new and polished, a school desk and a U-Boat
periscope, an abandoned sneaker lies on a witness stand, a five-
string banjo and a Dodgers' cap, a battered phone booth;
twenty-two clocks, all of them with a different time and all of
them wrong, a straw hat, a derby, a steel safe with a doily and a
bowl of flowers on it, the cabin of a ferris wheel, a rotting B.L.T.
and a rocking chair. The objects stand in some order, ready for
use. As always, I'm sure there is a pattern to this debris, and as
always I don't know what it is. In the wings an ancient stage
hand sits with half a pastrami sandwich, dozing; he awakens
briefly, smiles at me, offers a wink of recognition and whispers
the word "schmuck." He is my muse. He whispers the word
again; I tell him that I am a playwright. There is always a confusion between us on this issue. Actors and actresses of various
ages and in various shapes and sizes wait in positions around the

stage, in doorways, at the top of stairways, one is behind the wheel of a taxi and another is mumbling under a trapdoor at my feet. "Please wait," I say, "I'll be ready soon." In the back of the theatre a white-haired man is speaking calmly into a walkie-talkie, arranging a lawsuit. He is the producer. "Please wait," I shout to him, "I'll be ready soon." I hold onto the card table and we shake together. I look down at the manuscript; it is entitled "Please Wait." I feel a strange mixture of terror and comfort, I am in that familiar, anxious place: a theatre. I am where I have always wanted to be, wondering what I will do there. A barefoot tap dancer with marvelous plans, a hopeful amnesiac waiting to remember. The conspiracy is clear and the dream is complete; the players, the playgoers and the playwright wait for the play.

The editor of this volume, a hopeful and kindly fellow, has been waiting for this introduction for two months. I have offered him a series of deadlines, lies, promises and apologies which we have both decided to believe. How do I explain that I write plays, that I speak in the voices of other people because I don't know my own; that I write in the second person because I don't know the first; that I have been writing plays most of my adult life waiting to become both an adult and a playwright, and that it takes me so many years to write anything that I am forced to refer to myself during these periods as a playwrote? I have tried to write this introduction at desks, in taxis, on long plane rides; I have worked on it at thirty-thousand feet and in bathtubs; I have spoken it into tape-recorders and the ears of friends and loved ones. There are several problems: I can't seem to invent the character who says the lines; I am writing words that won't be spoken aloud and in a strange language, English—my first, last, and only language; and, most importantly, I cannot offer an explanation for why I wrote these plays because there is none. Playwriting is an irrational act. It is the Las Vegas of art forms, and the odds are terrible. A curious trade in which optimism, like any three-year-old's, is based on a lack of information, and integrity is based on the fact that by the time you decide to sell your soul no devil is interested. Your days are spent making up things that no one ever said to be spoken by people who do not exist for an audience that may not come. The most personal thoughts, arrived at in terrible privacy, are interpreted by strangers for a group of other strangers. The fear that no one will put your plays on is quickly replaced by the fear that someone will. It's hard to live with yourself and even harder for people to live with you: how do you ask a Kamakazi Pilot if his work is going well? The word "Playwright" looks terrible on passports, leases, and credit applications; and even worse in newspaper articles alternately titled "Where Did These Playwrights Go?" and "Why Don't These Playwrights Go Away?," usually appearing in what the New York *Times* whimsically refers to as The Leisure Section. The most difficult problem, of course, is that I love it.

God help me, I love it. Because it's alive. And because the theatre is alive, exactly what is terrible is wonderful, the gamble, the odds. There is no ceiling on the night and no floor either; there is a chance each time the curtain goes up of glory and disaster, the actors and the audience will take each other somewhere, neither knows where for sure. Alive, one time only, that night. It's alive, has been alive for a few thousand years, and is alive tonight, this afternoon. An audience knows it's the last place they can still be heard, they know the actors can hear them, they make a difference; it's not a movie projector and they are not at home with talking furniture, it's custom work. Why do playwrights, why do we outsiders and oddballs who so fear misunderstanding use a medium where we are most likely to be misunderstood? Because when this most private of enterprises goes public, and is responded to, we are not alone. Home is where you can tell your secrets. In a theatre, the ones in the dark and the ones under the lights need each other. For a few hours all of us, the audience, the actors, the writer, we are all a little more real together than we ever were apart. That's the ticket; and that's what the ticket's for.

Some words of advice about reading these plays. Sometimes I'm out in the street and I think of a character or a scene; on the way upstairs to my desk I lose fifty per cent. While translating these captionless pictures into intelligible language I lose another twenty-five. A good actor can put back the seventy-five per cent I lost on the way to my desk. So I ask you, for whatever might be good in these plays, read them like good actors; because a play on paper is only a code book, signals, notes for emotions, vague road maps for countries in constant border dispute, and nothing without you. Also, of course, none of these plays is finished; but please wait, I'll be ready soon.

Herb Gardner
New York City
January 1979

A Thousand Clowns

A Thousand Clowns was first presented by Fred Coe and Arthur Cantor at the Eugene O'Neill Theatre, New York City, April 5, 1962. It was directed by Fred Coe, with scenery and lighting design by George Jenkins and costumes by Ruth Morley. The cast was as follows:

Nick Burns	Barry Gordon
Murray Burns	Jason Robards, Jr.
Albert Amundson	William Daniels
Sandra Markowitz	Sandy Dennis
Arnold Burns	A. Larry Haines
Leo Herman	Gene Saks

ACT ONE

In complete darkness, before the curtain goes up, we hear the voice of Chuckles the Chipmunk.

CHUCKLES' VOICE: (*Intimately, softly*) Goshes and gollygoods, kidderoonies; now what're all us Chippermunkies gonna play first this fine mornin'?

CHORUS OF KIDS: Gonna play Chuckle-Chip Dancing.

CHUCKLES' VOICE: And with who?

CHORUS OF KIDS: With you!

CHUCKLES' VOICE: (*Louder*) And who is me?

CHORUS OF KIDS: (*Screaming*) Chuckles the Chippermunkie! Rayyyyyyyyyyyyyyy.

The curtain goes up on this last screaming syllable, revealing Murray Burns' one-room apartment. The voices of Chuckles and the kids continue but are now coming from an ancient table-model T.V. set at the left. The set is facing away from the audience and is being watched by Nicholas Burns, a twelve-year-old. The apartment is on the second floor of a brownstone on the lower West Side of Manhattan. It consists of one large, high-

*ceilinged room in which borrowed furniture rambles in no mean-
ingful arrangement—some gaudy, some impractical, no matching
pieces. It is obvious from Murray Burns' apartment that he is a
collector, though it is not entirely clear just what he is a collector
of. All about the room, on the floor, on the coffee table, on
dresser tops, is Murray's collection: eighteen broken radios, some
with interesting cathedral-style cabinets; over two dozen elaborately disabled clocks of different sizes, some of them on the
wall; parts of eight Victrolas, mostly cabinets; a variety of hats,
including a Prussian helmet and a deerstalker; a pirate pistol; a
bugle; a megaphone; and stacks of magazines and books. It is
somehow, though, a very comfortable-looking apartment. There
is an alcove at the left, with a small bed, a child's desk and some
bookshelves. This is Nick's part of the place and it is very neat,
ordered, organized, seeming almost to have nothing to do with
the main room. There is a bathroom door at left below the small
alcove. Right of the alcove are three large windows and a built-
in window seat. A closed venetian blind covers all three windows. At center is a large, comfortable rumpled bed with an
elaborate wooden headboard running up the wall almost to the
ceiling. The headboard is loaded with clocks, radios, and two
lamps. At right is the entrance door to the apartment. To the left
of the door are two large office-style filing cabinets in which
Murray keeps some of his clothes, and to the right is a bureau
covered with knickknacks on which Murray's hats are hung.
Downstage right is the kitchen door; to the left of it is a desk
buried under papers, and built-in bookshelves stuffed with a
jumble of books and nonsense. There is a closet to the left of the
desk. A Morris chair and an armless swivel chair are on either
side of a small table at right and there is a brightly colored
beach chair at left in front of the windows.*

*At rise: It is eight-thirty on a Monday morning, it is rather
dark, the only real light is a scattered haze from the television
set. The chorus of kids is now singing the "Chuckles Song." Nick
watches expressionlessly.*

CHORUS OF KIDS: (*Singing*) Who's whitcha at—eight-thirty?
Who's face is so—so dirty?
Who's sparky—who's spunky?
Chip, Chip, Chip, Chip—Chippermunkie!

NICK: (*Quietly*) Oh, this is terrible. This is rotten.

CHORUS OF KIDS: Who's always good—for funnin'?
Whose scooter-bike—keeps runnin'?
(*Murray enters from the kitchen carrying a cup of coffee; he is in his mid-thirties. He is wearing shorts and an undershirt and is not quite awake yet*)

MURRAY: (*Walking across to the bed*) Get those kids outa here. (*Sits on the bed*) Nick, what'd I tell you about bringing your friends in here this early in the morning?

NICK: It's not my friends; it's the T.V.

MURRAY: Play with your friends outside. Get those kids out of here. (*Nick turns the set off. Murray looks over at the front door, waves at it and shouts*) Good. And none of you kids come back here till this afternoon.

NICK: It wasn't my friends. It was Chuckles the Chipmunk.

MURRAY: (*Sleepily*) That's very comforting.

NICK: (*Brings a pack of cigarettes to Murray*) Boy, it's a terrible program now. It was a much better show when you were writing it.

MURRAY: When Sandburg and Faulkner quit, I quit. What kind of a day is it outside?

NICK: (*Going to the kitchen*) It's a Monday.

MURRAY: I mean warm or cold or sunny is what I mean.

NICK: I haven't been outside yet.

MURRAY: (*He pulls the blind up revealing the windows; there is no change whatever in the lighting, the room remains dark. The windows have no view other than the gray blank wall of the building a few feet opposite)* Ah, light. (*He leans out of the window, cranes his head around to look up at the sky)* Can't see a thing. Not a thing. (*Pulls his head back in)* No matter what time of day or what season, we got a permanent fixture out there; twilight in February.

NICK: (*Bringing the coffee pot out of the kitchen and filling Murray's cup)* You better call the weather record like always.

MURRAY: One morning I'll wake up and that damn building'll have fallen down into Seventh Avenue so I can see the weather. (*Picks up the phone; dialing)* Using a machine to call up another machine. I do not enjoy the company of ghosts. (*Into the phone)* Hello, Weather Lady! Well, I'm just fine, and how is your nasal little self this morning? What's the weather? Uh-huh. That high? And the wind, which way does the wind blow this morning? Ah, good. Uh-huh, all the way to East Point and Block Island. Humidity? Very decent. Whoops, oh, there you go again. You simply *must* learn not to repeat yourself. I keep telling you every morning that once is enough. You'll never learn. (*Hangs up)* Women seldom sense when they have become boring. (*Goes to the window again, leans out, raises his voice, shouting out of the window)* Neighbors, I have an announcement for you. I have *never seen* such a collection of dirty windows. Now I want to see you all out there on the fire escape with your Mr. Clean bottles, and let's snap it up . . .

NICK: Gee, Murray, you gotta shout like that every morning?

MURRAY: It clears my head. (*After glancing around clock-filled apartment)* What time is it?

NICK: It's eight-forty.

MURRAY: Well, what're you doing here? Why aren't you in school?

NICK: It's a holiday. It's Irving R. Feldman's birthday, like you said.

MURRAY: Irving R. Feldman's birthday is my own personal national holiday. I did not open it up for the public. He is proprietor of perhaps the most distinguished kosher delicatessen in this neighborhood and as such I hold the day of his birth in reverence.

NICK: You said you weren't going to look for work today because it was Irving R. Feldman's birthday, so I figured I would celebrate too, a little.

MURRAY: Don't kid *me*, Nick, you know you're supposed to be in school. I thought you *liked* that damn genius' school—why the hell—

NICK: Well, I figured I'd better stay home today till you got up. (*Hesitantly*) There's something I gotta discuss with you. See, because it's this special school for big brains they watch you and take notes and make reports and smile at you a lot. And there's this psychologist who talks to you every week, each kid separately. He's the biggest smiler they got up there.

MURRAY: Because you got brains they figure you're nuts.

NICK: Anyway, we had Show and Tell time in Mrs. Zimmerman's class on Monday; and each kid in the class is supposed to tell about some trip he took and show pictures. Well, y'remember when I made you take me with you to the El Bambino Club over on Fifty-second?

MURRAY: Nick . . . you showed and you told.

NICK: Well, it turned out they're very square up at the Revere School. And sometimes in class, when we have our Wednesday Free-Association-Talk Period, I sometimes quote you on different opinions . . .

MURRAY: That wasn't a good idea.

NICK: Well, I didn't know they were such nervous people there. Murray, they're very nervous there. And then there was this composition I wrote in Creative Writing about the advantages of Unemployment Insurance.

MURRAY: Why did you write about that?

NICK: It was just on my mind. Then once they got my record out they started to notice what they call "significant data." Turns out they've been keeping this file on me for a long time, and checking with that Child Welfare place; same place you got those letters from.

MURRAY: I never answer letters from large organizations.

NICK: So, Murray . . . when they come over here, I figure we'd better . . .

MURRAY: When they come over here?

NICK: Yeah, this Child Welfare crowd, they want to take a look at our environment here.

MURRAY: Oh, that's charming. Why didn't you tell me about this before, Nick?

NICK: Well, y'know, the past coupla nights we couldn't get together.

MURRAY: That was unavoidable. You know when I have a lot of work you stay up at Mrs. Myers'.

NICK: (*Pointing at the dresser*) Murray; your work forgot her gloves last night.

MURRAY: That's very bright.

NICK: Anyway, for this Child Welfare crowd, I figure we better set up some kind of story before they get here.

MURRAY: You make it sound like a vice raid.

NICK: I mean, for one thing, you don't even have a job right now.

MURRAY: Look, you want me to put up some kind of front when they get here? O.K., I will. Don't worry, kid. I'll snow 'em good.

NICK: I thought maybe you could at least look in the papers for a job, this morning before they get here. So we could tell them about your possibilities.

MURRAY: (*Without much conviction*) I look every day.

NICK: Couldn't I just read you from the *Times* again like last week? While you get dressed?

MURRAY: O.K., read me from the paper.
(*He starts to get dressed*)

NICK: And then, maybe, you'll take a shave?

MURRAY: All right, all right.

NICK: (*Picking up the* Times *from the swivel chair*) This paper is three days old.

MURRAY: So what do you want me to do, bury it? Is it starting to rot or something? Read me from the paper.

NICK: But most of these jobs, somebody must have taken them. Look, I'll go down and get a newer—

MURRAY: We do *not* need a newer paper. All the really important jobs stay forever. Now start on the first page of Help-Wanted-Male and read me from the paper.

NICK: O.K. (*Puts on his glasses; reads aloud*) "Administ, Exoppty. To ninety dollars." What's that?

MURRAY: Administrative Assistant, excellent opportunity. Nothing. Keep reading.

NICK: But ninety dollars would be ninety dollars more than nothing. Nothing is what you make now.

MURRAY: Have you ever considered being the first twelve-year-old boy in space?

NICK: But, ninety dollars . . .

MURRAY: *You* go be an Administ, Exoppty. They *need* men like you. Read further.

NICK: (*Reading from the paper*) "Versatile Junior, traffic manager, industrial representative organization. One hundred to one hundred twenty-five dollars. Call Mr. Shiffman."

MURRAY: (*Picks up the cardboard from his shirt collar and talks into it*) Hello, Mr. Shiffman? I read your name in the New York *Times,* so I know you must be real. My name is Mandrake the Magician. I am a versatile Junior and I would like to manage your traffic for you. You see, sir, it has long been my ambition to work in a pointless job, with no future and a cretin like you as my boss . . .

NICK: But, Murray, it says "one hundred twenty-five dollars," that's a lot of . . .

MURRAY: Just read the ads. No editorial comment or personal recommendations. When I need your advice, I'll ask for it. Out of the mouths of babes comes drooling.

NICK: You said that last week. Murray, you don't want a job is the whole thing.

MURRAY: Would you just concentrate on being a child? Because I find your imitation of an adult hopelessly inadequate.

NICK: You want to be your own boss, but the trouble with that is you don't pay yourself anything. (*Nick decides that what he has just said is very funny. He laughs*) Hey—you don't pay yourself anything—that's a good line—I gotta remember that.

MURRAY: That's what *you* said last week.

NICK: Look, Murray. (*He puts the paper down and stands up*) Can I speak to you man to man?

MURRAY: That was cute about a year ago, buddy, but that line has got to go.

NICK: (*Takes off his glasses*) Murray, I am upset. For me as an actual child the way you live in this house and we live is a dangerous thing for my later life when I become an actual person. An unemployed person like you are for so many months is bad for you as the person involved and is definitely bad for me who he lives with in the same house where the rent isn't paid for months sometimes. And I wish you would get a job, Murray. Please.

(*Murray tries to control himself but cannot hide his laughter; he sees that Nick is offended by this and tries to stop. Nick walks away from him, goes to his alcove*)

MURRAY: (*Goes to Nick in the alcove*) Kid, I know. I'm sorry. You're right. You are. This *is* terrible.

NICK: You're not kidding.

MURRAY: Nick.

NICK: Yeah?

MURRAY: Nick, y'know when I said I was looking for work last week? (*Somewhat ashamed*) Well, I went to the movies. Every day. In the afternoon.

NICK: *Murray*, you mean you really . . .

MURRAY: Now don't give me any of that indignant crap. I happen to be admitting something to you, and it is bad enough I should have to discuss my adult problems with a grotesque cherub, without you giving me dirty looks on top of it. Swell crowd in the movies on a weekday working afternoon. Nobody sits next to anybody, everybody there figures that everybody else is a creep; and *all* of them are right. (*Suddenly smiling, taking Nick's arm, trying to change the subject*) Have you ever been to the top of the Empire State Building?

NICK: Yes. Six times. With you. In November.

MURRAY: Oh, really? Have you ever been to the Statue of Liberty?

NICK: No.

MURRAY: Today is Irving R. Feldman's birthday. We will go to the top of the Statue of Liberty and watch the *Queen Elizabeth* come in, full of those tired, poor, huddled masses yearning to breathe free.

NICK: Murray, why did you go to the movies in the middle of the afternoon when you said you were looking for work?

MURRAY: There's a window right in her navel, we will look out and see . . .

NICK: What is it? Were you very tired, or what?

MURRAY: (*Sits down in his chair*) See, last week I was going to check with Uncle Arnie and some of the other agents about writing for some of the new T.V. shows. I was on the subway, on my way there, and I got off at Forty-second Street and went to the movies. (*He leans back in his chair, lights a cigarette; Nick sits opposite him on the bed*) There are eleven movie houses on that street, Nick. It is Movieland. It breathes that seductive, carpety, minty air of the inside of movie houses. Almost as irresistible for me as pastrami. Now, there is the big question as you approach the box office, with the sun shining right down the middle of a working day, whether everybody going in is as embarrassed as you are. But once you are past the awkward stage, and have gotten your ticket torn by the old man inside, all doubts just go away. Because it is dark. And inside it is such a scene as to fracture the imagina-

tion of even a nut like yourself, Nick, because inside it is
lovely and a little damp and nobody can see you, and the dialogue is falling like rain on a roof and you are sitting deep in
front of a roaring, color, Cinemascope, stereophonic, nerve-
cooling, heart-warming, spine-softening, perfect-happy-ending
picture show and it is Peacefulville, U.S.A. There are men
there with neat mustaches who have shaved, and shined their
shoes and put on a tie even, to come and sit alone in the
movies. And there are near-sighted cute pink ladies who eat
secret caramels; and very old men who sleep; and the *ushers;*
buddy, you are not kidding *these* boys. They know you are not
there because you are waiting for a train, or you are on a vaca-
tion, or you work a night job. They know you are there to *see*
the *movie*. It is the business and the purpose of your day, and
these boys give you their sneaky smile to show you that they
know. (*Depressed by his own words; quietly, almost to himself*) Now the moral question for me here, is this: When one is
faced with life in the bare-assed, job-hunting raw on the one
hand, and eleven fifty-cent double features on the other, what
is the mature, sensible, and mentally healthy step to take?

(*He is slumped in his chair now*)

NICK: (*Seeing Murray's depression; softly, with concern*)
What's wrong, Murray?

MURRAY: (*Walks slowly to the window, leans against the wall,
looks sadly out of the window; speaks quietly*) I don't know.
I'm not sure.

NICK: Hey, Murray, you all right . . . ? (*He goes to Murray,
touches his arm. Then smiling suddenly in an attempt to cheer
him*) Murray, let's go to the Statue of Liberty.
(*Murray turns, laughs in agreement, and Nick starts for his
jacket while Murray puts his binoculars around his neck and
begins putting on his jacket. The doorbell rings. Nick looks
at Murray, then goes to answer it. Nick is holding the front
door only part-way open, hesitating to let in two people we*

now see standing outside in the hall. They are Albert Amundson and Sandra Markowitz. Albert, graduate of N.Y.U.'s School of Social Work, is a middle-aged man of twenty-eight. Sandra, though a pretty girl of twenty-five, wears clothes obviously more suited to a much older woman. Albert carries a small briefcase and Sandra carries two manila file envelopes and a gigantic handbag)

ALBERT: Hello, young man, I am Mr. Amundson, this is Miss Markowitz. We would like to speak to your uncle.

NICK: *(Still not opening the door all the way)* Well, I don't know if . . .

ALBERT: Isn't he in?

MURRAY: Hello.

ALBERT: How do you do, Mr. Burns. Miss Markowitz and I are a Social Service unit assigned to the New York Bureau of Child Welfare. We have been asked by the Bureau to— May we come in?

MURRAY: Certainly.
(Nick opens the door all the way, letting them both into the main room)

ALBERT: We, Miss Markowitz and I, have been asked by the B.C.W. to investigate and examine certain pupils of the Revere School. There is certain information which the school and the city would like to have, regarding young Nicholas.

MURRAY: Sit down, Miss Markowitz, please. Mr. Amundson. I'll just get rid of these things.
(Murray takes pants, shirts, a bugle, a clock, a yoyo, a half-empty bag of peanuts and an ash tray off the chairs, and with one sweeping movement puts all of them on the bed. The three of them take seats around the coffee table, Nick standing nervously off to one side)

ALBERT: I'd like to explain just why we are here, Mr. Burns . . .

NICK: Would anybody like some coffee?

ALBERT: Why, thank you, Nicholas. Miss Markowitz?

SANDRA: Yes, thank you.

NICK: (*Whispering to Murray on his way to the kitchen*)
Watch it.

ALBERT: (*Smiling politely*) It might be best, Mr. Burns, for the
child, if perhaps you sent him downstairs to play or something,
while we have our discussion. Your case is . . .

MURRAY: Our "case." I had no idea we were a "case."

ALBERT: We do have a file on certain students at Revere.

MURRAY: So we're on file somewhere. Are we a great, big, fat
file, or a li'l teeny file?

ALBERT: Due to the fact that you have chosen not to answer our
letters and several of our phone calls, there are many areas in
which the file is incomplete, several questions— Mr. Burns, it
might be better if the child went outside . . .

MURRAY: You gonna talk dirty?

ALBERT: It would be more advisable for the child not to be present, since Miss Markowitz, who will be discussing the psychological area . . . that is, we will be discussing certain matters
which . . .

NICK: (*From the kitchen*) Cream and sugar for everybody?

ALBERT: (*To the kitchen*) Yes, Nicholas. (*To Murray again*)
Mr. Burns, it's going to be awkward, with the child present,
to . . .

MURRAY: (*To Sandra*) Miss Markowitz, may I know your first
name?

SANDRA: Sandra.

MURRAY: And you are the psychologist part of this team, Sandy?

SANDRA: That's right, Mr. Burns.

MURRAY: (*To Albert*) And you, I take it, are the brawn of the outfit?

ALBERT: Perhaps I should explain, Mr. Burns, that the Social Service teams which serve Revere School are a carefully planned balance of Social Case Worker, such as myself, and Psychological Social Worker, such as Miss Markowitz, or, actually, *Dr.* Markowitz. (*Nick enters from the kitchen with four cups, gives one each to Albert, Sandra, Murray; keeps one for himself*) Mr. Burns, it is not easy to define those elements, those influences and problems which go into the make-up of a young boy.

MURRAY: I thought it was just frogs and snails and puppy dogs' tails.

ALBERT: (*Using once again his polite smile*) I appreciate the informality with which you approach this meeting, Mr. Burns, but on the more serious side, if I may, Miss Markowitz and I have a few matters . . .

NICK: Is the coffee any good?

ALBERT: Yes, very good. Thank you, Nicholas.

SANDRA: Very nice, Nicholas. (*She sees the cup in Nick's hand, speaks with professional interest*) Are you drinking coffee, Nicholas? Don't you think it would be better if . . .

NICK: No. Milk. I like to drink it from a cup.

MURRAY: (*To Sandra, smiling*) Now aren't you ashamed of yourself?

ALBERT: (*Taking a rather large file out of his briefcase*) Now, to plunge right in here . . .

MURRAY: Sometimes I put his milk in a shot glass. Better for getting him to drink it than adding chocolate syrup.

SANDRA (*Firmly*) Mr. Burns, Mr. Amundson and I have several cases to examine today, and we would appreciate a certain amount of cooperation . . .

MURRAY: (*To Nick*) East Bronx, Mosholu Parkway.

NICK: (*Looks at Sandra, then to Murray*) With a couple of years in maybe Massachusetts.

MURRAY: No Massachusetts at all. Complete Bronx.

SANDRA: I don't understand what . . .

MURRAY: (*Sitting on the beach chair*) Oh, excuse me. Nick and I are merely testing our sense of voice and accent. Nick insists he's better at it than I am.

SANDRA: (*Smiling*) As a matter of fact, the Bronx is right, but it's Grand Concourse.

MURRAY: The Massachusetts thing, way off, right?

SANDRA: Actually I took my graduate work with a professor, a man with a very strong New England accent, who could very well've influenced my speech. Nick is quite right.

NICK: (*Proudly*) Thank you, lady.

SANDRA: You certainly have a fine ear for sound, Nick. Do you and your uncle play many of these sorts of games together?

NICK: Oh, yes. We play many wholesome and constructive-type games together.

MURRAY: You're a big phony, Nick. Miss Markowitz has beautiful hazel eyes that have read many case histories and are ever watchful, and even clever little boys are not going to snow her. The lady is here for the facts.

ALBERT: Quite so, Mr. Burns. But facts alone cannot complete our examination. (*He takes out a pen, opens to a blank page in the file*) We wish to understand . . .

NICK: (*To Sandra, showing off for her*) Jersey City, maybe Newark. And . . . a little bit of Chicago.

MURRAY: Uh-huh. Think you've hit it, Nick.

SANDRA: That's really quite remarkable. Albert—Mr. Admundson *is* from New Jersey, and he went to Chicago University for several . . .

ALBERT: (*Firmly*) This is really quite beside the point, Sandra . . .

SANDRA: I just think it's quite remarkable, Albert, the boy's ability to . . .

ALBERT: (*Purposely interrupting her*) Suppose I just plunge right in here, before Dr. Markowitz begins her part of the interview . . .
　　(*There is a noise at the front door and Arnold Burns enters. He is carrying a medium-sized grocery delivery carton filled with a variety of fruit. He makes a rather incongruous delivery boy in that he is in his early forties and dressed in expensive, distinguished clothes, top coat, and hat. He is Murray's older brother, and his agent. It is obvious in the way he enters and automatically sets the delivery carton down on the desk that this is a daily ritual enacted at this same time every day and in this same manner. Murray does not even look up to greet him and Nick makes some casually mumbled greeting in his direction*)

ARNOLD: The honeydew melon's in season again but not really ripe yet so . . . (*He turns, sees that there are strangers there*) Oh, sorry. Didn't know you had company . . . (*Turns, goes to the door*) See you, Nick.

NICK: Yeah, see you, Uncle Arnie.
　　(*Arnold exits*)

ALBERT: (*Looking at the door*) There is somebody else living here with you?

MURRAY: No. That's just my brother Arnold. He brings fruit every morning on his way to the office. He's a fruit nut.

ALBERT: I see here in the file that our research team spoke to your brother; your agent, I believe. We also called the people at your last business address, N.B.C. . . .

MURRAY: (*Rising*) You really do a lot of that stuff, calling people, going into my personal . . .

ALBERT: You've refused for quite some time, Mr. Burns, to answer any of our regular inquiries. We understand that you have been unemployed at this point for nearly five months.

NICK: (*To Albert*) He has an excellent opportunity to be an administrative assistant . . .

ALBERT: (*Pressing forward*) Other than your activities as freelance script writer, I understand that you wrote regularly for an N.B.C. program for several years.

MURRAY: I was chief writer for Leo Herman, better known as Chuckles the Chipmunk, friend of the young'uns, and seller of Chuckle-Chips, the potato chips your friend Chuckles the Chipmunk eats and chuckles over.

ALBERT: And the circumstances under which you left the employ of . . .

MURRAY: I quit.

ALBERT: You felt that this was not the work you . . .

MURRAY: I felt that I was not reaching all the boys and girls out there in Televisionland. Actually it was not so much that I wasn't reaching the boys and girls, but the boys and girls were starting to reach *me*. Six months ago, a perfectly adult bartender asked me if I wanted an onion in my martini, and I said, "Gosh n' gollies, you betcha." I knew it was time to quit.

ALBERT: May I ask if this is a pattern; that is, in the past, has there been much shifting of position?

MURRAY: I *always* take an onion in my martini. This is a constant and unswerving . . .
   (*Nick, concerned with Murray's behavior, goes toward him in an attempt to quiet him down*)

SANDRA: (*Firmly, standing*) Mr. Burns. Perhaps you are not aware of just how serious your situation is. This entire matter is a subject of intense interest to the B.C.W. The circumstances of this child's environment, the danger of . . .

ALBERT: Our investigation, Mr. Burns, is the result of what the Bureau considers to be almost an emergency case.

NICK: He just likes to kid around, lady. But, see, we really got a great environment here . . .

MURRAY: (*To Nick*) Relax, kid. (*To Albert and Sandra*) Look, people, I'm sorry. Let's get back to the questions.

SANDRA: Fine. Nick, suppose you and I have a little chat right here.

NICK: (*As he sits down next to her*) Fine. I was gonna suggest that myself.

SANDRA: Nick, I bet you love to come home when you've been out playing and you get tired. You say to yourself, "Gee, I'd like to go home now."

NICK: Sure. Right. And I'm happy here. Boy, if you think I'm happy now, you should see me when I'm *really* happy.

MURRAY: (*To Sandra, sympathetically*) He's on to you, honey. You're gonna have to be a lot foxier than that . . .

SANDRA: And I'm sure that you and your uncle have a great deal of fun together.

NICK: It's not *all* laughs.

SANDRA: Oh, I'm sure there are times when the fun stops and you have nice talks and your uncle teaches you things, helps you to . . .

NICK: I can do a great Peter Lorre imitation. Murray taught me.

ALBERT: Nicky, what Miss Markowitz means, is that you and your uncle must sometimes . . .

NICK: (*In the voice of Peter Lorre, a rather good imitation*) You can't hang me . . . I didn't do it, I tell you . . . that's not my knife . . . I am innocent . . . it's all a mistake . .
    (*Murray beams, smiles proudly during imitation*)

ALBERT: Nicky, that's not what we meant, we . . .

MURRAY: What's the trouble? That happens to be a very good imitation.

ALBERT: Perhaps; but we are trying to . . .

MURRAY: Can *you* imitate Peter Lorre?

NICK: (*Confidentially, to Sandra*) I can do a pretty good James Cagney; I mean it's not fantastic like my Peter Lorre, but it . . .

ALBERT: (*Raising his voice a bit, somewhat commanding*) Nicholas, please. Try to pay attention. Now if I may proceed to . . .

SANDRA: (*Aside, to Albert, somewhat annoyed with him*) Albert, if you'll just let me handle this area. (*Then, to Nick*) Nick, let's talk about games. O.K.?

NICK: O.K.

SANDRA: Now, what kind of games do you like the best?

NICK: Mostly I like educational games and things like that. Murray gets me to develop my natural inquiring mind.

SANDRA: I wonder, do you have any favorite games or toys you'd like to show me? Some plaything that is just the most favorite one of all?

NICK: I just now threw away my collection of *National Geographics* and other educational-type magazines I had a whole collection of . . .

ALBERT: Nicky, Miss Markowitz is very interested in you and cares about you and everything. And if you brought out some of your favorite toys and playthings for her to see, I'm sure that she'd love them just as much as you do.

NICK: Well, there's Bubbles . . .
(*He gets up to get it for them*)

MURRAY: I don't think you'd be interested in seeing Bubbles . . .
(*Nick goes to a cardboard carton at the bureau, opens it, and takes out a twenty-four-inch-high plastic statue of a bare-chested hula girl. The statue is in bright colors and has an electric switch at its pedestal. Nick places the statue on the table between Albert and Sandra and turns it on*)

NICK: Bubbles is what you'd call an electric statue. (*The breasts of the statue light up and continue to blink on and off in spectacular fashion for the next part of the scene. Albert looks at the statue, begins busily going through the file on his lap. Sandra regards the statue scientifically, professionally. Nick smiles proudly over his possession*) It's got an electric battery timer in there that makes it go on and off like that.

SANDRA: Nick, is this your favorite toy?

NICK: Well, after a while it gets pretty boring. But it's a swell gimmick. There was another one in the store that was even better . . .

MURRAY: Anybody want orange juice or toast or anything?

SANDRA: Nick, tell me . . . do you like best the fact that the chest of the lady lights up?

NICK: Well, you got to admit, you don't see boobies like that every day. You want to see the effect when the lights are out? When the room is dark?

SANDRA: Tell me, Nick is *that* what you like best about it, that you can be alone in the dark with it.

NICK: Well, I don't know. But in the dark they really knock your eye out.

(*Albert is blinking nervously at the blinking lights of the statue*)

ALBERT: (*With strenuous calm*) Perhaps, don't you think we ought to switch it off, turn off the . . .

SANDRA: Nick, does Bubbles, does she in any way, does her face remind you at all of, oh, let me see, your mother, for example?

NICK: (*He looks at the face of the statue*) No. I mean, it's just a doll, it's not a statue of anybody I know. I got it in this store downtown.

SANDRA: Her chest, is that something which . . .

NICK: (*Smiling broadly*) It's *something* all right, isn't it?

SANDRA: When you think of your mother, do you . . .

NICK: I don't think about her much.

SANDRA: But when you *do* think of her, do you remember her face best, or her *hands,* or . . .

NICK: I remember she has this terrific laugh. The kind of laugh that when she laughs it makes you laugh too. Of course, she overdoes that a lot.

SANDRA: I mean, physically, when you think of her, do you, well, when you see Bubbles, and Bubbles goes on and off like that . . .

MURRAY: Sandra, his mother's chest did not light up. Let's get that settled right now; mark it down in the file.

ALBERT: (*Nervously; pointing at the blinking statue*) Nicky, I wonder if you would turn those off . . . I mean, turn *it* off, turn her off, unplug it . . .
(*Murray turns the statue off, puts it back into the box*)

SANDRA: Nicky, when you bought this doll . . .

MURRAY: Sandy, why don't I save you a lot of time. Nick is a fairly bright kid and he knows that girls are *not* boys. Other than that his interest in ladies is confined right now to ones that light up or don't light up.

NICK: I mostly like to read books that are healthy, constructive, and extremely educational for a person.

MURRAY: Don't push it, Nick. He does not have any unusual fixations, Sandy. He is no more abnormally interested in your bust than Mr. Amundson is.

ALBERT: Mr. Burns, it is not necessary to . . .

MURRAY: Of course, I might be wrong about that.

ALBERT: Our interest in that doll . . .

MURRAY: You really *are* interested in that doll, Albert.

ALBERT: Our interest . . .

NICK: (*To Albert*) I'll sell it to you for two dollars. That's fifty cents less than I paid for it.
(*Sandra is unable to suppress her amusement and laughs happily*)

ALBERT: (*Quite annoyed with her*) Sandra, I fail to see . . .

SANDRA: (*Controlling herself again, but still smiling*) It's just that it was funny, Albert.

ALBERT: (*Taking command*) Suppose *I* pursue, then, the psychological part of . . .

SANDRA: (*Bristling at him*) Excuse me, Albert, I really do feel it would be better if *I* were to . . .

MURRAY: Albert, the lady was just laughing because something funny happened. That's actually the best thing to do under the circumstances.

ALBERT: Mr. Burns . . .

MURRAY: How would you all like to go to the Statue of Liberty? I have it on good authority from the Weather Lady that today is a beautiful day.

ALBERT: Is it at all possible, Mr. Burns, for you to stick to the point?

MURRAY: Albert, I bet you'd make Sandy a lot happier if you took her off somewhere once in a while. Doesn't have to be the Statue of Liberty; actually any . . .

ALBERT: My relationship with Dr. Markowitz is of no . . .

MURRAY: Well, there's obviously some relationship. When Nick asked you if you'd have sugar in your coffee before, Albert, you answered for Sandy.

ALBERT: Mr. Burns, this entire interview has reached a point . . .

NICK: I'm going to get my educational books. I left them out on the street.
(*He leaves the apartment, his exit unnoticed by the others*)

ALBERT: This entire interview, Mr. Burns, has . . .

SANDRA: Mr. Burns, I . . .

ALBERT: Damn it, Sandra, don't interrupt me!

SANDRA: Albert, for goodness sakes, you . . .

ALBERT: (*Stands up*) Sandra, perhaps we . . . (*To Murray*) Would you excuse us for just a moment, Mr. Burns? I'd like to have a short conference with Sandra . . . Miss . . . *Dr.* Marko-witz for a moment. (*She gets up, Albert and Sandra walk over to the alcove, where Murray cannot hear them. Murray starts to peer at them through his binoculars until Albert turns and looks at him; he then goes to desk and tinkers with clock. Now alone with Sandra, Albert's manner changes somewhat. He speaks more softly and with more warmth, a departure from the stiff, professional manner he uses in dealing with Murray*) Sandra, what are you *doing*, have we lost all control?

SANDRA: Are you seriously talking to *me* about control?

ALBERT: Dear, I told *you* and I told Dr. Malko. It's much too soon for you to go out on cases. You need another year in the office, behind the lines, I told both of you. You're simply *not* ready.

SANDRA: Really, Albert, you hardly let me get started. I was at-tempting to deal with the whole child.

ALBERT: Three months out of grad school and you want to go right into the front lines. Not advisable.

SANDRA: (*Whispering angrily*) Don't you think that this is rather stupid and unprofessional? Right here in front of him you decide to have a conference.

ALBERT: A necessity. I am supposedly the leader of our examin-ing team . . .

SANDRA: Oh, *really* . . .

ALBERT: You get too *involved*, Sandra. Each case, you get much too emotionally involved. This is an exploratory visit, we are *scientists*, dear, you lose sight of the . . .

SANDRA: You make me sick today, Albert. This is no way to approach this man's problem. We . . .

ALBERT: (*Sighing*) Oh, fine. That's just fine. Well . . . fine . . . (*Murray, at the other side of the room, picks up a megaphone*)

MURRAY: (*Through the megaphone*) How are we doing? (*Puts the megaphone down, comes over to them in the alcove, sits between them; speaks sympathetically*) I personally don't feel that you're gonna work out your problems with each other. But I'm glad you came to me because I think I can help you. Al, Sandy is not going to respect you because you threaten her. Respect will have to come gradually, naturally, a maturing process . . .

ALBERT: Mr. Burns . . .

MURRAY: Sandy, I bet he's got a file on you.

ALBERT: Mr. Burns, according to the B.C.W., the child's continuance in your home is in serious and immediate doubt. I am trying to encourage your cooperation . . . (*He is making a genuine attempt to speak warmly, understandingly*) Aren't you at all willing to answer some questions, to give some evidence in your favor for our report, some evidence to support your competency as a guardian? The Board is thoroughly aware that Nicholas is not legally adopted.

MURRAY: He's my nephew. He's staying with me for a while. He's visiting.

ALBERT: How long has he been here?

MURRAY: Seven years.

ALBERT: So you see, the Child Welfare Board has, I assure you, the right to question . . .

MURRAY: (*Rises, faces Albert angrily*) You don't assure me of *any*thing, buddy, you make me damn nervous. Do you mean to tell me that four years at N.Y.U. has made you my judge? (*Albert shrugs, defeated; crosses to Morris chair for his coat, signals Sandra that they are leaving. Murray goes toward them; speaks quietly, apologetically*) O.K., all right. What do you want to know? I'll be cooperative.

(*Sandra and Albert sit down again*)

ALBERT: Nicholas' father, where is he?

MURRAY: That's not a *where* question. That's a *who* question.

ALBERT: I don't quite . . .

MURRAY: Nick's mother, she didn't quite either.

SANDRA: She is still living . . .

MURRAY: My sister is unquestionably alive.

SANDRA: But her responsibility to the child.

MURRAY: For five years she did everything she could for Nick . . . but get married. Now that's not easy to understand since she used to get married to *everybody*. But, somehow, having Nick matured her, she felt a responsibility not to get married to just *any*body any more, so she didn't marry Nick's father, nor was she married at the time he was born. You might call Nick a bastard, or "little bastard," depending on how whimsical you feel at the time. Is that the sort of information you wanted . . . Ah, this situation is the social workers' paradise. What a case history, huh? . . . My sister Elaine showed up here one day with two suitcases, a hatbox, a blue parakeet, a dead gold fish, and a five-year-old child. Three days later she went downstairs to buy a pack of filter tip cigarettes . . . (*Murray shrugs*) Six years later she returned for the suitcases and the hatbox . . . the parakeet I had given away, the gold fish I had long since flushed down the toilet, and the five-year-old child had, with very little effort, become six years older.

When Elaine returned for her luggage I reminded her of the child and the pack of filter-tip cigarettes and suggested that this was perhaps the longest running practical joke in recent history. She was accompanied by a tall chap with sunglasses who was born to be her fifth divorce and who tried to start a small conversation with me. At this point I slapped my sister, Fifth Divorce slugged me, Sister cried, stopped quite suddenly, and then proceeded to explain to me, briefly, her well-practiced theory on the meaning of life, a philosophy falling somewhere to the left of Whoopie. At which point, I remember, I started laughing and then we all laughed and said "good-bye" like people at the end of a long party. That was almost a year ago. And I've still got Nick.

(*Sandra is obviously sympathetic to this situation, emotionally involved in the story; Albert continues his cool professionalism, here and there jotting notes in the file*)

SANDRA: But . . . but I'm sure she must have had *some* concern about Nicholas . . . about the child . . .

MURRAY: His name is not Nicholas. I will admit that he has stayed with that name much longer than the others . . . no, actually he was "Bill" for almost eight months . . .

SANDRA: I'm sure, on his birth certificate . . .

MURRAY: Certainly an elusive document. Not having given him a last name, Elaine felt reticent about assigning him a first one. When Nick first came here this presented a real difficulty. Nick answered to nothing whatsoever. Even the parakeet recognized its own name. Nick only knew I was calling him when he was positive there was no one else in the room.

SANDRA: (*Very much emotionally involved in this now*) Well, how did you communicate with . . .

MURRAY: I made a deal with him when he was six, up to which time he was known rather casually as Chubby, that he could try out any name he wished, for however long he wished, until his thirteenth birthday, at which point he'd have to decide on a name he liked permanently. He went through a long period of dogs' names when he was still little, Rover and King having a real vogue there for a while. For three months he referred to himself as Big Sam, then there was Little Max, Snoopy, Chip, Rock, Rex, Mike, Marty, Lamont, Chevrolet, Wyatt, Yancy, Fred, Phil, Woodrow, Lefty, The Phantom . . . He received his library card last year in the name of Raphael Sabatini, his Cub Scout membership lists him as Barry Fitzgerald, and only last week a friend of his called asking if Toulouse could come over to his house for dinner. Nick seems to be the one that'll stick, though.

SANDRA: His mother . . . ?

MURRAY: His mother, when last heard, was studying mime in Paris, having been given a sort of scholarship by a twenty-two-year-old handbag heir named Myron, who seems to believe strongly in the development of talent and student exchange. Well, I don't believe I've left anything out.

ALBERT: I was not aware that Nick was an O.W. child.

MURRAY: O.W.?

ALBERT: Out of wedlock.

MURRAY: For a moment I thought you meant Prisoner of War. I think it's that natural warmth of yours that leads me to misunderstand.

ALBERT: But as concerns the child . . . (*Looks around the room*) Where *is* the child?

SANDRA: You preferred not having him here anyway, Albert.

ALBERT: (*Sharply*) I am perfectly aware, Sandra, of what I *prefer*, and what I do *not* prefer.

SANDRA: (*Sharply*) I don't care for that tone of voice at *all*, Albert.

ALBERT: (*Rises, begins to put on his coat; calmly*) Sandra, I understand perfectly what has happened. We have allowed this man to disturb us and we have *both* gotten a bit upset. Now, I really do feel that it's time we got over to that family problem in Queens. It's there in your file, the Ledbetters, the introverted child. We've really given an unreasonable amount of time to this case. This interview, I'm afraid, Mr. Burns, has reached a point . . .

SANDRA: (*Attempting to sound authoritative*) Albert, I personally feel that it would not be advisable to leave this particular case, at this point.

ALBERT: Sandra, we have done here this morning all we . . .

SANDRA: I feel that we have not really given Mr. Burns a chance to . . .

ALBERT: Sandra, it's really time we left for Queens . . .

SANDRA: (*Hands Albert one of her two file envelopes*) Here's the Ledbetter file, I'm staying here.

ALBERT: (*Raising his voice a little*) Sandra.

SANDRA: I have decided to pursue this case.

ALBERT: (*Almost shouting*) Sandra, have we lost all professional control?

SANDRA: (*Angry, flustered*) You just . . . you just go yourself to the Leadbellies . . . you go on to Queens.

ALBERT: (*Takes her by the arm, gently, but firmly*) May I just talk to you for a moment?
(*Albert leads Sandra over to the alcove*)

MURRAY: Time out for signals again?

ALBERT: (*Away from Murray, now he speaks softly, less stiffly, though still angry*) What *is* this, dear? What has happened to you today? What are you doing?

SANDRA: I'm doing what I think is right.

ALBERT: I know how you feel, Sandra, but there is no more we can do here.

SANDRA: (*Emotionally*) I just . . . I just don't understand your behavior when you're on a case. We're supposed to be of some help, he . . .

ALBERT: Of course I want to help. But don't forget that the child is the one who needs protection, who needs . . .

SANDRA: Are you really going to leave that man here like that? You're not going to even try to help him or tell him what to do about the Board separating him from the child . . . I mean . . . just so cold.

ALBERT: (*Takes her hand*) Dear, you spent much too much time at that graduate school and not enough time in the field. That's your whole trouble. You've got to learn your job, Sandra . . .

SANDRA: (*Angry, frustrated*) Oh *really*, is that so? Albert Amundson, don't give me any of that nonsense.

ALBERT: (*Glancing over at Murray*) Please, Sandra . . . dear, this is not the time or the place for . . .

SANDRA: (*Shouting*) Graduate school wouldn't have done *you* any harm, Albert, believe *me!* Oh, this is the most terrible thing . . . (*Very close to tears*) You mean . . . you're just going to leave . . . ? Do you know what you are . . . ? you're a . . . I don't know; . . . but I'll think of something . . .
(*Albert walks away, leaving her in the alcove, goes into the main room, calmly picks up his briefcase*)

ALBERT: (*Retaining his control, but just a little shaken. To Murray*) Mr. Burns . . . You can assume at this point that Miss Markowitz is no longer involved with your case. The Board will be informed that she is no longer involved with this particular case. Her continuing here, to discuss your case . . . at this point . . . is entirely unofficial. You can dismiss any conference . . . that may resume after I leave . . . when I leave here, from your mind. And, regardless of what you think of me . . .

MURRAY: I think you're a dirty O.W.
(*Some of Sandra's file papers slip from her hand and fall to the floor*)

ALBERT: And . . . and do you know what *you* are? (*Readying himself to deliver a crushing insult to Murray*) Maladjusted! (*Goes to the door, opens it*) Good afternoon, Mr. Burns. Good afternoon, Sandra.

MURRAY: Good afternoon, Mr. Amundson. Watch out crossing the street.
(*Albert exits, closing door sharply behind him. Sandra stands for a moment in the alcove, then begins to pick up the papers she had dropped on the floor*)

SANDRA: Mr. Burns . . . (*She is making a very strong attempt to control herself, but she is obviously on the verge of tears. She goes into the main room, begins to collect her things to leave*) Mr. Burns, I must apologize to you. We . . . we have put you . . . you have been put at a disadvantage this morning. You have been involved in a personal problem that has nothing to do whatsoever with your particular case. It is entirely wrong for me to give you this impression of our . . . of our profession. (*She can no longer control herself and becomes, suddenly, a sort of child. She stands quite still, with her hands at her sides, and cries. It is not loud, hysterical crying, but inter-*

mittent and disorganized sobs, squeaks, whines, sniffles and assorted feminine noises which punctuate her speech) Do you know what? I just lost my job. This is awful. He's right, you know. I'm not suited to my work. I get too involved. That's what he said and he's right. (*Rummaging through her purse for Kleenex*) Please don't look at me. Do you *have* to stand there? Please go away. Still, he didn't have to talk to me like that. This is the first *week* we've ever gone on cases together. I didn't think he'd behave that way. That was no way. Why don't I ever have any Kleenex? (*He gives her the closest thing at hand to blow her nose in, his undershirt from the bed*) Thank you. (*She sits down on the bed*) Do you know that even with two fellowships it still cost me, I mean my parents mostly, it cost them seven thousand two hundred and forty-five dollars for me to go through school. I was the eighth youngest person to graduate in New York State last year and I can't stop crying. Maybe if I hurry, if I took a cab, I could still meet him in Queens.

MURRAY: You can't. Queens is closed. It's closed for the season.

SANDRA: Do you know what?
    (*Her crying lets up a bit*)

MURRAY: What?

SANDRA: (*With a new burst of sobs*) I hate the Ledbetters.

MURRAY: Then I'm sure once I got to know them I'd hate them too.

SANDRA: Mr. Burns, you don't understand. Some of the cases I love and some of them I hate, and that's all wrong for my work, but I can't help it. I hate Raymond Ledbetter and he's only nine years old and he makes me sick and I don't give a damn about him.

MURRAY: (*Pointing to the file on her lap*) You can't like everybody in your portfolio.

SANDRA: But some of them I like too much and worry about them all day . . . (*She is making an attempt to control her tears*) It is an obvious conflict against all professional standards. I didn't like Raymond Ledbetter so I tried to understand him, and now that I understand him I hate him.

MURRAY: I think that's wonderful. Can I get you a cup of coffee?

SANDRA: (*She turns to Murray as if to answer him, but instead bursts into fresh tears*) He's gone to Queens and I'll never hear from him again. I wrote out what my married name would be after dinner last night on a paper napkin, Mrs. Albert Amundson, to see how it would look. You know what I think I am, I think I'm crazy.

MURRAY: Well, then, I can talk to you.

SANDRA: We were going to get married. It was all planned, Mrs. Albert Amundson on a napkin. You have to understand Albert. He's really a very nice person when he's not on cases. He's a very intelligent man but last month I fell asleep twice while he was talking. I know him for so long. (*She tries once again to stop crying but the effort only increases her sobs*) Mr. Burns, don't look at me. Why don't you go away?

MURRAY: But I live here.

SANDRA: I would like everybody to go away.

MURAY: (*Attempting to comfort her*) Can I get you a pastrami sandwich?

SANDRA: Oh, I don't know you and I'm crying right in front of you. Go away.

MURRAY: Couldn't you just think of this as Show-and-Tell time?

SANDRA: (*Turning away again, still seated on the bed*) The minute I got out of school I wanted to go right back inside. (*With a great sob*) Albert is gone and I just lost my job.

MURRAY: (*He walks over to her*) Now, you're really going to have to stop crying, because I am going out of my mind.

SANDRA: I cry all the time and I laugh in the wrong places in the movies. I am unsuited to my profession and I can't do anything right. Last night I burned an entire chicken and after seven years of school I can't work and I've got no place to go. An entire chicken.

MURRAY: If I do my Peter Lorre imitation, will you stop crying?

SANDRA: (*She pokes the file-envelope in her lap*) Look what I've done, I've cried on one of my files. The ink is running all over the Grumbacher twins . . .

MURRAY: (*In the voice of Peter Lorre, a decent imitation*) It was all a mistake, I didn't stab Mrs. Marmalade . . . it was my knife, but someone else did it, I tell you . . .

SANDRA: That's an awful imitation, Mr. Burns . . .
(*She turns away from him and sobs into the bedclothes. He takes the Bubbles statue out of the box, switches it on, places it on the floor near the bed; it starts to blink on and off. Her face peeks out, she sees the blinking statue and puts her face back into the bedclothes, but we hear some giggles mixing with her sobs now, and then overtaking them, until she finally lifts her face and we see that she is laughing*)

MURRAY: (*Smiling*) There. Progress. (*He turns off the statue*) Would you like a cup of coffee, or a pastrami sandwich or something?

SANDRA: No, thank you. (*Sandra begins to compose herself, she has stopped crying completely and is wiping her eyes with the undershirt he gave her. Then she begins to fold the undershirt neatly, smoothing it out into a nice little square on her lap*) This is absolutely the most unprofessional experience I have ever had.

MURRAY: People fall into two distinct categories, Miss Markowitz; people who like delicatessen, and people who don't like
delicatessen. A man who is not touched by the earthy lyricism
of hot pastrami, the pungent fantasy of corned beef, pickles,
frankfurters, the great lusty impertinence of good mustard . . .
is a man of stone and without heart. Now, Albert is obviously
not a lover of delicatessen and you are well rid of him.
    (*Sandra is still on the bed, her hands folded neatly in her
    lap on top of her files and his undershirt*)

SANDRA: What am I going to do? This is an awful day.

MURRAY: (*He sits on the swivel chair next to the bed*) Miss
Markowitz, this is a beautiful day and I'll tell you why. My
dear, you are really a jolly old girl and you are well rid of Albert. You have been given a rare opportunity to return the
unused portion and have your money refunded.

SANDRA: But . . . my work . . . what am I going to . . .

MURRAY: You are a lover, Dr. Markowitz, you are a lover of
things and people so you took up work where you could get as
many of them as possible; and it just turned out there were too
many of them and too much that moves you. Damn it, please
be glad that it turned out you are not reasonable and sensible.
Have all the gratitude you can, that you are capable of embarrassment and joy and are a marathon crier.

SANDRA: (*Looking directly at him*) There is a kind of relief that
it's gone . . . the job, and even Albert. But I know what it is,
it's just irresponsible . . . I don't have the vaguest idea who I
am . . .

MURRAY: (*He takes her hand*) It's just there's all these Sandras
running around who you never met before, and it's confusing
at first, fantastic, like a Chinese fire drill. But god *damn*, isn't it
great to find out how many Sandras there are? Like those little

cars in the circus, this tiny red car comes out and putters around, suddenly its doors open and out come a thousand clowns, whooping and hollering and raising hell.

SANDRA: (*She lets go of his hand in order to pick up the undershirt in her lap*) What's this?

MURRAY: That's my undershirt. How's about going to the Empire State Building with me?

SANDRA: I'll have that coffee now.

MURRAY: You didn't answer my question. Would you like to visit the Empire State Building?

SANDRA: No, not really.

MURRAY: Well, then how about the zoo?

SANDRA: Not just now.

MURRAY: Well, then will you marry me?

SANDRA: What?

MURRAY: Just a bit of shock treatment there. I have found after long experience that it's the quickest way to get a woman's attention when her mind wanders. Always works.

SANDRA: Mr. Burns . . .

MURRAY: Now that you've cried you can't call me Mr. Burns. Same rule applies to laughing. My name is Murray.

SANDRA: Well, Murray, to sort of return to reality for a minute . . .

MURRAY: I will only go as a tourist.

SANDRA: Murray, you know, you're in trouble with the Child Welfare Board. They could really take Nick away. Murray, there's some things you could try to do . . . to make your case a little stronger . . .

MURRAY: Sandra, do you realize that you are not wearing your shoes?

SANDRA: (*She looks down at her bare feet*) Oh.
(*The front door opens and Nick bursts into the room, laden with books*)

NICK: Well, here I am with all my favorite books, *Fun in the Rain, The Young Railroader, Great Philosophers, Science for Youth,* a Spanish dictionary. What I did was I left them out in the street when I was playing, and I went down to . . .

MURRAY: Nick, you just killed a month's allowance for nothing. Miss Markowitz isn't even on our case any more.

NICK: I shouldn't have left. You got angry and insulted everybody.

MURRAY: Don't worry about it, Nick, we'll work it out.
(*He goes over to the closet for something*)

NICK: (*Dropping his books regretfully on the chair*) Four dollars right out the window. (*To Sandra*) Y'know, I really do read educational books and am encouraged in my home to think.

SANDRA: I'm sure that's true, Nicholas, but I'm not in a position to do you much official good any more.

NICK: We're in real trouble now, right? (*He turns to Murray who has taken two ukuleles from the closet and is coming toward Nick*) I figured it would happen; you got angry and hollered at everybody.

MURRAY: Nick, we have a guest, a music lover. . . . (*He hands the smaller of the two ukuleles to Nick*) We've got to do our song. I am sure it will be requested.

NICK: (*Protesting, gesturing with his ukulele*) Murray, stop it . . . we—this is no time to sing songs, Murray. . . .

MURRAY: (*Striking a downbeat on his ukulele*) Come on, where's your professional attitude?

(*Murray starts playing "Yes Sir, That's My Baby" on the ukulele, then sings the first line. Nick turns away at first, shaking his head solemnly at Murray's behavior. Murray goes on with the second line of the song. Reluctantly, Nick begins to pick out the melody on his ukulele, then he smiles in spite of himself and sings the third line along with Murray.*

They really go into the song now, singing and playing "Yes, Sir, That's My Baby," doing their routine for Sandra. She sits in front of them on the bed, smiling, enjoying their act. Nick is in the spirit of it now and having a good time. In the middle of the song Nick and Murray do some elaborate soft-shoe dance steps for a few lines, ukuleles held aloft. This is followed by some very fast and intricate two-part ukulele harmony on the last few lines of the song for a big finish.

Sandra applauds.

Murray and Nick, singing and strumming ukes, go into a reprise of the song, Murray moving forward and sitting down on the bed next to Sandra. Nick, left apart from them now, does a line or two more of the song along with Murray, then gradually stops. Nick considers them both for a moment as Murray goes on doing the song alone now for Sandra. Nick nods to himself, circles around in front of them and, unnoticed by them, puts his uke down on the window seat, goes to his alcove, gets school briefcase and pajamas from his bed. Murray is still playing the uke and singing the song to Sandra as Nick goes past them on his way to the front door, carrying his stuff)

NICK: (*Pleasantly, to Sandra*) Nice to meet you, lady. I'll see you around.

MURRAY: (*Stops singing, turns to Nick*) Where you off to, Nick?

NICK: Gonna leave my stuff up at Mrs. Myers'. (*Opens the door*) I figure I'll be staying over there tonight.

(*Nick exits, waving a pleasant good-bye to Sandra. Sandra looks at the front door, puzzled; then she looks at Murray, who resumes the song, singing and strumming the uke*)

Curtain

ACT TWO

Scene: *Murray's apartment, eight* A.M. *the following morning.*

At rise: *The phone is ringing loudly on the window seat. Murray enters from the bathroom with his toothbrush in his mouth, grabs the phone. The room is as it was at the end of Act One except that there is a six-foot-high folding screen placed around the bed, hiding it from view, and the shades are drawn again on the windows.*

MURRAY: (*Speaks immediately into the phone*) Is this somebody with good news or money? No? Good-bye. (*He hangs up*) It's always voices like that you hear at eight A.M. Maniacs. (*He pulls up the shade to see what kind of a day it is outside. As usual the lighting of the room changes not at all with the shade up, as before he sees nothing but the blank, grayish wall opposite*) Crap. (*With a sigh of resignation, he picks up the phone, dials, listens*) Hello, Weather Lady. I am fine, how are you? What is the weather? Uh-huh . . . uh-huh . . . uh-huh . . . very nice. Only a *chance* of showers? Well, what exactly does that . . . Aw, there she goes again . . . (*He hangs up*) Chance of showers. (*The phone rings. He picks it up, speaks immediately into it*) United States Weather Bureau forecast for New York City and vicinity: eight A.M. temperature, sixty-five degrees, somewhat cooler in the suburbs, cloudy later today with a chance of . . . (*Looks incredulously at the phone*) He hung up. Fool. Probably the most informative phone call he'll make all day. (*He stands, opens the window, leans out, raising his voice, shouting out the window*) This is your neighbor speaking! Something must be done about your garbage cans in the alley here. It is definitely second-rate garbage! By next week I want to see a better class of garbage, more empty champagne bottles and caviar cans! So let's *snap* it up and get on the *ball!*

(*Sandra's head appears at the top of the screen, like a puppet's head. She is staring blankly at Murray. Murray steps toward her, she continues to stare blankly at him. Her head suddenly disappears again behind the screen. The screen masks the entire bed and Sandra from his view, and the view of audience. We hear a rustle of sheets and blankets, silence for a couple of seconds, and then Sandra's voice; she speaks in a cold, dignified, lady-like voice, only slightly tinged with sleep, impersonal, polite, and distant, like one unintroduced party guest to another*)

SANDRA: Good morning.

MURRAY: Good morning.

SANDRA: How are you this morning?

MURRAY: I am fine this morning. How are you?

SANDRA: I am fine also. Do you have a bathrobe?

MURRAY: Yes, I have a bathrobe.

SANDRA: May I have your bathrobe, please?

MURRAY: I'll give you Nick's. It'll fit you better.

SANDRA: That seems like a good idea.
(*He takes Nick's bathrobe from the hook in the alcove, tosses it over the top of the screen*)

MURRAY: There you go.

SANDRA: (*Her voice from behind the screen is getting even colder*) Thank you. What time is it?

MURRAY: It is eight-fifteen and there is a chance of showers. Did you sleep well?

SANDRA: Yes. How long have you been up?

MURRAY: Little while.

SANDRA: Why didn't you wake me?

MURRAY: Because you were smiling. (*Silence for a moment*) How does the bathrobe fit?

SANDRA: This bathrobe fits fine. (*After a moment*) Did you happen to see my clothes?

MURRAY: (*Starts for the bathroom*) They're in the bathroom. Shall I get them?

SANDRA: No, thank you. (*She suddenly pops out from behind the screen and races across the room into the kitchen at right, slamming the kitchen door behind her. We hear her voice from behind the door*) This isn't the bathroom. This is the kitchen.

MURRAY: If it *was* the bathroom then this would be a very extreme version of an efficiency apartment. (*He goes to the bathroom to get her clothes, brings them with him to the kitchen door. He knocks on the door*) Here are your clothes. Also toothpaste and toothbrush.
(*The kitchen door opens slightly, her hand comes out. He puts the stuff in it, her hand goes back, the door closes again*)

SANDRA: Thank you.

MURRAY: Sandy, is everything all right?

SANDRA: What?

MURRAY: I said, is everything all right?

SANDRA: Yes. I'm using the last of your toothpaste.

MURRAY: That's all right. There's soap by the sink.

SANDRA: I know. I found it.

MURRAY: That's good.

SANDRA: It was right by the sink.

MURRAY: Suppose we broaden this discussion to other matters . . .

SANDRA: I saw the soap when I came in.
(The front door opens and Arnold Burns enters as he did before, carrying a grocery carton filled with varieties of fruit. He sets it down on the desk)

ARNOLD: Morning, Murray.

MURRAY: (*Without turning to look at him*) Morning, Arnold.

ARNOLD: Murray, Chuckles called again yesterday. I told him I'd talk to you. And Jimmy Sloan is in from the coast; he's putting a new panel-show package together . . .

MURRAY: Arnold, you have many successful clients . . .

ARNOLD: Murray . . .

MURRAY: With all these successful people around, where are all of our new young failures going to come from?

ARNOLD: Murray, those people I saw here yesterday; they were from the Welfare Board, right? I tried to warn you . . .

MURRAY: Nothing to worry about.

ARNOLD: These Welfare people don't kid around.

MURRAY: Arnold, I don't mind you coming with fruit if you keep quiet, but you bring a word with every apple . . . Everything's fine. You'll be late for the office.

ARNOLD: Is Nick all right?

MURRAY: Fine.

ARNOLD: O.K., good-bye, Murray.

MURRAY: Good-bye, Arnold. (*Arnold exits. Murray talks to the closed kitchen door again*) There's coffee still in the pot from last night, if you want to heat it up.

SANDRA: I already lit the flame.

MURRAY: Good. The cups are right over the sink. Will you be coming out soon?

SANDRA: I found the cups.

MURRAY: Do you think you will be coming out soon?

SANDRA: Yes, I think so. Cream and sugar in your coffee?

MURRAY: Yes, thank you.

SANDRA: Murray.

MURRAY: Yes.

SANDRA: I'm coming out now.

MURRAY: That's good.

SANDRA: I'm all finished in here so I'm coming out now.

MURRAY: That's very good.
(*The kitchen door opens. Sandra, dressed neatly, comes out of the kitchen, carrying two cups of coffee and Nick's bathrobe*)

SANDRA: (*Pausing at kitchen doorway, smiles politely*) Well, here I am. (*She goes to Murray, gives him a cup, sits on swivel chair. He sits next to her, on the stool. She takes a sip of coffee, straightens her hair. She is quite reserved, though pleasant; she behaves as though at a tea social)* You know, yesterday was the first time I've ever been to the Statue of Liberty. It's funny how you can live in a city for so long and not visit one of its most fascinating sights.

MURRAY: That is funny. *(He sips his coffee)* This coffee isn't bad, for yesterday's coffee.

SANDRA: I think it's very good, for yesterday's coffee. *(Takes another sip)* What kind of coffee is it?

MURRAY: I believe it's Chase and Sanborn coffee.

SANDRA: "Good to the last drop," isn't that what they say?

MURRAY: I think that's Maxwell House.

SANDRA: Oh yes. Maxwell House coffee. "Good to the last drop."

MURRAY: It's Chase and Sanborn that used to have the ad about the ingredients: "Monizalles for mellowness" was one.

SANDRA: They used to sponsor Edgar Bergen and Charlie McCarthy on the radio.

MURRAY: Yes. You're right.

SANDRA: "Monizalles for mellowness." I remember. That's right. *(She finishes her coffee, puts her cup down on the table. Then, after a moment)* I have to leave now.

MURRAY: Oh?

SANDRA: Yes. I'll have to be on my way.
(She stands, takes her pocketbook, puts on her shoes and starts to exit)

MURRAY: *(Takes her files from the floor, hands them to her)* Don't forget your files.

SANDRA: Oh yes. My files. (*She takes them from him, stands looking at him*) Well, good-bye.

MURRAY: Good-bye, Sandra.

SANDRA: Good-bye.
(*She walks out of the apartment, and closes the door behind her. Alone in the apartment now, Murray stands for a moment looking at the door. He then runs to open the door; she has had her hand on the outside knob and is dragged into the room as he does so*)

MURRAY: (*Laughing, relieved*) You nut. I was ready to kill you.

SANDRA: (*Throws her arms around him, drops her bag and files on floor*) What happened? You didn't say anything. I was waiting for you to say something. Why didn't you say something or kiss me or . . .

MURRAY: I was waiting for *you*, for God's sake.
(*He kisses her*)

SANDRA: I didn't know *what* was going on. (*She kisses him, their arms around each other; he leans away from her for a moment to put his coffee cup on the table*) Don't let me go . . .

MURRAY: I was just putting my coffee cup down . . .

SANDRA: Don't let me go. (*He holds her tightly again*) Murray, I thought about it, and I probably love you.

MURRAY: That's very romantic. I probably love you too. You have very small feet. For a minute yesterday, it looked like you only had four toes, and I thought you were a freak. I woke up in the middle of the night and counted them. There are five.

SANDRA: I could have told you that.

MURRAY: (*He sits in the swivel chair; she is on his lap*) You knocked down maybe seven boxes of Crackerjacks yesterday. You are twelve years old. You sleep with the blanket under your chin like a napkin. When you started to talk about the coffee before, I was going to throw you out the window except there'd be no place for you to land but the trash can from the Chinese restaurant.

SANDRA: You mean that you live above a Chinese restaurant?

MURRAY: Yes. It's been closed for months, though.

SANDRA: Do you mean that you live above an abandoned Chinese restaurant?

MURRAY: Yes, I do.

SANDRA: That's wonderful. (*She kisses him; jumps up from his lap happily excited about what she has to say. Takes off her jacket and hangs it on the back of the Morris chair*) I didn't go to work this morning and I simply can't tell you how fantastic that makes me feel. I'm not going to do a *lot* of things any more. (*Picks at the material of her blouse*) This blouse I'm wearing, my mother picked it out, everybody picks out things for me. She gets all her clothes directly from Louisa May Alcott. (*Picks up the stool, changes its position in the room*) Well, we've all seen the last of this blouse anyway. Do you realize that I feel more at home here after twenty-four hours than I do in my parents' house after twenty-five years? Of course, we'll have to do something about curtains . . . and I hope you didn't mind about the screen around the bed, I just think it gives such a nice, separate bedroomy effect to that part of the room . . . (*Picks up her bag and files from the floor where she dropped them, puts them in the closet. She is moving in*) Oh, there are so many wonderful tricks you can try with a one-room apartment, really, if you're willing to use your imagination . . . (*He watches helplessly as she moves happily about the apartment judging it with a decorator's eye*) I don't

care if it sounds silly, Murray, but I was projecting a person-
ality identification with the Statue of Liberty yesterday . . .
courageous and free and solid metal . . . (*She kisses him, then
continues pacing happily*) I was here with you last night and I
don't give a damn who knows it or what anybody thinks, and
that goes for Dr. Malko, Albert, my mother, Aunt Blanche . . .
Oh, I'm going to do so many things I've always wanted to do.

MURRAY: For example.

SANDRA: Well . . . I'm not sure right now. And that's marvelous
too, I am thoroughly enjoying the idea that I don't know what
I'm going to do next. (*Stops pacing*) Do you have an extra
key?

MURRAY: What?

SANDRA: An extra key. Altman's has this terrific curtain sale,
thought I'd go and . . .

MURRAY: Well, then I'd better give you some money . . .

SANDRA: No, that's all right. (*Holds out her hand*) Just the key.

MURRAY: Oh.
(*He looks at her blankly for a moment, then reaches into his
pocket slowly, finds the key, slowly hands it to her*)

SANDRA: (*Snatches up the key, goes on delightedly pacing up
and down*) Murray, did we bring back any Crackerjacks?

MURRAY: (*Pointing to some packages on the desk*) Only stuff
we brought back was that cleaning equipment. I'll admit this
place is a little dirty, but all that stuff just for . . .
(*The doorbell rings. Sandra flinches for a moment, but then
smiles and stands firmly*)

SANDRA: You'd better answer it, Murray.

MURRAY: Sandra, would you prefer to . . .

(He indicates the kitchen as a hiding place, but she stands right where she is, refusing to move)

SANDRA: I've got no reason to hide from anybody.
(Murray goes to the front door and opens it halfway, but enough for us to see the visitor, Albert Amundson. Albert cannot see beyond the door to where Sandra is standing)

ALBERT: Good morning, Mr. Burns.

MURRAY: Albert, how are you?
(Sandra, hearing Albert's voice, and realizing who it is, goes immediately into the closet, closing the door behind her)

ALBERT: May I come in?

MURRAY: Sure.
(Murray opens the front door all the way, allowing Albert into the main room. Murray closes the door, then follows Albert into the room. Murray smiles to himself when he sees that Sandra is not there and then glances at the closet door)

ALBERT: I called you twice this morning, Mr. Burns.

MURRAY: That was you.

ALBERT: That was me. Miss Markowitz did not show up in Queens yesterday.

MURRAY: So?

ALBERT: Her parents are quite upset. I am quite upset. Where is she?

MURRAY: She's hiding in the closet.

ALBERT: We're really all quite anxious to know where she is.

MURRAY: I'm not kidding. She's in the closet.

(*Albert goes to the closet, opens the door, sees Sandra, then closes the door. Albert comes back to Murray*)

ALBERT: She *is* in the closet.

MURRAY: I wouldn't lie to you, Albert.

ALBERT: Why is she in the closet?

MURRAY: I don't know. She's got this thing about closets.

ALBERT: That's a very silly thing for her to be in that closet.

MURRAY: Don't knock it till you've tried it. Now, what else can I do for you?

ALBERT: That's a difficult thing for me to believe. I mean, that she's right there in the closet. You are not a person, Mr. Burns, you are an experience.

MURRAY: (*Goes into the kitchen*) That's very nice, Albert, I'll have to remember that.

ALBERT: Actually, Dr. Markowitz is not the reason for my visit today. I came here in an official capacity.

MURRAY: (*From the kitchen*) You don't wear an official capacity well, Albert. Coffee?

ALBERT: No, thank you.
(*Murray brings the pot out, fills the two cups on the table; brings one of the cups of coffee to the closet and hands it through the partly open door*)

MURRAY: (*Returns to the table, sits opposite Albert*) What have you got on your mind, Albert?

ALBERT: (*Sits; begins hesitantly*) Burns, late yesterday afternoon the Child Welfare Board made a decision on your case. Their decision is based on three months of a thorough study;

our interview yesterday is only a small part of the . . . I want you to understand that I am not responsible, personally, for the decision they've reached, I . . .

MURRAY: Relax, Albert, I won't even hold you responsible for the shadow you're throwing on my rug.

ALBERT: For eleven months you have avoided contact with the Board, made a farce of their inquiries. You are not employed, show no inclination to gain employment, have absolutely no financial stability . . .

MURRAY: Look, Albert, I . . .

ALBERT: Months of research by the Board and reports by the Revere School show a severe domestic instability, a libertine self-indulgence, a whole range of circumstances severely detrimental to the child's welfare . . .

MURRAY: Look, stop the tap-dancing for a second, Albert; what's going on, what . . .

ALBERT: It is the Board's decision that you are unfit to be the guardian of your nephew, and that action be taken this Friday to remove the child from this home and the deprivation you cause him.

MURRAY: You mean they can really . . . (*Sips his coffee, putting on an elaborate display of calm, showing no emotion*) Where'd they get this routine from, Charles Dickens?

ALBERT: The Board is prepared to find a more stable, permanent home for your nephew, a family with whom he will live a more wholesome, normal . . .

MURRAY: Look, Albert, there must be some kind of a hearing or something, where I'll have a chance to . . .

ALBERT: You will have the opportunity Thursday to state your case to the Board. If there is some substantial change in your circumstances, some evidence they're not aware of; if you can demonstrate that you are a responsible member of society . . .

MURRAY: It's Tuesday; what the hell am I supposed to do in two days, win the Nobel Peace Prize? They sent you here to tell me this?

ALBERT: No, you were to be informed by the court. But in view of the confusion which took place here yesterday, for which I consider myself responsible, I felt it my duty to come here and explain . . .

MURRAY: Buddy, you speak like you write everything down before you say it.

ALBERT: Yes, I do speak that way, Mr. Burns. I wish that I spoke more spontaneously. I realize that I lack warmth. I will always appear foolish in a conversation with a person of your imagination. Please understand, there is no vengeance in my activities here. I love my work, Mr. Burns. I believe that you are a danger to this child. I wish this were not true, because it is obvious that you have considerable affection for your nephew. It is in your face, this feeling. I admire you for your warmth, Mr. Burns, and for the affection the child feels for you. I admire this because I am one for whom children do not easily feel affection. I am not one of the warm people. But your feeling for the child does not mollify the genuinely dangerous emotional climate you have made for him. (*He moves toward Murray*) I wish you could understand this, I would so much rather you understood, could really hear what I have to say. For yours is, I believe, a distorted picture of this world.

MURRAY: Then why don't you send *me* to a foster home?

ALBERT: I was right. You really can't listen to me. You are so sure of your sight. Your villains and heroes are all so terribly clear to you, and I am obviously one of the villains. (*Picks up*

his briefcase) God save you from your vision, Mr. Burns. (*Goes to the front door, opens it*) Good-bye.
    (*Albert exits*)

MURRAY: (*Stands at the window with his coffee cup in his hand, looking out at gray, blank wall of the building opposite*) Hey, courageous, free one, you can come out now.
    (*Sandra comes out of closet carrying her coffee cup; Murray does not look at her*)

SANDRA: I'm sorry, Murray. I'm really very embarrassed. I don't know what happened. I just ran into the closet. And . . . and once I was in there, I just didn't want to come out. I'm sorry, Murray . . .

MURRAY: Don't be nervous, lady, you're just going through an awkward stage. You're between closets. (*Quietly, calmly*) Look, if Nick has to leave, if he goes, he goes, and my life stays about the same. But it's no good for *him*, see, not for a couple of years, anyway. Right now he's still ashamed of being sharper than everybody else, he could easily turn into another peeled and boiled potato. Are you listening to me?

SANDRA: Yes, of course . . .

MURRAY: Well, make some kind of listening noise then, will you? Wink or nod your head or something.

SANDRA: But, I'm . . .

MURRAY: (*Casually; gesturing with his coffee cup*) Tell you the truth, it's even a little better for me if he goes. I mean, he's a middle-aged kid. When I signed with the network he sat up all night figuring out the fringe benefits and the pension plan. And he started to make *lists* this year. Lists of everything; subway stops, underwear, what he's gonna do next week. If somebody doesn't watch out he'll start making lists of what he's gonna do next year and the next ten years. Hey, suppose they put him in with a whole family of listmakers? (*Angrily*) I didn't spend six years with him so he should turn into a listmaker. He'll learn to know everything before it happens, he'll learn to plan, he'll learn how to be one of the nice dead people. Are you listening?

SANDRA: Of course, I told you, Murray, I . . .

MURRAY: Then stamp your feet or mutter so I'll know you're there, huh? (*Still speaking quite calmly*) I just want him to stay with me till I can be sure he won't turn into Norman Nothing. I want to be sure he'll know when he's chickening out on himself. I want him to get to know exactly the special thing he is or else he won't notice it when it starts to go. I want him to stay awake and know who the phonies are, I want him to know how to holler and put up an argument, I want a little guts to show before I can let him go. I want to be sure he sees all the wild possibilities. I want him to know it's worth all the trouble just to give the world a little goosing when you get the chance. And I want him to know the subtle, sneaky, important reason why he was born a human being and not a chair. (*Pause*) I will be very sorry to see him go. That kid was the best straight man I ever had. He is a laugher, and laughers are rare. I mean, you tell that kid something funny . . . not just any piece of corn, but something funny, and he'll give you your money's worth. It's not just funny jokes he reads, or I tell him, that he laughs at. Not just set-up funny stuff. He sees street jokes, he has the good eye, he sees subway farce and crosstown-bus humor and all the cartoons that people make by being alive. He has a good eye. And I don't want him to leave until I'm certain he'll never be ashamed of it. (*Still quite calmly, unemotionally*) And in addition to that . . . besides that . . . see (*Suddenly; loudly*) Sandy, I don't want him to go. I like having him around here. What should I do, Sandy? Help me out. (*Suddenly slumps forward in his chair, covers his face with his hands; very quietly*) I like when he reads me from the want ads.

SANDRA: (*Takes his hands*) Murray, don't worry, we'll do something. I know the Board, their procedure, there's things you can do . . .

MURRAY: (*Quietly, thoughtfully*) What I'll do is I'll buy a new suit. The first thing is to get a dignified suit.

SANDRA: If you could get some kind of a job, get your brother to help you.

MURRAY: Right. Right.

SANDRA: Is there something you can get in a hurry?

MURRAY: Sure, one of those summer suits with the ready-made cuffs . . .

SANDRA: No, I mean a job. If we could just bring some proof of employment to the hearing, Murray, show them how anxious you are to change. We'll show them you want to be reliable.

MURRAY: (*Brightening*) Yeah, reliable . . . (*Rises; going toward the phone*) Sandy, we will put on a God-damned show for them. Spectacular reliability; a reliability parade; bands, floats, everything. (*Starts to dial*) Sandy, go to the files and pick me out a tie that is quiet but at the same time projects a mood of inner strength. (*Into the phone*) Arnold Burns' office, please.

SANDRA: (*On her way to the file cabinet*) One quiet tie with a mood of inner strength.

MURRAY: (*Into the phone*) Hello, Margot? It's Murray. Oh, well, when Arnie comes in here's what you do. First you tell him to sit down. Then you tell him I want to get a job. When he has recovered sufficiently from that shock, tell him . . . (*Sandra comes to him with a tie*) Excuse me a second, Margot . . . (*To Sandra, indicating the tie*) Yes, quiet but with strength. (*Sandra laughs*) Sandy, that is the greatest happy laugh I ever heard on a lady. Do that again. (*She laughs*

again) Great. Keep that laugh. I'll need it later. (*Into the phone*) Margot, tell him I'm going downtown to pick up a new suit for myself and a beautiful pineapple for him, call him back in about an hour, O.K.? Thanks, Margot.
(*Puts the phone down, goes to get his jacket*)

SANDRA: Can I come with you? I'd love to buy a suit with you.

MURRAY: (*Putting on his jacket*) Better not, Sandy. Gotta move fast. These shoes look O.K.? (*She nods, he takes her hand*) Look, don't go away.

SANDRA: I won't.
(*She kisses him*)

MURRAY: (*Goes to the front door; turns to her, smiles*) Say "Good luck."

SANDRA: Good luck.

MURRAY: (*Opening the door*) Now say "You are a magnificient human being."

SANDRA: You are a magnificent human being.

MURRAY: (*As he exits*) I *thought* you'd notice.
(*She stands in door and watches him go as the lights fade out quickly. Immediately, as the lights fade, we hear the voice of Chuckles the Chipmunk (Leo Herman)*)

LEO'S VOICE: Hi there, kidderoonies; there's nothin' more lonelier than a lonely, little looney Chippermunk. So won't ya please come on along with me fer a fun hour, 'cuz that loneliest, littlest, looniest Chippermunk, is *me* . . . Chuckles. (*Lights come up now in Arnold Burns' office, later that afternoon. The office is part of a large theatrical agency of which Arnold is a rather successful member; modern, wood-paneling, nonobjective paintings and framed photographs of his clients on the wall, a spectacularly large window behind the desk with a*

*twenty-second-floor skyline view. A large bowl of fruit is on
an end table near the door. One of the two phones on Arnold's
desk is a special speaker-phone, consisting of a small loud-
speaker box on the desk which amplifies clearly the voice of
whoever is calling. It can also be spoken into from almost any
point in the room if one is facing it. As the following scene
progresses the speaker-phone is treated by those present as if
it were a person in the room, they gesture to it, smile at it. Arnold is alone in his office, leaning against his desk, listening to
the speaker-phone, from which we continue to hear the voice
of Leo Herman)* God damn it, Arn; that's the intro Murray
wrote for me two *years* ago, and it's still lovely, still warm. It's
the way the kids know me, the way I say "Hello, kids"; he's a
sweetie of a writer.

ARNOLD: That was *last* year he won the sweetie award, Leo.

LEO's VOICE: (*Laughs good-naturedly*) Please excuse my little
words. They slip out of my face once in a while. Arn, you got
my voice comin' out of that speaker-phone in your office, huh?
Comes out like the biggest phony you ever met, right? That's
how I sound, don't I? Big phony.

ARNOLD: No, Leo.

LEO's VOICE: I'm getting sick of myself. Hey, Arn, you figure
there's a good chance of Murray comin' back with me on the
show?

ARNOLD: Can't guarantee it, Leo; I've sent him to one other appointment today, fairly good offer . . .

LEO's VOICE: Well, I'm hopin' he comes back with *me*, Arn.
Funny bit you being the agent for your own brother—what
d'ya call that?

ARNOLD: It's called incest. (*The intercom buzzes; Arnold picks it
up*) O.K., send him in. (*Into the speaker-phone*) Got a call,
fellah; check back with you when Murray shows.

LEO's VOICE: Right, 'bye now.

(*Murray enters wearing a new suit and carrying a beautiful pineapple*)

MURRAY: Good afternoon, Mr. Burns.

ARNOLD: Good afternoon, Mr. Burns. Hey, you really did get a new suit, didn't you? How'd the appointment go with . . .

MURRAY: (*Putting the pineapple on the desk, gestures around at the office*) Arnold, every time I see you, the agency's put you on a higher floor. I swear, next time I come you'll be up in a balloon.

ARNOLD: Murray, the appointment . . .

MURRAY: Can't get over this office, Arnie. (*Goes to the window, looks out*) Twenty-second floor. You can see everything. (*Shocked by something he sees out of the window*) My God, I don't believe it: it's King Kong. He's sitting on top of the Time-Life Building. He . . . he seems to be crying. Poor gorilla bastard, they shoulda told him they don't make those buildings the way they used to . . .

ARNOLD: (*Raising his hand in the air*) *Hello*, Murray, hello there . . . here we are in my office. Welcome to Tuesday. Now, come *on*, how'd it go with Jimmy Sloan?

MURRAY: He took me to lunch at Steffanos, East Fifty-third. Christ, it's been a coupla years since I hustled around lunch-land. There is this crazy hum that I haven't heard for so long, Arnie; eight square yards of idea men, busily having ideas, eating away at their chef's salad like it's Crackerjacks and there's a prize at the bottom.

ARNOLD: And Sloan . . . ?

MURRAY: (*Sitting on the sofa*) Sloan lunches beautifully, can out-lunch anybody. He used to be a Yes-man but he got himself some guts and now he goes around bravely saying "maybe" to everybody. And a killer, this one, Arnie; notches on his attaché case. Told me this idea he had where I'd be a lovable eccentric on his panel show. This somehow led him very logically to his conception of God, who he says is "probably a really fun guy."

ARNOLD: What'd you tell him about the offer?

MURRAY: I told him good-bye. I don't think he noticed when I left; he focuses slightly to the right of you when he talks, just over your shoulder, so if you stay out of range he can't tell that you're gone. Probably thinks I'm still there.

ARNOLD: Murray, you told me this morning to get any job I could; Sloan's offer wasn't so bad . . .

MURRAY: Sloan is an idiot.

ARNOLD: (*Sitting next to him on the sofa; angrily, firmly*) Listen, cookie, I got *news* for you, right now you *need* idiots. You got a bad reputation for quitting jobs; I even had trouble grabbing Sloan for you. Why did you have to go and build your own personal blacklist; why couldn't you just be blacklisted as a Communist like everybody else?

MURRAY: Don't worry, Arnie; I figured I'd go back with Chuckles. He's ready to take me back, isn't he?

ARNOLD: Yeah, he's ready. I just spoke to him. (*Solemnly*) Hey, Murray, Leo says he came up to your place last January, a week after you quit him, to talk you into coming back with the show. And right in the middle you went into the kitchen and started singing "Yes, Sir, That's My Baby." Just left him standing there. Your way of saying "good-bye."

MURRAY: Well, that was five months ago, Arnie . . .

ARNOLD: (*Attempts to conceal his amusement, then turns to Murray, smiling*) So, what'd you do with him, just left him standing there? (*He laughs*) Like to have been there, seen that, must have been great.

MURRAY: Arnie, it was beautiful.

ARNOLD: (*Still laughing*) It's about time somebody left Leo Herman standing around talking to himself. (*Rubbing his head*) I wish to God I didn't enjoy you so much. Crap, I don't do you any good at all. (*Then, solemnly again*) Murray, no fun and games with Leo today, understand? He is absolutely *all* we got left before the hearing Thursday.

MURRAY: Yes, I understand.

ARNOLD: (*Goes to pick up the phone on the desk*) I wish we coulda got something better for you, kid, but there just wasn't any time.

MURRAY: Well, Chuckles won't be so bad for a while . . .

ARNOLD: No, Murray. (*Puts phone down firmly*) Not just for a while. You'll really have to stick with Chuckles. I had our agency lawyer check the facts for me. Most the Board'll give you is a probationary year with Nick; a trial period. The Board's investigators will be checking on you every week . . .

MURRAY: That's charming.

ARNOLD: . . . checking to see if you've still got the job, checking with Leo on your stability, checking up on the change in your home environment.

MURRAY: Sounds like a parole board.

ARNOLD: (*Into the intercom phone*) Margot; get me Leo Herman on the speaker-phone here, his home number. Thanks. (*Puts the phone down*) He's waiting for our call. Look, Murray, maybe he's not the greatest guy in the world; but y'know, he really *likes* you, Murray, he . . .

MURRAY: Yeah. I have a way with animals.

ARNOLD: (*Pointing at Murray*) That was your last joke for today. (*A click is heard from speaker-phone; Arnold turns it on*) You there, Leo?

LEO'S VOICE: Right, Arn. I'm down here in the basement, in my gymnasium: lot of echoing. Am I coming through, am I coming through O.K.?

ARNOLD: Clearly, Leo. Murray's here.

LEO'S VOICE: Murray! Murray the wonderful wild man; fellah, how are ya?

MURRAY: (*Takes his hat off, waves hello to the speaker-phone*) O.K., Leo, how're you doing?

LEO'S VOICE: Oh, you crazy bastard, it's damn good to hear that voice again. You're an old monkey, aren't ya?

MURRAY: You sound about the same too, Leo.

LEO'S VOICE: Not the same. I'm *more impossible* than I used to be. Can you imagine that?

MURRAY: Not easily, Leo; no.

LEO'S VOICE: Murray, I need you, fellah; I need you back with the show. Murr', we'll talk a while now, and then I'll come over to your place tonight, go over some idea for next week's shows. It'll be great, sweetie . . . Oh, there's that word again. "Sweetie." I said that word again. Oh, am I getting *sick* of myself. Big phony. The truth, fellah, I'm the biggest phony you ever met, right?

MURRAY: Probably, Leo.

LEO'S VOICE: (*After a pause; coldly*) Probably, he says. There he goes, there goes Murray the old joker, right? You're a jester, right? Some fooler. You can't fool with a scheduled show, Murray; a scheduled show with a tight budget. (*Softly, whispering*) Murray, come closer, tell you a secret . . . (*Murray comes closer to the box*) You're gonna hate me, Murray; I gotta tell you something and I know you're gonna hate me for it, but we can't have the same Murray we used to have on the

show. Who appreciates a good joke more than anybody? *Me.*
But who jokes too much? (*Suddenly louder*) *You!*

MURRAY: Leo, couldn't we talk about this tonight when we get
together . . .

LEO'S VOICE: (*Softly again*) It hurt me, Murr', it hurt me what
you used to do. When all those thousands of kids wrote in asking for the definition of a chipmunk and you sent back that
form letter sayin' a chipmunk was a . . . was a what?

MURRAY: A cute rat.

LEO'S VOICE: (*Still soft*) A cute rat; yeah. I remember my skin
broke out somethin' terrible. Some jester you are, foolin'
around at the script conferences, foolin' around at the studio.
Now, we're not gonna have any more of that, are we?

MURRAY: (*Subservient, apologetic*) No, we won't, I'm sorry,
Leo.

LEO'S VOICE: Because we can't fool with the innocence of children, can we? My God, they believe in the little Chipmunk,
don't ask me why; I'm nothing; God, I know that. I've been
damned lucky. A person like me should get a grand and a half
a week for doin' nothin'. I mean, I'm one of the big no-talents
of all time, right?

MURRAY: Right . . . I mean, no, Leo, no.

LEO'S VOICE: Oh, I know it's the truth and I don't kid myself
about it. But there'll be no more jokin'; right, Murr'? Because
I'll tell you the truth, I can't stand it.

MURRAY: Right, Leo.

LEO'S VOICE: (*Softly*) Good. Glad we cleared that up. Because
my skin breaks out somethin' terrible. (*Up again*) You're the
best, Murray, such talent, you know I love ya, don't ya? You
old monkey.

MURRAY: (*To Arnold*) Please, tell him we'll talk further tonight, too much of him all at once . . .

ARNOLD: Say, Leo, suppose we . . .

LEO'S VOICE: Murray, I want you to put some fifteen-minute fairy tales into the show. You've got your Hans Christian Andersen's there, your Grimm Brothers, your Goldilocks, your Sleepin' Beauties, your Gingerbread Men, your Foxy-Loxies, your legends, your folk tales . . . do I reach ya, Murr'?

MURRAY: (*Quietly*) Yeah, Leo . . .

LEO'S VOICE: Now, what I want in those scripts is this, Murray, I want you to give 'em five minutes a action, five minutes a poignancy and than five minutes of the moral message; race-relations thing; world-peace thing; understanding-brings-love thing. I don't know. Shake 'em up a little. Controversy. Angry letters from parents. Kid's show with something to say, get some excitement in the industry, wild . . .

MURRAY: (*He leans over very close to speaker-phone; whispers into it*) Hey, Leo, I might show up one day with eleven minutes of poignancy, no action and a twelve-second moral message . . .

ARNOLD: Murray, stop it . . .

MURRAY: (*Shouting into the speaker-phone*) And then where would we be?
    (*There is a pause. No sound comes from the speaker-phone. Then:*)

LEO'S VOICE: See how he mocks me? Well, I guess there's plenty to mock. Plenty mocking. Sometimes I try to take a cold look at what I am. (*Very soft*) Sweaty Leo jumping around in a funny costume trying to make a buck out of being a chipmunk. The Abominable Snowman in a cute suit. But I'll tell you something, Murray . . . sit down for a minute. (*Murray is standing; Leo's voice is still fairly pleasant*) Are ya sitting down, Murray? (*Murray remains standing; Leo's voice is suddenly loud, sharp, commanding*) Murray, sit down! (*Murray sits down*) Good. Now I'm gonna tell you a story . . .

MURRAY: (*Softly, painfully*) Arnold, he's gonna do it again . . . the story . . .

LEO'S VOICE: Murray . . .

MURRAY: (*Softly, miserably*) The story I got tattooed to my skull . . .

LEO'S VOICE: On June the third . . .

MURRAY: (*Hunching over in his chair, looking down at the floor*) Story number twelve . . . the "Laughter of Children" story . . . again . . .

LEO'S VOICE: I will be forty-two years old . . .

MURRAY: (*To Arnold; painfully, pleading*) Arnie . . .

LEO'S VOICE: And maybe it's the silliest, phoniest, cop-out thing . . .

LEO'S VOICE and MURRAY: (*In unison*) . . . you ever heard, but the Chipmunk, Chuckles, the little guy I pretend to be, is real to me . . .

LEO'S VOICE: . . . as real to me as . . . as this phone in my hand; those children, don't ask me why, God I don't know, but they believe in that little fellah . . . (*Murray looks up from the floor now and over at the speaker-phone, which is on the other side of the room; his eyes are fixed on it*) Look, Murr', I do what I can for the cash-monies; but also, and I say it without embarrassment, I just love kids, the laughter of children, and we can't have you foolin' with that, Murr', can't have you jokin' . . . (*Murray stands up, still looking at the speaker-phone*) because it's this whole, bright, wild sorta child kinda thing . . . (*Murray is walking slowly toward the speaker-*

phone now; Arnold, watching Murray, starts to rise from his chair) it's this very up feeling, it's all young, and you can't joke with it; the laughter of children; those warm waves, that fresh, open, spontaneous laughter, you can feel it on your face . . .

MURRAY: (*Picking the speaker-phone up off the desk*) Like a sunburn . . .

LEO's VOICE: Like a sunburn . . .

ARNOLD: (*Coming toward Murray as if to stop him*) Murray . . . wait . . .

LEO's VOICE: And it's a pride thing . . . (*Murray turns with the speaker-phone held in his hands and drops it into the wastepaper basket next to the desk. He does this calmly. Arnold, too late to stop him, stands watching, dumbly paralyzed. Leo, unaware, goes right on talking, his voice somewhat garbled and echoing from the bottom of the wastepaper basket*) . . . so then how lovely, how enchanting it is, that I should be paid so well for something I love so much . . . (*Pause*) Say, there's this noise . . . there's this . . . I'm getting this crackling noise on my end here. . . . What's happened to the phone?

ARNOLD: (*Sadly, solemnly; looking down into the basket*) Leo, you're in a wastepaper basket.

LEO's VOICE: That you, Murray? . . . There's this crackling noise. . . . I can't hear you. . . . Hello? . . . What's going on? . . .

ARNOLD: Leo, hold it just a minute, I'll get you.

LEO's VOICE: There's this funny noise. . . . Where'd everybody go? Where is everybody? . . . Hello, Murray . . . hello . . . come back . . . come back . . .

ARNOLD: (*Fishing amongst the papers in basket for the speaker-phone*) I'll find you, Leo, I'll find you. . . . (*Finally lifts the speaker out of the basket, holds it gently, tenderly in his hands like a child, speaks soothingly to it)* Look, Leo . . . Leo, we had a little . . . some trouble with the phone, we . . . (*Realizes that he is getting no reaction from the box*) Leo? . . . Leo? . . . (*As though the box were a friend whom he thinks might have died, shaking the box tenderly to revive it*) Leo . . . Leo, are you there? . . . Are you there? . . . It's dead. (*Turning to look at Murray, as though announcing the demise of a dear one*) He's gone.

MURRAY: Well, don't look at me like that, Arnie; I didn't *kill* him. He doesn't *live* in that box. . . . Or maybe he does.

ARNOLD: A man has a job for you so you drop him in a basket.

MURRAY: Arnie, I quit that nonsense five months ago . . .

ARNOLD: Murray, you're a *nut*, a man has a job for you, there's a hearing on Thursday . . .

MURRAY: A fool in a box telling me what's funny, a Welfare Board checking my underwear every week because I don't look good in their files . . . and *I'm* the nut, right? *I'm* the crazy one.

ARNOLD: Murray, you float like a balloon and everybody's waitin' for ya with a pin. I'm trying to put you in *touch*, Murray . . . with *real things;* with . . .

MURRAY: (*Angrily, taking in the office with a sweep of his hand*) You mean like this office, *real* things, like this office? The world could come to an end and you'd find out about it on the phone. (*Pointing at two framed photographs on Arnold's desk*) Pictures of your wife six years ago when she was still a piece, and your kids at their cutest four years ago when they looked best for the office. . . . Oh, you're in *touch* all right, Arnie.

ARNOLD: (*Softly, soothing*) Murray, you're just a little excited, that's all, just relax, everything's gonna be fine . . .

MURRAY: (*Shouting*) Damn it . . . get angry; I just insulted you, personally, about your wife, your kids; I just said lousy things to you. Raise your voice, at least your eyebrows . . . (*Pleading painfully*) Please, have an argument with me . . .

ARNOLD: (*Coaxing*) We'll call Leo back, we'll apologize to him . . . (*Murray goes to the end table, picks up an apple from the bowl of fruit*) Everything's gonna be just fine, Murray, you'll see . . . just fine.

MURRAY: Arnie?

ARNOLD: Huh?

MURRAY: Catch.
(*Tosses the apple underhand across the room. Arnold catches it. Murray exits*)

ARNOLD: (*His hand out from catching the apple*) Aw, Murray . . . (*Lowers his hand to his side; speaks quietly, alone now in the office*) Murray, I swear to you, King Kong is *not* on top of the Time-Life Building . . .
(*Arnold discovers the apple in his hand; bites into it. The lights fade quickly. As they dim, we hear Nick humming and whistling "Yes, Sir, That's My Baby." The lights go up on Murray's apartment. Nick's humming and whistling fades back so that it is coming from outside the window; the humming grows louder again after a second or two as, it would seem, he descends the fire-escape ladder from Mrs. Myers' apartment. It is early evening. No one is onstage. The apartment has been rather spectacularly rehabilitated by Sandra since we saw it last. The great clutter of Murray's nonsense collection, clocks, radios, knickknacks, has been cleared away, the books have been neatly arranged in the bookcases, a hat rack has been placed above the bureau and Murray's hats are placed neatly on it. There are bright new bedspreads on the two beds and brightly colored throw*

*pillows, one new curtain is already up at the windows and
a piece of matching material is over the Morris chair. The
beach chair and swivel chair are gone and the wicker chair
has been painted gold, the table has a bright new cloth
over it. Pots of flowers are on the table, the bookshelves,
the file cabinets, headboard and desk; and geraniums are in
a holder hanging from the window molding. The whole
place has been dusted and polished and gives off a bright
glow. After two lines or so of the song, Nick enters through
the window from the fire escape, carrying his pajamas and
school books. Nick sees the new curtain first, and then,
from his position on the window seat, sees the other changes
in the apartment and smiles appreciatively. Sandra enters
from the kitchen, carrying a mixing bowl and a spoon. She
smiles, glad to see Nick)*

SANDRA: Hello, Nick . . .

NICK: Hello, lady. I came in from the fire escape. Mrs. Myers
lives right upstairs. I went there after school, I . . . (*Indicating
her work on the apartment*) Did . . . did you do all this?

SANDRA: Yes, Nick; do you like it?

NICK: (*Goes to her, smiling*) I think it's superb. I mean, imagine
my surprise when I saw it. (*Pause*) Where's Murray?

SANDRA: (*Happily telling him the good news*) Nick . . . Murray
went downtown to see your Uncle Arnold. He's going to get a
job.

NICK: That's terrific. Hey, that's just terrific. (*Sandra goes to the
folded new curtains on the bed, sits down on the bed, unfolds
one of the curtains, begins attaching curtain hooks and rings
to it; Nick sits next to her, helping her as they talk together*)
See, lady, he was developing into a bum. You don't want to
see somebody you like developing into a bum, and doing nutty

things, right? You know what he does? He hollers. Like we were on Park Avenue last Sunday, it's early in the morning and nobody is in the street, see, there's just all those big quiet apartment houses; and he hollers "Rich people, I want to see you all out on the street for volley ball! Let's snap it up!" And sometimes, if we're in a crowded elevator some place, he turns to me and yells "Max, there'll be no *more* of this self-pity! You're forty, it's time you got *used* to being a midget!" And everybody stares. And he has a wonderful time. What do you do with somebody who hollers like that? Last week in Macy's he did that. (*He laughs*) If you want to know the truth, it was pretty funny. (*Sandra smiles*) I think you're a very nice lady.

SANDRA: Thank you, Nick.

NICK: What do you think of me?

SANDRA: I think you're very nice also.

NICK: A very nice quality you have is that you are a good listener, which is important to me because of how much I talk. (*She laughs, enjoying him*) Hey, you're some laugher, aren't you, lady?

SANDRA: I guess so, Nick.

NICK: (*Trying to make her feel at home*) Would you like some fruit? An orange maybe?

SANDRA: No thank you, Nick.

NICK: If you want to call your mother or something, I mean, feel free to use the telephone . . . or my desk if you want to read a book or something . . . or *any* of the chairs . . .

SANDRA: I will, Nick, thank you.

NICK: O.K. (*Pause*) Are you going to be staying around here for a while?

SANDRA: I might, yes.

NICK: (*He rises, picks up the pajamas and books he brought in with him; indicates apartment*) Has . . . has Murray seen . . . all this?

SANDRA: No, not yet.

NICK: (*Nods*) Not yet. Well . . . (*Goes to the window, steps up on window seat*) Good luck, lady.
(*He exits through the window, carrying his pajamas and school books, goes back up the fire escape. Sandra crosses to window seat, smiling to herself. Murray enters, unnoticed by her*)

MURRAY: (*Standing still at the front door, glancing around at the apartment; to himself*) Oh God, I've been attacked by the *Ladies Home Journal.*
(*Sandra hears him, goes to him happily*)

SANDRA: Murray, what a nice suit you bought. How is everything, which job did . . .

MURRAY: (*Looking around at her work on the apartment*) Hey, look at this. You've started to get rid of the Edgar Allan Poe atmosphere.

SANDRA: Don't you like it?

MURRAY: (*Looking around, noticing his knickknacks are missing*) Sure. Sure. Lotta work. Place has an unusual quality now. Kind of Fun Gothic.

SANDRA: Well, of course I'm really not done yet, the curtains aren't all up, and this chair won't look so bad if we reupholster . . . Come on, Murray, don't keep me in suspense, which one of the jobs did you . . .

MURRAY: (*Takes her arm, smiles, seats her on the chair in front of him*) I shall now leave you breathless with the strange and wondrous tale of this sturdy lad's adventures today in down-town Oz. (*She is cheered by his manner and ready to listen*) Picture, if you will, me. I am walking on East Fifty-first Street an hour ago and I decided to construct and develop a really decorative, general-all-purpose apology. Not complicated, just the words "I am sorry," said with a little style.

SANDRA: Sorry for what?

MURRAY: Anything. For being late, early, stupid, asleep, silly, alive . . . (*He moves about now, acting out the scene on the street for her*) Well, y'know when you're walking down the street talking to yourself how sometimes you suddenly say a coupla words out loud? So I said, "I'm sorry," and this fella, complete stranger, he looks up a second and says, "That's all right, Mac," and goes right on. (*Murray and Sandra laugh*) He automatically forgave me. I communicated. Five-o'clock rush-hour in midtown you could say, "Sir, I believe your hair is on fire," and they wouldn't hear you. So I decided to test the whole thing out scientifically, I stayed right there on the corner of Fifty-first and Lex for a while, just saying "I'm sorry" to everybody that went by. (*Abjectly*) "Oh, I'm so sorry, sir . . ." (*Slowly, quaveringly*) I'm terribly sorry, madam . . ." (*Warmly*) Say there, miss, I'm sorry." Of course, some people just gave me a funny look, but Sandy, I swear, seventy-five percent of them *forgave* me. (*Acting out the people for her*) "Forget it, buddy" . . . "That's O.K., really." Two ladies for-gave me in unison, one fella forgave me from a passing car, and one guy forgave me for his dog. "Poofer forgives the nice man, don't you, Poofer?" Oh, Sandy, it was fabulous. I had tapped some vast reservoir. Something had happened to all of them for which they felt *some*body should apologize. If you went up to people on the street and offered them money, they'd refuse it. But everybody accepts apology immediately. It is the most negotiable currency. I said to them, "I am sorry." And they were all so generous, so kind. You could give 'em love and it wouldn't be accepted half as graciously, as unquestioningly . . .

SANDRA: (*Suspiciously, her amusement fading*) That's certainly
. . . that's very interesting, Murray.

MURRAY: Sandy, I could run up on the roof right now and
holler, "I am sorry," and half a million people would holler
right back, "That's O.K., just see that you don't do it again!"

SANDRA: (*After a pause*) Murray, you didn't take any of the
jobs.

MURRAY: (*Quietly*) Sandy, I took whatever I am and put a suit
on it and gave it a haircut and took it outside and that's what
happened. I know what I said this morning, what I promised,
and Sandra, I'm sorry, I'm very sorry. (*She just sits there before
him and stares at him expressionlessly*) Damn it, lady,
that was a beautiful apology. You gotta love a guy who can
apologize so nice. I rehearsed for over an hour. (*She just looks
at him*) That's the most you should expect from life, Sandy, a
really good apology for all the things you won't get.

SANDRA: Murray, I don't understand. What happens to Nick?
What about the Welfare Board?

MURRAY: (*He takes her hand*) Sandra . . .

SANDRA: I mean, if you don't like the jobs your brother found for
you, then take *any* job . . .

MURRAY: (*He takes both of her hands and kneels next to her
chair*) Oh, Sandy . . . (*Softly, pleading for her to understand*)
Nick, he's a wonderful kid, but he's brought the God-damned
world in on me. Don't you understand, Sandy, they'd be
checking up on me every week; being judged by people I
don't know and who don't know me, a committee of ghosts;
gimme a month of that and I'd turn into an ash tray, a bowl of

corn flakes, I wouldn't know me on the street. . . . (*Looks under chair*) Have you seen Murray? He was here just a minute ago. . . . (*Looks at her, smiles*) Hey, have you see Murray? (*Pleading for her to understand*) I wouldn't be of any use to Nick or you or anybody . . .

(*Sandra moves away from him, goes to the window seat, leaves him kneeling at the chair. She is still holding the curtain she had been working on*)

SANDRA: (*Quietly*) I've had no effect on you at all. I've made no difference. You have no idea what it feels like to have no effect on people. I am not a leader. I scored very low in leadership in three different vocational aptitude tests. When I point my finger, people go the other way . . .

(*Absently, she begins to fold the curtain neatly in her lap*)

MURRAY: Sandra . . .

SANDRA: In grad school they put me in charge of the Structured-Childs-Play-Analysis session one day . . . (*She shrugs*) and all the children fell asleep. I am not a leader.

MURRAY: (*Going to her at the window seat; warmly, with love*) Oh, Sandy, you are a cute, jolly lady . . . please understand.

SANDRA: When you left this morning, I was so sure . . .

MURRAY: This morning . . . (*He sits next to her on the window seat, his arm around her, his free hand gesturing expansively, romantically*) Oh, Sandy, I saw the most beautiful sailing this morning . . . The *Sklardahl*, Swedish liner, bound for Europe. It's a great thing to do when you're about to start something new; you see a boat off. It's always wonderful; there's a sailing practically every day this time of year. Sandy, you go down and stand at the dock with all the well-wishers and throw confetti and make a racket with them. . . . Hey, bon voyage, Charley, have a wonderful time. . . . It gives you a genuine

feeling of the beginning of things. . . . There's another one
Friday, big French ship, two stacker . . .

(*Sandra has been watching him coldly during this speech;
she speaks quietly; catching him in mid-air*)

SANDRA: Nick will have to go away now, Murray. (*She looks
away from him*) I bought new bedspreads at Altman's, I
haven't spoken to my mother in two days, and you went to see
a boat off. (*She pauses; then smiles to herself for a moment*)
My goodness; I'm a listmaker. (*She leaves him alone in the
window seat*) I have to have enough sense to leave you, Murray. I can see why Nick liked it here. I would like it here too if
I was twelve years old.

(*She puts the folded curtain down on a chair, picks up her
jacket*)

MURRAY: (*Coming toward her, warmly*) Come on, stick with
me, Dr. Markowitz, anything can happen above an abandoned
Chinese restaurant. . . .

SANDRA: (*Looking directly at him; quietly*) Maybe you're won-
derfully independent, Murray, or maybe, maybe you're the
most extraordinarily selfish person I've ever met.

(*She picks up her hand bag and starts toward the door*)

MURRAY: (*Tired of begging; angrily, as she walks toward the
door*) What're you gonna do now, go back and live in a
closet? It's really gonna be quite thrilling, you and Albert,
guarding the Lincoln Tunnel together.

SANDRA: (*Turning at the door to look at him*) I think, Murray,
that you live in a much, much larger closet than I do.

MURRAY: (*Painfully*) Lady, lady, please don't look at me like
that . . .

SANDRA: (*Looking about the apartment; very quietly*) Oh, there are so many really attractive things you can do with a one-room apartment if you're willing to use your imagination. (*Opens the door*) Good-bye, Murray.

(*She exits. Murray stands still for a moment; then rushes forward to the closed door, angrily*)

MURRAY: (*Shouting*) Hey, damn it, you forgot your files! (*Picks up her files from the bureau, opens the door; but she is gone*) The management is not responsible for personal property! (*Closes the door, puts the files back on the bureau; stands at the door, looking around at the apartment*) And what the hell did you do to my apartment? Where are my clocks? What'd you do with my stuff? Where's my radios? (*His back to the audience, shouting*) What've we got here; God damn Sunnybrook Farm?! What happened to my place? (*Suddenly realizing he is still wearing a new suit, he pulls off his suit jacket, rolls it up into a tight ball, and throws it violently across the room. A moment; then he relaxes, walks casually to the window, puts his favorite hat on, sits, leans back comfortably in the window seat and smiles. He talks out of the window in a loud mock-serious voice*) Campers . . . the entertainment committee was quite disappointed by the really poor turn-out at this morning's community sing. I mean, where's all that old Camp Chickawattamee spirit? Now, I'd like to say that I . . . (*He hesitates; he can't think of anything to say. A pause; then he haltingly tries again*) I'd like to say right now that I . . . that . . . that I . . . (*His voice is soft, vague; he pulls his knees up, folds his arms around them, his head bent on his knees; quietly*) Campers, I can't think of anything to say . . .

(*A moment; then*)

Curtain

ACT THREE

In the darkness, before the curtain goes up, we hear an old recording of a marching band playing "Stars and Stripes Forever." This goes on rather loudly for a few moments. The music diminishes somewhat as the curtain goes up; and we see that the music is coming from an old phonograph on the wicker chair near the bed. It's about thirty minutes later and, though much of Sandra's work on the apartment is still apparent, it is obvious that Murray has been busy putting his place back into its old shape. The curtains are gone, as is the tablecloth and the material on the Morris chair. All the flower pots have been put on top of the file cabinet. The swivel chair and the beach chair are back in view. Cluttered about the room again is much of Murray's nonsense collection, clocks, radios, knickknacks and stacks of magazines.

As the curtain goes up, Murray has just retrieved a stack of magazines, the megaphone and the pirate pistol from the closet where Sandra had put them; and we see him now placing them back around the room carefully, as though they were part of some strict design. Arnold enters, carrying his attaché case; walks to the beach chair, sits, takes his hat off. The two men do not look at each other. The music continues to play.

ARNOLD: (*After a moment*) I didn't even bring a tangerine with me. That's very courageous if you think about it for a minute. (*Looks over at Murray, who is not facing him, points at record player*) You wanna turn that music off, please? (*No reply from Murray*) Murray, the music; I'm trying to . . . (*No reply from Murray, so Arnold puts his attaché case and hat on table, goes quickly to the record player and turns the music off; Murray turns to look at Arnold*) O.K., I'm a little slow. It takes me an hour to get insulted. Now I'm insulted. You walked out of my office. That wasn't a nice thing to do to me, Murray . . . (*Murray does not reply*) You came into my office like George God; everybody's supposed to come up and audition for Human Being in front of you. (*Comes over closer to him, takes his arm*) Aw, Murray, today, one day, leave the dragons alone, will ya? And look at the dragons you pick on; Sloan, Leo, me; silly old arthritic dragons, step on a toe and we'll start to cry. Murray, I called Leo back, I apologized, told him my phone broke down; I got him to come over here tonight. He's anxious to see you, everything's O.K. . . .

MURRAY: Hey, you just never give up, do you, Arnie?

ARNOLD: Listen to me, Murray, do I ever tell you what to do . . .

MURRAY: Yes, all the time.

ARNOLD: If you love this kid, then you gotta take any kinda stupid job to keep him . . .

MURRAY: Now you're an expert on love.

ARNOLD: Not an expert, but I sure as hell value my amateur standing. Murray, about him leaving, have you told him yet?

MURRAY: (*Softly; realizing Arnold's genuine concern*) Arnie, don't worry, I know how to handle it. I've got a coupla days to tell him. And don't underrate Nick, he's gonna understand this a lot better than you think.

ARNOLD: Murray, I finally figured out your problem. There's only one thing that really bothers you . . . (*With a sweep of his hand*) Other people. (*With a mock-secretive tone*) If it wasn't for them other people, everything would be great, huh, Murray? I mean, you think everything's fine, and then you go out into the street . . . and there they all *are* again, right? The Other People; taking up space, bumping into you, asking for things, making lines to wait on, taking cabs away from ya . . . The Enemy . . . Well, *watch* out, Murray, they're *every*where . . .

MURRAY: Go ahead, Arnie, give me advice, at thirty thousand a year you can afford it.

ARNOLD: Oh, I get it, if I'm so smart why ain't I poor? You better get a damn good act of your own before you start giving *mine* the razzberry. What's this game you play gonna be like ten years from now, without youth? Murray, Murray, I can't *watch* this, you gotta *shape* up . . .

MURRAY: (*Turning quickly to face Arnold; in a surprised tone*) Shape *up?* (*Looks directly at Arnold; speaks slowly*) Arnie, what the hell happened to you? You got so old. I don't know you any more. When you quit "Harry the Fur King" on Thirty-eighth Street, remember?

ARNOLD: That's twenty years ago, Murray.

MURRAY: You told me you were going to be in twenty businesses in twenty years if you had to, till you found out what you wanted. Things were always going to change. Harry said you were not behaving maturely enough for a salesman; your clothes didn't match or something . . . (*Laughs in affectionate memory of the event*) So the next day, you dressed perfectly, homburg, gray suit, cuff links, carrying a briefcase and a rolled umbrella . . . and you came into Harry's office on roller skates. You weren't going to take crap from *any*body. So that's the business you finally picked . . . taking crap from *every*body.

ARNOLD: I don't do practical jokes any more, if that's what you mean . . .

MURRAY: (*Grabs both of Arnold's arms tensely*) Practical, that's right; a way to stay alive. If most things aren't funny, Arn, then they're only exactly what they are; then it's one long dental appointment interrupted occasionally by something exciting, like waiting or falling asleep. What's the point if I leave everything exactly the way I find it? Then I'm just adding to the noise, then I'm just taking up some more room on the subway.

ARNOLD: Murray, the Welfare Board has these specifications; all you have to do is meet a couple specifications . . .

(*Murray releases his grip on Arnold's arms; Murray's hands drop to his sides*)

MURRAY: Oh, Arnie, you don't understand any more. You got that wide stare that people stick in their eyes so nobody'll know their head's asleep. You got to be a shuffler, a moaner. You want me to come sit and eat fruit with you and watch the clock run out. You start to drag and stumble with the rotten weight of all the people who should have been told off, all the things you should have said, all the specifications that aren't yours. The only thing you got left to reject is your food in a restaurant if they do it wrong and you can send it back and make a big fuss with the waiter. . . . (*Murray turns away from Arnold, goes to the window seat, sits down*) Arnold, five months ago I forgot what *day* it was. I'm on the subway on my way to work and I didn't know what day it was and it scared the hell out of me. . . . (*Quietly*) I was sitting in the express looking out the window same as every morning watching the local stops go by in the dark with an empty head and my arms folded, not feeling great and not feeling rotten, just not feeling, and for a minute I couldn't remember, I didn't know, unless I really concentrated, whether it was a Tuesday or a Thursday . . . or a . . . for a minute it could have been *any* day, Arnie . . . sitting in the train going through any day . . . in the dark through any year. . . . Arnie, it scared the hell out of me. (*Stands up*) You got to know what day it is. You got to know what's the name of the game and what the rules are with nobody else telling you. You have to own your days and name them, each one of them, every one of them, or else the years go right by and none of them belong to you. (*Turns to look at Arnold*) And that ain't just for weekends, kiddo . . . (*Looks at Arnold a moment longer, then speaks in a pleasant tone*) Here it is, the day after Irving R. Feldman's birthday, for God's sake . . . (*Takes a hat, puts it on*) And I never even congratulated him . . .

(*Starts to walk briskly toward the front door. Arnold shouts in a voice stronger than we have ever heard from him*)

ARNOLD: Murray!

(*Murray stops, turns, startled to hear this loud a voice from Arnold. Arnold looks fiercely at Murray for a moment, then Arnold too looks surprised, starts to laugh*)

MURRAY: What's so funny?

ARNOLD: Wow, I scared myself. You hear that voice? Look at that, I got you to stop, I got your complete, full attention, the floor is mine now . . . (*Chuckles awkwardly*) And I can't think of a God-damned thing to say . . . (*Shrugs his shoulders; picks up his hat from the table*) I have long been aware, Murray . . . I have long been aware that you don't respect me much. . . . I suppose there are a lot of brothers who don't get along. . . . But in reference . . . to us, considering the factors . . . (*Smiles, embarrassed*) Sounds like a contract, doesn't it? (*Picks up his briefcase, comes over to Murray*) Unfortunately for you, Murray, you want to be a hero. Maybe if a fella falls into a lake, you can jump in and save him; there's still that kind of stuff. But who gets opportunities like that in midtown Manhattan, with all that traffic. (*Puts on his hat*) I am willing to deal with the available world and I do not choose to shake it up but to live with it. There's the people who spill things, and the people who get spilled on; I do not choose to notice the stains, Murray. I have a wife and I have children, and business, like they say, is business. I am not an exceptional man, so it is possible for me to stay with things the way they are. I'm lucky. I'm gifted. I have a talent for surrender. I'm at peace. But you are cursed; and I like you so it makes me sad, you don't have the gift; and I see the torture of it. All I can do is worry for you. But I will not worry for myself; you cannot convince me that I am one of the Bad Guys. I get up, I go, I lie a little, I peddle a little, I watch the rules, I talk the talk. We fellas have those offices high up there so we can catch the wind and go with it, however it blows. But, and I will not apologize for it, I take pride; I am the best possible Arnold Burns. (*Pause*) Well . . . give my regards to Irving R. Feldman, will ya?

(*He starts to leave*)

MURRAY: (*Going toward him*) Arnold . . .

ARNOLD: Please, Murray . . . (*Puts his hand up*) Allow me once to leave a room before you do.
(*Arnold snaps on record player as he walks past it to the front door; he exits. Murray goes toward the closed door, the record player has warmed up and we suddenly hear "Stars and Stripes Forever" blaring loudly from the machine again; Murray turns at this sound and stands for a long moment looking at the record player as the music comes from it. Nick enters through the window from the fire escape, unnoticed by Murray. Nicks looks about, sees that the apartment is not quite what it was an hour before*)

NICK: Hey, Murray . . .

MURRAY: (*Turns, sees Nick*) Nick . . .
(*Turns the record player off; puts the record on the bed*)

NICK: Hey, where's the lady?

MURRAY: Well, she's not here right now . . .

NICK: (*Stepping forward to make an announcement*) Murray, I have decided that since *you* are getting a job today then I made up my mind it is time for *me* also to finish a certain matter which I have been putting off.

MURRAY: Nick, listen, turned out the only job I could get in a hurry was with Chuckles . . .

NICK: (*Nodding in approval*) Chuckles, huh? Well, fine. (*Then, grimly*) Just as long as I don't have to watch that terrible program every morning. (*Returning to his announcement*) For many months now I have been concerned with a decision, Murray . . . Murray, you're not listening.

MURRAY: (*Distracted*) Sure I'm listening, yeah . . .

NICK: The past couple months I have been thinking about different names and considering different names because in four weeks I'm gonna be thirteen and I gotta pick my permanent name, like we said.

MURRAY: Why don't you just go on calling yourself Nick? You've been using it the longest.

NICK: Nick is a name for a short person. And since I am a short person I do not believe I should put a lot of attention on it.

MURRAY: Whaddya mean, where'd you get the idea you were short?

NICK: From people who are taller than I am.

MURRAY: That's ridiculous.

NICK: Sure, standing up there it's ridiculous, but from down here where I am it's not so ridiculous. And half the girls in my class are taller than me. Especially Susan Bookwalter.
  (*Nick sits dejectedly in the swivel chair*)

MURRAY: (*Crouching over next to him*) Nick, you happen to be a nice medium height for your age.

NICK: (*Pointing at Murray*) Yeah, so how is it everybody crouches over a little when I'm around?

MURRAY: (*Straightening up*) Because you're a kid. (*Sits next to him*) Listen, you come from a fairly tall family. Next couple years you're gonna grow like crazy. Really, Nick, every day you're getting bigger.

NICK: So is Susan Bookwalter. (*Stands*) So for a couple of months I considered various tall names. Last month I considered, for a while, Zachery, but I figured there was a chance Zachery could turn into a short, fat, bald name. Then I thought about Richard, which is not really tall, just very thin with glasses. Then last week I finally, really, decided and I took out a new library card to see how it looks and today I figured I would make it definite and official.

(*He takes a library card out of his pocket, hands it to Murray*)

MURRAY: (*Looks at the card, confused*) This is *my* library card.

NICK: No, that's the whole thing; it's mine.

MURRAY: But it says "*Murray* Burns" on it . . .

NICK: Right, that's the name I picked. So I took out a new card to see how it looks and make it official.

MURRAY: (*Looks at the card, is moved and upset by it, but covers with cool dignity; stands, speaks very formally*) Well, Nick, I'm flattered . . . I want you to know that I'm . . . very flattered by this. (*Nick goes to the alcove to put his school books and pajamas away*) Well, why the hell did you . . . I mean, damn it, Nick, that's too many Murrays, very confusing . . . (*Murray begins to shift the card awkwardly from one hand to the other, speaks haltingly*) Look, why don't you call yourself George, huh? Very strong name there, George . . .

NICK: (*Shaking his head firmly*) No. We made a deal it was up to me to pick which name and that's the name I decided on; "Murray."

MURRAY: Well, what about Jack? What the hell's wrong with Jack? Jack Burns . . . sounds like a promising heavyweight.

NICK: I like the name I picked better.

MURRAY: (*Very quietly*) Or Martin . . . or Robert . . .

NICK: Those names are all square.

LEO's VOICE: (*From behind the door, shouting*) Is this it? Is this the Lion's Den, here? Hey, Murr'!

MURRAY: (*Softly*) Ah, I hear the voice of a chipmunk.

NICK: (*Going into the bathroom*) I better go put on a tie.

MURRAY: (*Goes to the door; stands there a moment, looks over to the other side of the room at Nick, who is offstage in the bathroom; smiles, speaks half to himself, very softly*) You coulda called yourself Charlie. Charlie is a very musical name.
(*Then, he opens the door. Leo Herman enters. He wears a camel's-hair coat and hat. The coat, like his suit, is a little too big for him. He is carrying a paper bag and a large Chuckles statue—a life-size cardboard cutout of himself in his character of Chuckles the Chipmunk; the statue wears a blindingly ingratiating smile*)

LEO: (*With great enthusiasm*) Murray, there he is! There's the old monkey! There's the old joker, right?

MURRAY: (*Quietly, smiling politely*) Yeah, Leo, here he is. (*Shakes Leo's hand*) It's . . . it's very nice to see you again, Leo, after all this time.

LEO: (*Turning to see Nick, who has come out of the bathroom wearing his tie*) There he is! There's the little guy! (*Goes to Nick carrying the statue and the paper bag*) Looka here, little guy . . . (*Setting the statue up against the wall next to the window*) I gotta Chuckles statue for you.

NICK: (*With his best company manners*) Thank you, Mr. Herman; imagine how pleased I am to receive it. It's a very artistic statue and very good cardboard too.

LEO: (*Taking a Chuckles hat from the paper bag; a replica of the furry, big-eared hat worn by the statue*) And I gotta Chuckles hat for you too, just like the old Chipmunk wears.
(*He puts the hat on Nick's head*)

NICK: Thank you.

LEO: (*Crouching over to Nick's height*) Now that you've got the Chuckles hat, you've got to say the Chuckles-hello.

NICK: (*Confused, but anxious to please*) The what?

LEO: (*Prompting him*) "Chip-chip, Chippermunkie!"
(*He salutes*)

NICK: Oh, yeah . . . "Chip-chip, Chippermunkie!"
(*He salutes too*)

LEO: May I know your name?

NICK: It's Nick, most of the time.

LEO: Most of the . . . (*Pulling two bags of potato chips from his overcoat pockets*) Say, look what I've got, two big bags of Chuckle-Chip potato chips! How'd ya like to put these crispy chips in some bowls or somethin' for us, huh? (*Nick takes the two bags, goes to the kitchen*) And take your time, Nick, your uncle 'n' me have some grown-up talkin' to do. (*After Nick exits into the kitchen*) The kid hates me. I can tell. Didn't go over very well with him, pushed a little too hard. He's a nice kid, Murray.

MURRAY: How are *your* kids, Leo?

LEO: Fine, fine. But, Murray, I swear, even *they* don't like my show since you stopped writing it. My youngest one . . . my six-year-old . . .

(*He can't quite remember*)

MURRAY: Ralphie.

LEO: Ralphie; he's been watching the Funny Bunny Show now every morning instead of me. (*Begins pacing up and down*) Oh *boy*, have I been bombing out on the show. Murray, do you know what it *feels* like to bomb out in front of children? You flop out in front of kids and, Murray, I swear to God, they're ready to *kill* you. (*Stops pacing*) Or else, they just stare at you, that's the worst, that hurt, innocent stare like you just killed their pup or raped their turtle or something. (*Goes over to Murray*) Murray, to have you back with me on the show, to see you at the studio again tomorrow, it's gonna be *beautiful*. You're the *best*.

MURRAY: I appreciate your feeling that way, Leo.

LEO: This afternoon, Murray, on the phone, you hung up on me, didn't you?

MURRAY: I'm sorry Leo, I was just kidding . . . I hope you . . .

LEO: (*Sadly*) Murray, why do you do that to me? Aw, don't tell me, I know, I make people nervous. Who can listen to me for ten minutes? (*Begins pacing up and down again, strokes his tie*) See *that?* See how I keep touching my suit and my tie? I keep touching myself to make sure I'm still there. Murray, I get this feeling, maybe I vanished when I wasn't looking.

MURRAY: Oh, I'm sure that you're here, Leo.

LEO: (*Pointing at Murray*) See how he talks to me? A little nasty. (*Smiles suddenly*) Well, I like it. It's straight and it's real and I like it. You know what I got around me on the show? Finks, dwarfs, phonies and frogs. No Murrays. The show: boring, boredom, bore . . . (*Cups his hands around his mouth and shouts*) boring, boring . . .

(*During these last few words, Sandra has entered through the partly open door. Murray turns, sees her.*)

SANDRA: (*Staying near the doorway; reserved, official*) Murray, I believe that I left my files here; I came to get my files; may I have my files, please. I . . . (*She sees Leo, comes a few feet into the room*) Oh, excuse me . . .

MURRAY: (*Cordially, introducing them*) Chuckles the Chipmunk . . . this is Minnie Mouse.

LEO: (*Absently*) Hi, Minnie . . .

SANDRA: (*Looking from one to the other, taking in the situation, smiles; to Leo*) You must be . . . you must be Mr. Herman.

LEO: (*Mumbling to himself*) Yeah, I must be. I must be him; I'd rather not be, but what the hell . . .

SANDRA: (*Smiling, as she turns right around and goes to the door*) Well, I'll be on my way . . .

(*She exits. Murray picks up her files from the bureau, goes to the door with them*)

LEO: (*Interrupting Murray on his way to the door*) Very attractive girl, that Minnie; what does she do?

MURRAY: She's my decorator.

LEO: (*Looking around the apartment*) Well, she's done a *wonderful* job! (*Indicating the apartment with a sweep of his hand*) This place is great. It's loose, it's open, it's free. Love it. Wonderful, crazy place. My God . . . you must make out like mad in this place, huh? (*Murray closes door, put the files back on the bureau; Leo is walking around the apartment*) How come I never came here before?

MURRAY: You were here last January, Leo.

Leo: Funny thing, work with me for three years and I never saw
your apartment.

Murray: You were here last January, Leo.

Leo: (*Stops pacing, turns to Murray*) Wait a minute, wait a
minute, wasn't I here recently, in the winter? Last January, I
think . . . (*Goes over to Murray*) Oh, I came here to get you
back on the show and you wouldn't listen, you went into the
kitchen, sang "Yes, Sir, That's My Baby." I left feeling very
foolish, like I had footprints on my face. . . . You old monkey.
(*Smiles, musses up Murray's hair*) You're an old monkey,
aren't ya? (*Starts pacing again*) You know what I got from
that experience? A rash. I broke out something terrible. . . .
Minnie Mouse! (*Stops pacing*) Minnie *Mouse!* (*Laughs
loudly, points at the door*) You told me her name was Minnie
Mouse! I swear to God, Murray, I think my mission in life is to
feed you straight-lines . . . (*Taking in the apartment with a
sweep of his hand*) It's kind of a fall-out shelter, that's what
you got here, Murr', protection against the idiots in the atmosphere. Free, freer, freest . . . (*Cups his hands around his
mouth, shouts*) Free! Free! (*Takes off his coat*) Another year
and I'm gonna cut loose from the God damn Chipmunk show.
Binds me up, hugs me. Finks, dwarfs, phonies and frogs . . .
(*Following Murray to the window seat*) Two of us should do
something new, something wild; new kind of kid's show, for
adults maybe . . .

Murray: (*Sitting on the window seat*) You told me the same
thing three years ago, Leo.

Leo: (*Sits next to Murray*) Well, whaddya want from me? I'm a
coward; everybody knows that. (*Suddenly seeing the
Chuckles statue against the wall next to him*) Oh God! (*Points
at the statue; in anguish*) Did you ever see anything so *im-
modest?* I bring a big statue of myself as a gift for a child! I
mean, the *pure ego* of it . . . (*Covers his face with his hands*)
I am ashamed. Murray, could you throw a sheet over it or

something . . . (*Sees Nick, who has just come out of the kitchen with two bowls of potato chips*) Mmmm, good! Here they are. (*Grabs one bowl from Nick's hand, gives it to Murray. Then Leo turns to Nick, assumes the character and the voice of Chuckles the Chipmunk; a great mock-frown on his face, he goes into a routine for Nick*) Oh, goshes, kidderoonies, look at your poor Chippermunk friend; he got his mouff stuck. No matter how hard I try I can't get my mouth unstuck. But maybe—if you Chippermunks yell, "Be happy, Chuckles," maybe then it'll get unstuck . . . (*Leo waits. Nick does not react. Leo prompts Nick in a whisper*) You're supposed to yell, "Be happy, Chuckles."

Nick: Oh yeah . . . sure . . . (*Glances quickly at Murray; then, a little embarrassed, he yells*) Be happy, Chuckles!

Leo: Oh boy! (*His frown changes to a giant smile*) You *fixed* me! Looka my mouff! (*He jumps in the air*) Now I'm all fixed! (*Gets no reaction from Nick. Nick stands patiently in front of Leo*)

Nick: (*Offering the other bowl of potato chips to Leo, trying to be polite*) Mr. Herman, don't you want your . . .

Leo: (*Not accepting the potato chips, speaking in his own voice again, stroking his tie nervously*) That was a bit from tomorrow morning's show. You'll know it ahead of all the kids in the neighborhood.

Nick: Thank you.

Leo: That . . . that was one of the funny parts there, when I couldn't move my mouth.

Nick: Yeah?

Leo: Didn't you think it was funny?

Nick: Yeah, that was pretty funny.

LEO: (*Smiling nervously*) Well, don't you laugh or something when you see something funny?

NICK: It just took me by surprise is all. So I didn't get a chance. (*Offering him the potato chips, politely*) Here's your . . .

LEO: Another funny part was when I jumped up with the smile there, at the end there. That was another one.

NICK: Uh-huh.

LEO: (*Pressing on, beginning to get tense*) And the finish on the bit, see, I've got the smile . . . (*Nick, looking trapped, stands there as Leo switches back to his Chipmunk voice and puts a giant smile on his face*) Now I'm aaaall fixed, Chippermunks! (*Sudden mock-pathos in his eyes*) Oooops! *Now* I got stuck the *other* way! Oh, *oh,* now my face is stuck the *other* way!
  (*Throws up his arms, does a loose-legged slapstick fall back onto the floor. Remains prone, waiting for Nick's reaction. Nick stands there looking at Leo quite solemnly*)

NICK: (*Nods his head up and down approvingly*) That's terrific, Mr. Herman. (*With admiration*) That's all you have to do, you just get up and do that and they pay you and everything.

LEO: You didn't laugh.

NICK: I was waiting for the funny part.

LEO: (*Sits up*) That was the funny part.

NICK: Oh, when you fell down on the . . .

LEO: When I fell down on the floor here.

NICK: See, the thing is, I was . . .

LEO: (*Gets up from the floor, paces up and down tensely*) I know, waiting for the funny part. Well, you missed another funny part.

NICK: Another one. Hey, I'm really sorry, Mr. Herman, I . . .

LEO: Forget it . . . I just happen to know that that bit is very *funny.* I can prove it to you. (*Takes small booklet from pocket, opens it, shows it to Nick*) Now, what does that say there, second line there?

NICK: (*Reading from the booklet*) "Frown bit; eighty-five percent of audience; outright prolonged laughter on frown bit."

LEO: That's the analysis report the agency did for me on Monday's preview audience. The routine I just did for you, got outright prolonged laughter; eighty-five percent.

MURRAY: You could try him on sad parts, Leo; he's very good on sad parts.

LEO: (*Goes to Murray at the window seat, shows him another page in the booklet*) Matter fact, there's this poignant-type bit I did at the Preview Theatre: "Sixty percent of audience; noticeably moved."

MURRAY: They left the theatre?

LEO: (*Tensely, angrily*) There he is; there's the old joker; Murray the joker, right?

NICK: I do some routines. I can imitate the voice of Alexander Hamilton.

LEO: That's lovely, but I . . .

NICK: I do Alexander Hamilton and Murray does this terrific Thomas Jefferson; we got the voices just right.

MURRAY: (*In a dignified voice; to Nick*) Hello there, Alex, how are you?

NICK: (*In a dignified voice; to Murray*) Hello there, Tom; say, you should have been in Congress this morning. My goodness, there was quite a discussion on . . .

LEO: Now, that's *ridiculous*. You . . . you can't *do* an imitation of Alexander Hamilton; nobody knows what he *sounds* like . . .

NICK: (*Pointing triumphantly at Leo*) *That's* the *funny* part.

MURRAY: (*Shaking his head regretfully*) You missed the funny part, Leo.

LEO: (*Walking away from them*) I'm getting a terrible rash on my neck. (*Turns to them, growing louder and more tense with each word*) The routine I did for him was *funny*. I was workin' good in front of the kid, I know how to use my God-damn *warmth*, I don't go over with these odd kids; I mean, here I am right in *front* of him, in *person* for God's sake, and he's *staring* at me . . . (*Moves toward them, on the attack*) it's oddness here, Murray, *odd*ness. Alexander *Ham*ilton imitations! Jaded jokes for old men. Murray, what you've done to this kid. It's a damn shame, a child can't enjoy little animals, a damn shame . . . (*Really on the attack now; waving at the apartment, shouting*) The way you brought this kid up, Murray, grotesque atmosphere, *unhealthy*, and you're not even guilty about it, women in and out, *dec*orators; had he been brought up by a *normal* person and not in this *mad*house . . .

NICK: (*Quietly, going toward Leo*) Hey, don't say that . . .

LEO: A certain kind of freakish way of growing up . . .

NICK: (*Quietly*) Hey, are you calling me a freak? You called me a freak. Take back what you said.

LEO: (*Walks away from them, mumbling to himself*) On June third I will be forty-two years old and I'm standing here arguing with a twelve-year-old kid . . . (*Leo quiets down, turns, comes toward Nick, sits on bed, Nick standing next to him; speaks calmly to Nick*) See, Nicky, humor is a cloudy, wonderland thing, but simple and clear like the blue, blue sky. All

I want is your simple, honest, child's opinion of my routine; for children are too honest to be wise . . .

NICK: (*Looking directly at Leo, calmly, quietly, slowly*) My simple, child's reaction to what you did is that you are not funny. Funnier than you is even Stuart Slossman my friend who is eleven and puts walnuts in his mouth and makes noises. What is not funny is to call us names and what is mostly not funny is how sad you are that I would feel sorry for you if it wasn't for how dull you are and those are the worst-tasting potato chips I ever tasted. And that is my opinion from the blue, blue sky.

(*Nick and Leo stay in their positions, looking at each other. A moment; then Murray throws his head back and laughs unroariously. Leo stands; the bowl of potato chips tips over in his hand, the chips spilling onto the floor*)

LEO: (*Seeing Murray's laughter, goes to him at the Morris chair; angrily*) Murray the joker, right? You didn't want to come back to work for me, you just got me up here to step on my face again! (*Nick, unnoticed by Leo, has gone quickly into his alcove and comes out now with his ukulele, playing and singing "Yes, Sir, That's My Baby" with great spirit. Leo, hearing this, turns to look at Nick*) It's the *song*. It's the good-*bye* song. (*Leo grabs his hat and coat quickly, as Nick goes on playing, starts for front door, shouting*) Getting *out*, bunch of *nuts* here, *crazy* people . . .

MURRAY: Leo, wait . . . (*Goes to the door to stop Leo*) Leo, wait . . . I'm sorry . . . wait . . . (*Leo stops at the door; Murray goes down toward Nick, who is near the alcove, still playing the song*) Nick, you better stop now . . .

NICK: Come on, Murray, get your uke, we'll sing to him and he'll go away . . .

MURRAY: (*Quietly*) Nick, we can't . . . (*Gently taking the uke from Nick, puts it on the window seat*) Just put this down, huh?

NICK: (*Confused by this; urgently*) Come on, Murray, let him go away, he called us names, we gotta get rid of him . . .

MURRAY: Quiet now, Nick . . . just be quiet for a minute . . .
 (*Starts to go back toward Leo*)

NICK: (*Shouting*) Murray, please let him go away . . . (*Nick, seeing the Chuckles statue next to him against the wall, grabs it angrily, throws it down on the floor*) It's a crummy statue . . . that crummy statue . . . (*Begins to kick the statue fiercely, jumping up and down on it, shouting*) It's a terrible statue, rotten cardboard . . .
 (*Murray comes quickly back to Nick, holds both of his arms, trying to control him*)

MURRAY: Aw, Nick, please, no more now, stop it . . .
 (*There is a great struggle between them; Nick is fighting wildly to free himself from Murray's arms*)

NICK: (*Near tears, shouting*) We don't want jerks like that around here, Murray, let him go away, we gotta get rid of him, Murray, we gotta get rid of him . . .

MURRAY: (*Lifts the struggling Nick up into his arms, hugging him to stop him*) No, Nick . . . I'm sorry, Nick . . . we can't . . . (*Nick gives up, hangs limply in Murray's arms. Murray speaks quietly, with love*) I'm sorry . . . I'm sorry, kid . . . I'm sorry . . .
 (*He puts Nick down, still holding him*)

NICK: (*After a pause; quietly, in disbelief*) Murray . . .

MURRAY: You better go to your room.

NICK: This is a one-room apartment.

MURRAY: Oh. Then go to your alcove. (*Nick waits a moment, then turns, betrayed, walks over to his alcove, lies down on the bed. Murray looks over at Leo, who is standing at the front door. He walks slowly over to Leo, looking down at the floor; humbly*) Leo . . . hope you didn't misunderstand . . . we were just kidding you . . . we . . .

LEO: (*Coming toward Murray, apologetically*) I, myself, I got carried away there myself.

MURRAY: We all got a little excited, I guess. (*Reaches out to shake Leo's hand*) So, I'll see you at work in the morning, Leo.

LEO: (*Smiling, shaking Murray's hand*) Great to have you back, fellah. (*Pause*) You both hate me.

MURRAY: Nobody hates you, Leo.

LEO: I hollered at the kid, I'm sorry. I didn't mean to cause any upset. I don't get along too good with kids . . .

MURRAY: Don't worry about it.

LEO: Wanna come have a drink with me, Murray? We could . . .

MURRAY: No thanks; maybe another night, Leo.

LEO: Look, after I leave, you horse around a little with the kid, he'll feel better.

MURRAY: Right, Leo.

LEO: (*Pauses; then comes closer to Murray*) Murray . . . that bit I did was funny, wasn't it?

MURRAY: (*After a moment*) Yeah, Leo . . . I guess it was just a bad day for you.

LEO: (*Pointing at the Chuckles statue on the floor; quietly, but giving a command*) You don't want to leave that statue lying around like that, huh, Murray?

MURRAY: Oh, no. (*Goes to statue obediently, lifts it up off the floor, leans it upright against the wall*) There.

LEO: Fine.

MURRAY: See you tomorrow, Leo.

LEO: (*Smiles*) Yeah, see ya tomorrow at the studio . . . (*Ruffles up Murray's hair*) You old monkey. (*Goes to the door*) Hey, you're an old monkey, aren't you?
(*Leo exits. Murray stays at the door for a moment. Nick is sitting on the alcove step, his back to Murray*)

MURRAY: (*Walking over to Nick, trying to make peace with him*) Say, I could use a roast-turkey sandwich right now, couldn't you, Nick? On rye, with cole slaw and Russian dressing. . . .
(*Nick does not reply. Murray sits down next to him on the alcove step. Nick refuses to look at Murray. They are both silent for a moment*)

NICK: Guy calls us names. Guy talks to us like that. Shoulda got rid of that moron. Coulda fooled the Welfare people or something . . . (*Sandra enters through the partly open door, unnoticed by them; she stays up in the doorway, watching them*) We coulda gone to Mexico or New Jersey or someplace.

MURRAY: I hear the delicatessen in Mexico is terrible.

NICK: (*After a moment*) I'm gonna call myself *Theodore.*

MURRAY: As long as you don't call yourself Beatrice.

NICK: O.K., fool around. Wait'll you see a Theodore running around here. (*Silent for a moment, his back still to Murray; then, quietly*) Another coupla seconds he woulda been out the door . . . (*Turns to look at Murray*) Why'd you go chicken on me, Murray? What'd you stop me for?

MURRAY: Because your routines give me outright prolonged laughter, Theodore.

SANDRA: (*After a pause*) Four ninety-five for this tablecloth and you leave it around like this . . . (*Picks up the discarded tablecloth from the chair*) A perfectly new tablecloth and already there are stains on it . . . (*Sits on the Morris chair, starts to dab at the tablecloth with her handkerchief*) You know, it's very interesting that I left my files here. That I forgot them. I mean, psychologically, if you want to analyze that. Of course, last month I left my handbag in the Automat, and I have no idea what that means at all. (*Murray leaves alcove, starts toward her*) I think that the pattern of our relationship, if we examine it, is very intricate, the different areas of it, especially the whole "good-bye" area of it, and also the "hello" and "how-are-you" area . . . of it.

MURRAY: (*Standing next to her chair now, smiles warmly*) Hello, Sandy, and how are you?

SANDRA: (*Looks up at him, smiles politely*) Hello, Murray. (*Goes right back to her work, rubbing the tablecloth with her handkerchief*) You're standing in my light.

MURRAY: Oh.
(*He retreats a step*)

NICK: (*Walking over to her*) Hello, lady.

SANDRA: Hello, Nick.

NICK: (*Indicating her work on the tablecloth*) Lady, can I help you with any of that?

SANDRA: Matter of fact, Nick . . . (*She stands; her arm around Nick, she goes to center with him*) Nick, I don't think the effect, I mean, the overall design of this room, is really helped by all these . . . (*Gesturing to Murray's stuff around the bed*) these knickknacks.

NICK: You mean the junk?

SANDRA: Yes.

NICK: Yeah, not too good for the overall design.

SANDRA: If you'd just put them away in that carton there.
(*She indicates a carton near the bed*)

NICK: Sure, lady . . .
(*Nick goes quickly to the carton, begins to put Murray's junk into it—some radios, a megaphone, some clocks. Sandra starts putting the tablecloth on the table*)

MURRAY: (*Realizes that they are taking over, moves forward, trying to halt the proceedings*) Hey, Sandy, now wait a minute . . . (*She goes on with her work, putting a piece of material over the Morris chair. He turns at the sound of one of his radio cabinets being dropped into the carton by Nick*) Listen, Nick, I didn't tell you to . . . Nick . . .

NICK: (*Looking up from his work*) Wilbur . . . (*Drops a clock into the carton*) Wilbur Malcolm Burns.
(*Sandra is putting the flowers back around the room, picking up the magazines*)

MURRAY: (*Protesting*) Hey, now, both of you, will ya wait a minute here, will ya just wait . . . (*They ignore him, going on with their work. He shrugs, defeated; gives up, goes over to the windows, away from them, sits down sadly in the window seat*) Wonder what kind of weather we got out there tonight. (*Looks out of window; as usual, he can see nothing but the gray, blank wall of the building a few feet opposite; sadly, to himself*) Never can see the God-damned weather. We got a permanent fixture out there: twilight in February. Some day that damn building'll fall down into Seventh Avenue so I can see the weather. (*Leans over, begins to talk out the window*) Everybody onstage for the Hawaiian number, please . . .

(*Sandra, during these last few lines, has gone to phone, dialed, listened a few moments and hung up. Murray hears her hang up, turns to her*) What're you doing?

SANDRA: I just spoke to the Weather Lady. She says it's a beautiful day.

(*She goes back to her work on the apartment*)

MURRAY: (*He continues to talk out the window, softly at first*) Well, then, if you're not ready, we better work on the Military March number. Now the last time we ran this, let's admit it was pretty ragged. I mean, the whole "Spirit of '76" float was in disgraceful shape yesterday . . . O.K. now, let's go, everybody ready . . . (*As Murray continues to talk out the window, Nick looks up from his work, smiles, picks up a record from the bed, puts it on the record player, turns it on*) Grenadiers ready, Cavalry ready, Cossacks ready, Rough Riders ready, Minute Men ready . . . (*The record player has warmed up now and we hear "Stars and Stripes Forever." Murray hears the music, turns from the window, smiling, acknowledges Nick's assistance; turns to the window again, his voice gradually growing in volume*) O.K. now, let's go . . . ready on the cannons, ready on the floats, ready on the banners, ready on the flags . . . (*The music builds up with Murray's voice, Nick humming along with the band and Sandra laughing as Murray shouts*) Let's go . . . let's go . . . let's go . . .

(*His arms are outstretched*)

Curtain

Thieves

Thieves was first presented by Richard Scanga and Charles Grodin at the Broadhurst Theatre, New York City, April 7, 1974. It was directed by Charles Grodin, with sets by Peter Larkin, costumes by Joseph G. Aulisi, lighting by Jules Fisher, and sound by Sandy Hacker. The cast was as follows:

Street Man	William Hickey
Carlton Danfield II	Haywood Nelson
Man Above	Dick Van Patten
Harry	Pierre Epstein
Flo	Alice Drummond
Martin Cramer	Richard Mulligan
Sally Cramer	Marlo Thomas
Nancy	Ann Wedgeworth
Stanley	George Loros
Joe Kaminsky	Irwin Corey
Gordon	David Spielberg
Street Lady	Sudie Bond
Perez	Pierre Epstein
Policeman	George Loros
Devlin	Sammy Smith

The play takes place between one a.m. and seven a.m. on a warm June night in the upper East Side of Manhattan. We see pieces of a piece of the city; the upper reaches of the buildings rise directly out of the streets around them.

ACT ONE

Distantly, gracefully, someone is playing "The Streets of Laredo" on a flute. The melody drifts gently for a few moments, followed by the sound of city traffic, and then the curtain rises.

One A.M., mid-June, we see pieces of a piece of the city, the upper east side of Manhattan asleep in the heat. At Center is the entrance and the seventeenth and eighteenth-floor terraces of a modern luxury apartment building. A sign over the entrance says that this is "Riverview East," but the only view is of other terraces and the only sign of a river is in the name of the building. At Right and Far Left, we see the jutting terraces of two similar, Off Stage buildings. The columns of terraces face each other like the unmeshed teeth of opposing gears. Gordon's terrace at Far Left, Martin's terrace at Center in Riverview East, and Nancy's terrace at Right all have the same skeletal railings, plastic deck-chairs and redwood picnic-tables. Down Stage, the street level spills out onto the apron and down towards the audience. A ramp runs across, forward of the apron, from Center to Right, disappearing down into the pit, supposedly to the river level. At Right, under Nancy's terrace, is a park-bench, an open phone-booth and the ornate railing of a balcony over the unseen river. Up Left, between Gordon's terrace and Riverview East, is the indication of a dim alley or side-street.

At rise: Martin Cramer stands alone on his terrace at Center, playing his flute. He is about forty, wearing pajama-bottoms and an old, red N.Y.U. sweatshirt. He plays gently, with his eyes closed. Below him, on the side-street at Left is the indication of a Nineteen Forty-Eight DeSoto Sky-View Cab. The Driver is asleep on the front seat, cap pulled down, only the white stubble on his chin visible. At Center a very old Irish Doorman sleeps on a chair in the doorway of Riverview East, his ancient face in contrast to his shining new uniform. An old Bum sleeps on the bench at Right. A battered fishing-hat over his face to protect him from a recent rain. He wears an oversized double breasted jacket and stolen shoes.

After a moment there is the soft, cackling laughter of someone below the apron, and the crazy old Street Lady enters, coming up the ramp from below. She wears a ragged, floor-length velvet dress, a sailor's windbreaker, sneakers, a large straw sunhat, carries two huge shopping-bags, her face like a rouged antique. She stops at the top of the ramp, delicately picks up a discarded box of wooden matches, delighted by her treasure. She continues to rummage about the street for further prizes, her selections are thoughtful, her actions precise, items to be placed in her shopping-bags are chosen with a connoisseur's taste. She will laugh periodically at particular, secret jokes. Carlton Danfield, a twelve-year-old black kid, enters Up Left from the shadows of the side-street. He wears freshly laundered jeans and jean-jacket, a white polo shirt, lensless glasses, and carries two large children's books to complete his impersonation of an innocent schoolboy. He stops at the cab, his eyes flick professionally from the Driver's sleeping face to the coin-changer on the seat next to him and then back again. He checks the street, then reaches into his jean-jacket and takes out a wire coathanger which has been fashiond into a hook, his eyes never leaving the Driver's face. At Right, the Street Lady has moved up to the Bum on the bench, studying his hat. She wants it. The Driver stirs slightly; Carlton steps back, calmly adopting his schoolboy pose again. The Street Lady removes the fishing-hat from the sleeping Bum's face, puts it in her shopping-bag, chuckling softly. Martin turns Up Stage with his flute, swaying slightly with the music. A Man enters on the terrace above Martin carrying a small T.V. set and a bowl of soup, puts his things down on his picnic-table and reaches out over the edge of his terrace to feel for rain. Their terraces are constructed in such a way that Martin and the Man From Above can never see each other. Carlton reaches into the cab with the wire hook, removes the glistening coin-changer. The Street Lady moves from the Bum to the sleeping Doorman at Center, contemplates the um-brella under the Doorman's chair. Carlton opens one of his books, "The Wizard of Oz"; we see that it has been hollowed out, leaving only an outside frame of pages. He places the coin-changer quickly in the hollow space, puts the book under his arm and, adjusting his fake glasses, walks casually down towards the ramp. The Bum awakens, glances about for his hat, spots Carlton, watches him with great fascination as the kid sits at the edge of the stage, takes the coin-changer out of the book, begins to "click" out the coins, counting the loot. The Street Lady deftly removes the umbrella from under the Doorman's chair. The Bum leaves his bench, approaching the ramp as Carlton counts his coins. The Street Lady moves to the bench with her umbrella, opens it, laughing victoriously.

BUM: (*Shuffling over to Carlton.*) Lotta quarters, lotta quarters . . . (*Sits next to him.*) Some lotta quarters there, boy. (*Carlton calmly puts his hand into his jacket-pocket.*) I'm a com-mercial fisherman, see. Gotta get to Sheepshead Bay by four o'clock. Also, my eye-balls need fixin'. White Stallion is a very fine sauterne which is also a good eye-ball fixer. For one dollar and twenty-five I can get to the Bay and get my eye-balls fixed too. (*Silence.*) Total on that is one dollar and twenty-five. (*The old Bum and the twelve-year-old boy look into each other's eyes for several moments, judging.*) Quarters alone, you got nine, ten dollars in there, boy . . . (*Suddenly reaching for the book.*) Kid like you don't need all that—

CARLTON: (*Quickly, quietly, taking knife from his pocket.*) You lookin' to get cut, juice-head?

BUM: (*Studying the knife.*) No, sir. (*Shakes his head mournfully.*) Sweet Jesus, this has been a bad night. (*Rises, withdrawing into the shadows of the building.*) Never shoulda come uptown. Trouble with me, I never worked out no specialty for myself. You want to make it in this town, boy, you got to have a specialty . . .

MAN FROM ABOVE: (*Looks down in Martin's direction.*) My terrace is flooded from the rain. They forgot to put drains in these terraces. (*Silence. No reply.*) They build these buildings too quickly and they forget things. I was wondering if you had a similar problem down there. (*No reply. He goes to the plantbox at edge of terrace.*) Don't try to grow any vegetables out here. Especially tomatoes. What you get are these tough little New York tomatoes. Gotta chop half-way into the damn things before you get to a tomato. You feed them, you nurture them, you care for them, and you end up with a box full of little red handballs. (*Sits at picnic-table, turns on T.V. set.*) Forget tomatoes.

   (*Nancy Gresham, attractive, skimpy nightgown, comes out on terrace opposite Martin's in building at Right. She smiles at the flute music and the gentle night, holds her hand out delicately to feel for rain. Carlton continues to count his coins below.*)

STANLEY'S VOICE: (*From inside Nancy's terrace-doorway.*) Hon'? You up, hon'?

NANCY: (*Graceful Southern accent.*) Uh-huh. The rain woke me. The rain and the air-conditioners. Sounded like applause. I swear, love, like a standin' ovation. (*The Street Lady chuckles softly.*)

MAN FROM ABOVE: (*Eating his soup.*) Vichyssoise. Good. Cold soup on a hot night. Perfect.

(Gordon, moustached, early forties, bathrobe, appears in the light of a Japanese lantern on the highest terrace in the Far Left building. He is looking out at us through binoculars.)

GORDON: *(Quietly.)* God bless shortie nighties.

MAN FROM ABOVE: Another thing you can forget about in this building is good television reception. Every night it snows on Randolph Scott. *(Switches dial.)* Look, it's snowing on the Morning Prayer. It's snowing on the Rabbi.

HARRY'S VOICE: *(Approaching.)* Can you believe that, Flo? *(Harry and Flo, a middle-aged couple in formal party clothes, enter at Right, going towards the entrance. Harry is pointing at the sleeping Doorman.)* Look at that. Will you look at that, Flo?

FLO: *(Entering building.)* Come on, Harry.

BUM: *(approaching them)* Sir, pardon me, but could you spare thirty thousand dollars?

HARRY: Go away.

BUM: I'll settle for fifty cents.

HARRY: Go away, go away.

BUM: *(Drifting back into shadows of building.)* Gotta get myself a specialty . . .

HARRY: *(Leans close to sleeping Doorman.)* Devlin . . . Devlin, I want you to know how reassuring it is to see you asleep in front of this open doorway while approximately fifty thousand thieves, junkies, rapists, madmen and students are roaming the city. *(Leans closer.)* I want you to know that. *(Follows Flo into building.)* I told him, Flo, I told him . . .

FLO: Sure you told him. Because he's asleep. *(As they exit.)* Asleep or deaf or dead; that's when you tell them, Harry . . .
    (Carlton crosses quickly to the sleeping Doorman, feels

carefully along the pockets of the Doorman's jacket. The Street Lady on the bench and the Bum in the shadows observe with interest. Carlton slips his hand smoothly into one of Devlin's pockets, removes a large set of tinkling keys. The Street Lady chuckles approvingly. Carlton opens the entrance door with one of the keys, slips quietly into the building.)

BUM: (*Softly.*) Kid's gonna make it in this town; he's got himself a specialty.

MAN FROM ABOVE: Look. My Vichyssoise has turned black. Five minutes out here and it turned black. (*No reply.*) Please stop with the trumpet. Every night with the trumpet. You're making me crazy with that trumpet.

MARTIN: (*Stops playing.*) This is not a trumpet, sir.

MAN FROM ABOVE: Sure, talk tough. You're safe in your apartment. I know you people. I remember the voices . . . (*As Martin exits into his darkened apartment.*) I remember all the voices . . .

(Man From Above is lost in shadow as lights come up on Martin's apartment. The large bedroom is completely empty except for a stepladder with a geranium plant on it, a huge cardboard carton, a box-spring, a mattress and somebody asleep under the blanket, Martin gets into the bed, drifting towards sleep. Sally sits up, looks at his sleeping form for a moment, turns on the lamp which is set on a suitcase next to the bed. She is in her mid-thirties and has the kind of face that doesn't know how pretty it is. His eyes are closed. She studies his face for a moment.)

SALLY: Can I ask you a question?

MARTIN: Yes.

SALLY: Who are you?

MARTIN: Martin.

SALLY: (*Thoughtfully.*) Martin, Martin . . .

MARTIN: Martin Cramer.

SALLY: Martin Cramer. Right. (*After a moment.*) And where do I know you from?

MARTIN: I'm your husband. You know me from marriage.

SALLY: (*Nodding.*) Right, right . . .

MARTIN: (*Opens his eyes.*) Sally, the forgetting game. I hate it. You have no idea how much I hate it.

SALLY: O.K., O.K., I—

MARTIN: (*Sitting up at edge of bed.*) Sally, at least once a week now you wake me up in the middle of the night and ask me who I am. I hate it.

SALLY: You used to think it was charming.

MARTIN: I thought a lot of things were charming.

SALLY: (*Nodding thoughtfully.*) Dr. Mathew Spengler talks about this in his book, in "Marriage And Modern Society," he calls it "the inevitable decline from charm to nightmare . . ."

MARTIN: Sally, there is no such book and there is no Dr. Spengler.

SALLY: I know.

MARTIN: Sally, why do you keep—

SALLY: I do the best I can to class up the conversation.

MARTIN: But you don't just do it with me, you do it with everybody. Last month with my mother you made up a whole country. A whole country that doesn't exist.

SALLY: I thought she'd be happy there.

MARTIN: But there *is* none. There is no Hungarian West Indies.

SALLY: My countries, my books; you used to think they were funny . . .

MARTIN: I thought a lot of things were funny.

SALLY: What happened? We—

MARTIN: O.K., Sally. (*He rises decisively, goes to Center of room.*) I was going to wait till morning, but why wait . . .

SALLY: Let's wait.

MARTIN: First, Sally . . . First, I want you to know how much I appreciate the wonderful work you've done on our apartment here. How you've managed to capture, in only five short weeks, the subtle, elusive, yet classic mood previously found only in the Port Authority Bus Terminal. (*Pacing about the room.*) In addition, Sally, you have, somewhat mystically, lost or forgotten the name of the moving and storage company with whom you placed nearly fifty-five thousand dollars worth of our furniture.

SALLY: It's an Italian name, I know that. I'm working on that . . .

MARTIN: This, coupled with the fact that you disappeared eight days ago on what was ostensibly a trip to Gristede Brothers to buy some strawberry yogurt, and did not return until this evening, has led to a certain amount of confusion for me . . .

SALLY: I went to Gloria's place to think things out, to—

MARTIN: (*Opens crumpled letter.*) All confusion, of course, vanished with the arrival last week of this simple, touching, yet concise note from the Misters Morris, Klien, Fishback and Fishback . . . (*Reads, only the slightest tremor in his voice.*) "We have been retained by your wife, Sally Jane Cramer, hereinafter referred to as "Wife," to represent her in the matter of your divorce. Said wife having requested that her wherea-

bouts remain unknown to you at present, we therefore . . ."
(*Carefully folding letter into paper airplane.*) After eight days
of staring into the air-conditioner, wondering which Santini
Brother had my furniture, which Gristede Brother had my
wife, and which Fishback owned my soul, a light began to
dawn . . . or maybe one went out . . . and I realized that
nobody was hiding you from me, that your whereabouts, said
wife, have been unknown to me for years . . . that you make a
fine letter-writer, a great decorator, and a perfect stranger.
(*Going to terrace-doorway.*) You said you came back tonight
to talk about the divorce. You didn't mention it. Neither did I.
And the habit, the habit of being together, began again.
(*Turns to her.*) But I couldn't sleep. I couldn't sleep and I
thought about it and tonight, Sally, I have decided to retire
from the games. The Olympics are over, lady, the torch is out
. . . and you are free. (*He tosses the paper airplane through
the terrace-doorway, it sails into the street.*) Said husband,
hereinafter referred to as "gone," has had it. (*Martin goes out
onto the terrace. Below, the Street Lady scurries out of the
shadows to pick up the paper airplane, disappears again.*)

SALLY: (*After a moment, quietly.*) Marty, I came back tonight
because I'm pregnant and I'm terrified.

MARTIN: Can't hear you from out here.

SALLY: (*Rises from bed, wearing robe, going to terrace-doorway.*) Marty, I came back tonight . . . (*At doorway, after a
moment.*) Did I buy you that sweatshirt? (*No reply.*) It's a
size too big. If we're getting a divorce why did we make love
tonight?

MARTIN: Goddamn wine . . . why'd you bring a Goddamn bottle of wine to discuss a divorce?

SALLY: Why'd you light a candle?

MARTIN: It goes with the wine.

SALLY: (*She smiles. Remains in doorway, quietly.*) Marty, it was lovely tonight. Like a surprise party. Like a lovely party with two hosts . . . (*After a moment.*) If you've got any material of your own on this I'd be glad to hear it.

MARTIN: Look, it goes without saying—

SALLY: No, *don't* let it go, *not* without saying— (*Grabs his arm.*) Come on, keep me company, show an emotion! Emotions, Marty, *you* remember. Come on, scream at me for walking out! Holler, or cry, or—Christ, how many years since I've seen a tear outa ya!? (*Shaking him.*) Come on, Marty-baby, you can do it, break something, throw a plate at me—

MARTIN: I *can't* . . . They're all packed. (*He goes sadly back into the room.*) This beautiful place, you never moved in . . .

SALLY: (*Following him.*) You keep *moving* us, another room, a higher floor—

MARTIN: This beautiful place . . .

SALLY: Poor schmuck, we'd just be back up to our ass in French Provincial—

MARTIN: Do you have to talk like that, are you *compelled*—

SALLY: That's how I *always*—

MARTIN: When we're out with people, I cringe, I literally—

SALLY: I've seen ya, you go off in a corner and pretend you're an onion-dip—

MARTIN: All these years, that loud, embarrasing—

SALLY: That's how I talk to everybody—

MARTIN: What about at school, what about those little—

SALLY: P.S. Twenty-*Nine*, Marty, have you forgotten what those kids *sound* like down there? Canal Street, where you came from, you and the embarrassing lady here— (*He walks away.*)

Dummy, you bought yourself a new mouth and kept the same old wife. (*She follows him.*) It's *me*, Sally Jane Kaminsky, I know ya from before, fellah. I know ya from coppin' goodies off of every open counter in the neighborhood, I know ya from knockin' over DeSapio's Grocery with the Golden Avengers, I—

MARTIN: Sally, I was sixteen years old—

SALLY: (*Laughing.*) I remember your jacket, the red one with the big pockets sewn inside. You'd come draggin' outa Woolworth's, the only Jewish pelican in New York . . . (*Silence for a moment. He turns to her.*)

MARTIN: (*Quietly.*) I didn't think you even noticed me in those days.

SALLY: Sure I noticed you.

MARTIN: I mean, I thought it was years later that you . . .

SALLY: I was crazy about ya.

MARTIN: I always thought it was at Marilyn Krasney's party that you first— (*She shakes her head.*) All this time, how come you never talked about—

SALLY: Who talks? We don't talk, we move. We're movers. (*Goes towards him.*) I also saw ya following me home all the time.

MARTIN: I didn't.

SALLY: I saw ya.

MARTIN: You couldn't have. I cut in and outa doorways. (*He smiles.*) Peter Lorre taught me how.

SALLY: Woulda stopped and talked to you except I was scared of all you guys from the Golden Avengers. I mean, you weren't as tough as Whitey Arkish, but still I was scared. (*She puts her arms around him.*) Coulda had me at fifteen. How about that? We coulda been divorced by now.

MARTIN: (*His arms around her.*) Whitey Arkish wasn't so tough . . .

SALLY: (*Tenderly.*) First real date we had was four years later . . . we broke into Loew's Delancy with a crow-bar . . .

MARTIN: Take Whitey's knife away he fell apart . . .

SALLY: We pried open the fire-door at three in the morning, you put me in the middle of the eighth row . . . and then you got up on the stage and played your flute for me, "Blue-Tail Fly" and "The Streets of Laredo," fantastic repertoire . . . and over your head on the curtain, it said . . .

MARTIN: (*Softly.*) "Loew's Delancy, Home Of The Stars . . ."

SALLY: And then the cops came— (*Holds him tightly, inspired.*) Jesus, sirens . . . sirens and everything . . . runnin' through alleys, all those alleys, half-way across town, outa breath, gettin' away with it, gettin' away clean . . . (*Tenderly.*) Oh, Marty, how'd you do it?

MARTIN: What?

SALLY: Get to be so boring. (*He walks away, she pursues him.*) You had a knife and a flute and you wanted to be a teacher, you were a Goddamn interesting person—

MARTIN: What the hell is going *on* here, where's all this *coming* from!?

SALLY: We were gonna *stay* down there, we promised, we were gonna teach in the neighborhood—

MARTIN: Sally, that was *years* ago—

SALLY: (*Racing out onto terrace.*) And here he is, ladies and gentlemen— (*Announcing to the neighborhood.*) For the first time on any terrace—the principal of the Little Bluebell School

—see him pick up his check— (*He races after her.*) watch him do the totally unnecessary for the completely unneeding—

MARTIN: (*Pulling her back into room.*) Sally—

SALLY: You blew it, you lost your privates to a private school—

MARTIN: Damn it, the Little Bluebell School happens to be a first rate—

SALLY: My God, Marty, you sold your soul to Bugs Bunny for a five-room apartment!

MARTIN: (*Finally raising his voice.*) You're a bigot, Sally! You hate rich kids! Maybe that's why we don't have any. All we've got is Crazy Carmen and Danfield the Dealer—

SALLY: You only let Carlton stay a week, he really liked you—

MARTIN: I know he liked me. But he loved my typewriter; that's why he took it—

SALLY: He's intelligent, confused—

MARTIN: So was Willie Sutton—

SALLY: We're not alone here, Mister. You used to believe in something, you used to care. Just a few years ago, Civil Rights Day, you marched down Fifth Avenue with me—

MARTIN: Not a *few* years ago! Fifteen. That was fifteen *years* ago. I cared. Sure I cared. A long time ago. Another time. Marches that never got past the Six O'Clock News, carrying placards that nobody reads. You gotta be young, you gotta be in the world just long enough to think it's still worth saving. (*Pacing, loudly.*) *Canal* Street you're not teaching down there, you're a *cop.* You're a Goddamn policeman. I wait in terror every night for you to come home dead. Don't you know there's a Puerto Rican down there with your number on it? The neighborhood, the precious neighborhood, all I ever got from the neighborhood was four knife scars, two broken noses and a fruitcake wife! And they all hurt when it rains. (*Rushes to her, urgently.*) I got *out*, Sally, don't ya see? I got outa there alive and I won't go back. I'm too old to be a Golden Avenger, I'm too young to be Albert Schweitzer. I don't get hit anymore and I don't hit back, I don't change the world and it doesn't change me . . . (*Grips her arm, quietly.*) Don't you get it, Sally? Don't you know what's going on out there? This rotten little island is slowly sinking into the sea. Nobody listens, nobody cares, none of it's the same. It all got . . . older. The survivors are up here, lady, way up here. Please, Sally, the only kids I want to save are us. What's my crime, what's wrong with wanting something better for us? A new life, a view of the river—

SALLY: What river? (*Stalks out onto terrace.*) Show me the Goddamn river!

MARTIN: (*Shouting.*) O.K., forget it! Go back! Go back to our first place, Seventy-Eight Orchard Street, the one room roach festival!

SALLY: Glad you remember the address, Marty . . . because that's where I sent the furniture. (*Silence for a moment. She remains on terrace with her back to him.*)

MARTIN: (*Quietly, controlled.*) In other words, Sally, what you have done . . . what you have done is sent five rooms of antique furniture to a one room, cold water flat that we have not lived in for ten years. (*She nods.*) Unusual.

SALLY: Apartment Four B.

MARTIN: I think you're crazy.

SALLY: So did the old guy in Apartment Four B.

MARTIN: All . . . all of our furniture . . .

SALLY: Don't worry, I gave the old guy a coupla bucks to keep his eye on it. I mean, he can hardly *not* keep his eye on it, right?

MARTIN: (*Nodding.*) Right, fine, fine . . .

SALLY: (*Goes quickly to him.*) Four B, Marty—(*Holds his arm.*) We made terrific promises and gorgeous love there. And we had nice, loud fights and threw inexpensive things at each other and hugged a lot and . . . (*Sees his blank, unremembering face.*) Well, you had to be there. (*Moving about the large, bare room.*) I woke up in the middle of the night last week and I didn't know who we were. This empty room woke me like an alarm bell and for a minute I didn't know who we were. Without our coffee-table, I didn't know. Without our couch . . . And then I remembered. We're the Cramers. We're this couple. And we're staying together because we're expected to dinner next Friday by some other couples; and the next Friday we're expecting them. We're the Cramers. We don't love each other so we love other couples, and they love us. Held together by other couples, married to other marriages, travelling in fours, sixes, eights, shoulder to shoulder at each other's tables, boy, girl, boy, girl, boy, girl, close, close, so nobody slips away . . . (*She stands quite still.*) We're this couple; I remembered and I fell asleep . . . The next morning I heard somebody scream in the subway. Rush hour, the train stopped dead between Union Square and Canal and somebody blew. It was this high, nutsy scream, like somebody certain they're gonna die right there under the city. It scared the hell outa me and I put my hand to my throat and I felt it throbbing and I saw everybody looking and I knew it was me. It was me screaming, and I couldn't stop. And that night I went to Gristede Brothers and kept on walking. (*Silence for a moment.*) If you want to visit your furniture, the keys to the apartment are in the bookcase. (*Goes to pick up shoulder-bag on terrace picnic-table, as though to leave.*)

HARRY'S VOICE: (*From above.*) Finished. Finished. Finished. (*She looks up.*) Over. Over. Ended. Finished.

SALLY: Did you hire a narrator?

MARTIN: (*In terrace-doorway; gently.*) Sally, why did you come back tonight?

SALLY: (*Turns to him.*) Okay, Marty, I got some news for ya . . .

MAN FROM ABOVE: Hello? Hello? Hello there . . . ?

SALLY: Chrissake . . .

MAN FROM ABOVE: What do you people look like? Have I seen you in the lobby?

MARTIN: Sir, we would appreciate—

MAN FROM ABOVE: Are you the short people? Are you the midgets?

MARTIN: Look, Mister, we—

MAN FROM ABOVE: You're the midgets, aren't you? You sound like the midgets.

MARTIN: Please, sir—

MAN FROM ABOVE: One of you plays the trumpet and one of you giggles in the elevator. Why do you do that? Why is everybody so crazy? It wasn't always like this—

MARTIN: (*Shouting up.*) Damn it, will ya please—

MAN FROM ABOVE: You're angry. You're angry because you're short.
   (*Sally laughs. Martin chuckles in spite of himself, they suddenly hug each other, holding on silently.*)

NANCY: (*On her terrace.*) Hey, huggers . . .

STANLEY'S VOICE: What, hon'?

NANCY: Huggers, love. We got some huggers over there.

STANLEY'S VOICE: Huh?

NANCY: People huggin'.

STANLEY'S Voice: Oh.

MARTIN: Sally, what did you want to tell me?

MAN FROM ABOVE: Tell you the truth, I drink a little . . .

SALLY: There's something we oughta talk about . . .

MAN FROM ABOVE: Who am I kidding? I drink a lot. I sit out here with my Vodka and I try to understand what's going on. I'm sorry to intrude, but do you know what's going on? Do you know why everyone has gone mad? Would you like some Vodka?

MARTIN: Sally, what is it . . . ?

MAN FROM ABOVE: (*Whispering.*) I'm sorry, I'll go inside now . . . good night . . .

MARTIN: Have you been unfaithful to me? Is that it?

SALLY: Unfaithful sounds awesome. Ask if I've been foolin' around.

MARTIN: Have you?

SALLY: No. What about you?

MARTIN: I haven't been fooling around, either.

SALLY: How about unfaithful? (*Phone rings on picnic-table. She picks it up, whispers into it.*) No, Jim, no . . . I told you, not here, never here . . . (*Smiles, turns to him.*) I'm kidding, it's Gloria . . . (*Into phone.*) Sorry, Glo, I shouldn't've disappeared without telling you . . .

MARTIN: Tell her she'll get used to it . . .

SALLY: Good, let me speak to him . . . Barry! That's right, Barry, it's me. How ya doin', kid? Miss me? Sure, I miss you. Uh-huh . . . uh-huh . . . that sounds great. So what did . . . uh-huh. Yeah, just a sec' . . . (*To Martin*) Barry wants to speak to you . . .

MARTIN: I don't want to speak to Barry.

SALLY: Why not? He—

MARTIN: Sally, I would like to remind you that Barry is a German Shepherd. He does not speak, he barks. He barks because he is a dog. A very large—

SALLY: You wouldn't let him live in the new apartment with us, the least you could do is—

MARTIN: Hang up, it's a dog.

SALLY: (*Into phone.*) Just another sec', Barry . . . (*Covering phone.*) What should I tell him?

MARTIN: Don't tell him *any*thing! He's a *dog!* And he is a *great* dog, but he makes a *terrible person!*

MAN FROM ABOVE: My God, speak to the poor animal!

MARTIN: (*Shouting up.*) I thought you went inside!

MAN FROM ABOVE: I went inside. There's nobody there.

SALLY: He's heard your voice already, I can't just—

MARTIN: (*Shouting.*) Sally, stop it! For Chrissakes, we've got more important . . . (*She holds the phone out to him.*) Sally, we're right in the middle of a *very* important . . . (*Grabs phone.*) Okay, Okay, if you'll stop . . . (*Into phone, quickly.*) Hello, Barry, how are you? . . . Good . . . I'm fine. Okay, Barry, gotta go now; 'bye. (*Hangs up.*) I can't tell you how much that depresses me.

SALLY: You shouldn't just hang up on him like that.

MARTIN: I know I shouldn't. I'm not capable of a complete relationship.

SALLY: I don't think he's really happy with Gloria . . .

MARTIN: You and that dog, it's so damn sad.

SALLY: What's wrong? I love him. He loves me. He trusts me, he never asks—

MARTIN: (*Gently.*) Sally . . . you treat him like he's your child . . . you always have.

SALLY: Maybe we should do that.

MARTIN: What?

SALLY: Have some children. We'll start with one. (*Quietly; sitting at picnic-table.*) See, I've been thinking . . . I thought maybe, y'know, something new between us, a way to begin again . . .

MARTIN: All these years, you never—

SALLY: I wasn't sure.

MARTIN: And now that we're separating, now you're sure?

SALLY: (*After a moment.*) Sounds crazy, doesn't it?

MARTIN: I'm afraid so. (*Gently.*) Sally, look at us . . . we've been leaving each other for years . . . piece by piece. The way things are between us, a child would end up being a kind of souvenir.

SALLY: You're right, of course. (*They stand silently on the terrace for a few moments.*) Well, that doesn't leave us much more to talk about, does it?

MARTIN: I guess not.

SALLY: I better get dressed and go now. (*She goes through ter-*

race-doorway, exits through doorway at Left of main room,
where she has left her clothes. Martin, alone now, paces about
awkwardly, shifting his flute from one hand to the other. Then
he stands quite still, turns to doorway.)

MARTIN: Are you pregnant, Sally? (*No reply. She enters the*
main room, dressed to leave.)

SALLY: No.

Martin: Then why did you come back tonight?

SALLY: I guess it was a social call. (*She goes to front door; picks*
up suitcase. Martin remains in terrace-doorway, the large,
empty room between them.) Well, now we're at the goodbye
part. How do we do this?

MARTIN: I'm not sure.

SALLY: I guess we'll keep in touch.

MARTIN: Of course we will. You'll be staying at Gloria's, I imagine.

SALLY: For a while. And I guess you'll be staying here.

MARTIN: Yeah. (*After a moment.*) Sally . . . after Gloria's,
where will you go?

SALLY: I don't know. I'm not sure. (*Silence.*) You were crazy.
You were the craziest kid in the neighborhood. (*She exits.*)
    (*Martin sits at picnic-table; only the sound of distant, late-*
night traffic for a few moments.)

MAN FROM ABOVE: (*Softly.*) Martin, I think that you should
both seriously consider the—

MARTIN: (*Rising violently, flute held over his head like a*
weapon, screaming.) Shut up, will ya!!
    (*Sudden silence again. Lights up on Nancy's terrace as she*
moves to the edge, watching him, still wearing skimpy

*night-gown, a man's shirt over her arm. Martin sits down
again at picnic-table, pours glass of wine.*)

NANCY: They stopped huggin'.

STANLEY'S VOICE: (*From inside Nancy's terrace-doorway.*) Huh?

NANCY: The people who were huggin'. They ain't huggin' no
more. (*Lights up on Gordon's terrace, focusing binoculars on
Nancy.*)

STANLEY'S VOICE: Hon', I'll have to go home and get my pills.
I've got this thing with my back, see.

NANCY: She went away and he did his hollerin'. Sometimes
when he's alone he does this hollerin' . . .

GORDON: (*Whispering.*) Now just lean over a little, darlin' . . .

NANCY: They've got the same picnic-table I've got. Redwood.
(*Leans forward at railing.*)

GORDON: Forget the others, there is only you . . .

NANCY: Way they were huggin', Lord, I thought they were
gonna do it right there on the picnic-table. (*She starts to put
the shirt on.*)

GORDON: No, no, my love . . . I ask for so little really . . .

STANLEY'S VOICE: Thing is, hon', by the time I get down there
it'll be two o'clock and I've got to be up by seven.

NANCY: Y'know sometimes I come out here in the middle of the
night and I just stand here and think about all these buildin's
and all the people who must be doin' it at that exact moment . . .
   (*Gordon exits. Martin finishes his glass of wine, pours another. Although his actions remain muted his presence
should be felt through this scene.*)

STANLEY'S VOICE: So I think the sane thing'd be for me to stay down there, hon'.

NANCY: You see, in Daytona Beach, I thought I was the only one who did it. My momma gave me that impression. I mean, the only one who *wanted* to do it; I didn't *do* it in Daytona Beach, I only wanted to do it in Daytona Beach, I didn't start doin' it till I got to New York . . . Minute I got off that bus, I knew that everybody was doin' it in New York. It's a feeling you got. First job I had I knew that everybody in that office was doin' it. I mean, I wasn't really sure till I did it with some of them, but I had the feeling. I was in Daytona Beach for Thanksgiving and, I swear, they still don't do it there. It's very reassuring in New York. It's a comfort to know you're not alone.

STANLEY'S VOICE: Did you hear what I said, hon'?

NANCY: About what, love?

STANLEY'S VOICE: Well, I have to go home and get my pills, and the sensible thing'd be, since it's so late, that I stay there. Hey, I'll give you a wake-up call, a warm good morning. Would you like that?

NANCY: A warm good morning would be very nice.

STANLEY'S VOICE: Jesus, where's my shirt?

NANCY: (*She smiles, holds the collar of the shirt closer around her neck.*) What color are my eyes?

STANLEY'S VOICE: Your eyes? Your eyes, hon'? Blue. (*After a moment.*) Jesus, they're brown. I had it mixed up with your hair.

NANCY: (Pleasantly.) You thought I had blue hair? (*Quietly.*) Anyway, they're green; so now you lose your shirt.

STANLEY'S VOICE: Can't hear you, hon' . . .

NANCY: I said, we spilled some liquor on your shirt while we were doin' it so I threw it in the incinerator.

STANLEY'S VOICE: You threw it away? You threw my *shirt* away?

NANCY: 'Fraid that's what I did. (*Martin pours another glass of wine.*)

STANLEY'S VOICE: (*After a moment.*) Well, I think that was a very hostile thing to do, love.

NANCY: No, I know when I'm being hostile. My doctor tells me. I'm just havin' fun. Us blue haired ladies have all the fun.

STANLEY'S VOICE: Jesus, where . . . where the hell is my jacket? (*No reply.*) It's a checked sports jacket . . .

NANCY: What's my name, love?

STANLEY'S VOICE: Chrissake, *Nancy.*

NANCY: Nancy what?

STANLEY'S VOICE: Graham.

NANCY: Gresham. You lose.

STANLEY'S VOICE: (*After a moment; quietly.*) You're not gonna tell me you threw my jacket away too? You're not gonna tell me *that*, are ya . . . ? (*No reply.*) Oh, terrific. Getting a cab is gonna be just terrific . . . Running around half-naked on First Avenue . . . (*Closer; urgently.*) Listen to me, I've got . . . I've got to go home, see . . .

NANCY: I was smack in the middle of tellin' you about my life . . .

STANLEY'S VOICE: Nancy, the jacket . . .

NANCY: Okay, here's my story . . . (*She is silent for a moment.*) Oh, I guess I told you my story. I guess that's all there was. Your jacket is in the closet next to the kitchen.

STANLEY'S VOICE: Thank you.

NANCY: Goodness, finished my story and I didn't even know it. (*Martin moves off into his now darkened apartment, softly playing his flute.*)

STANLEY'S VOICE: Christ!

NANCY: What is it, love?

STANLEY'S VOICE: Christ, this *closet* . . . all these *shirts* . . .

NANCY: (*Smiling at flute music.*) He's playing his piccolo again . . .

STANLEY'S VOICE: Shirts, shirts, shirts . . .

NANCY: He plays so sweet . . .

STANLEY'S VOICE: Jesus Christ . . . it's like a Goddamn de*part*ment store in here . . .

NANCY: He plays so sweet, but so sad . . . maybe it's the rain . . .

STANLEY'S VOICE: (*Coming closer.*) Nancy, that's a creepy closet . . .

NANCY: Think of it this way, love, if you saved earrings, how many would you have?

STANLEY'S VOICE: Nancy, that closet is a pathological closet. I personally think you're in a lot of trouble . . .

NANCY: Come on, you figured me for a wacko up front; that's why you hit on me at the office this afternoon—

STANLEY'S VOICE: You're just being hostile because I can't remember the color of your Goddamn eyes.

NANCY: Okay now, Stan, you just go on home to your pills or whatever it is you're callin' your wife this year. Go home and wash me off and tell Mary-Lou how you lost your shirt gamblin'. Dawn's a long time comin' after you boys leave and I like thinkin' about that till I fall asleep. (*Goes to terrace-railing.*) So God damn my eyes and forget my name but never, never take me for a dumbo. I got smarts I ain't used yet, I am the Wonder Book of Knowledge, don't give me no wake-up calls, baby, I been up for hours . . . Looky here, come see the view; everybody's out there cheatin' t' beat hell. Everybody's out there cheatin' and I know it. Old city lookin' to get young, straights lookin' for crazy, low lookin' to get high, everybody lookin' to get out and I got the keys to the city. Ain't a marriage I can't get into, ain't a Mary-Lou I can't bust . . . Wowie, it's two A.M. in Manhattan, honey-babe, and everybody's lookin' for some nice, new, good old days. (*She is silent for a few moments. No sound from the doorway.*) I shall assume by your silence, sir, that you have decided to break off our engagement. (*No reply.*) Hey there, ol' Stan . . . Hey Stan? . . . (*No reply. She starts to unbutton the shirt.*) Listen, you can have your shirt back, I was only funnin' . . . (*No reply. She sees something far below in the street. She leans forward, squinting.*) Lord . . . (*Leans over the edge, shouts down.*) Hey! . . . Hey, you! . . . Hey, you without a shirt! (*Louder.*) Hey, you forgot to kiss me goodnight! You forgot! (*Martin stops playing his flute. Nancy takes the shirt off, rolls it angrily into a ball, and tosses it sharply down towards the street. She looks silently down into the street for several moments. Whispering.*) God damn . . . you didn't even kiss me goodnight.

> (*The Street Lady scurries out from the shadows below, snaps up Stanley's shirt, darts over to bench at Far Right, chuckling over her new treasure, sits on bench, putting shirt on over her coat. Martin moves out onto his terrace, playing his flute again . . . Nancy becomes aware of him, smiling at the gentle music, watching him, zeroing in . . . Lights up on Gordon watching them with binoculars.*)

GORDON: (*Quietly.*) Losing her . . . losing Shortie-Nightie . . .

CAMILLE'S VOICE: (*From inside Gordon's terrace-doorway.*) Gordon, let me give you a perfect example of how well I understand this relationship . . .

GORDON: What is this guy . . . some kinda Goddamn pied Piper . . . ?

CAMILLE'S VOICE: Monday night when I woke up and said these things were stabbing me and you said they were paperclips and I saw they were hairpins, I did not pursue the issue . . .

BUM'S VOICE: Hey, what's goin' on here, what time is it . . . ?
(*Lights up on Bum sprawled in shadows Down Left.*)

GORDON: I could play my guitar, but I'm too far away . . .
(*Lights up on Sally at open street-phone near Street Lady's bench at Far Right, her suitcase next to her, Street Lady listening with great interest. Martin moving to terrace-railing as he continues playing flute, Nancy watching him.*)

BUM: (*Quietly, to no one in particular.*) I'm a commercial fisherman, gotta get to Sheepshead Bay . . .

CAMILLE'S VOICE: I did not pursue the idiotic idea that you sleep in a bed full of paper-clips . . .

SALLY: (*Into phone, reading from notebook.*)
If you're a bird, be an early bird,
And be sure to fill your breakfast plate.
If you're a bird, be an early, early bird,
But if you're a worm, sleep late. (*She laughs, Street Lady laughs with her. Flute music and lights on Martin, Nancy and Gordon gradually fading during Sally's call.*) Nice, huh? Gloria, you have just been privileged to hear number One Hundred and Eighty-One in my ever-popular and yet to be published collection of children's poetry. I'm reading them to you because they protect me from muggers out here. It's like Wolfbane . . .

Bum: (*Takes tattered wristwatch from pocket.*) What time is it? I'm late, I'm late . . .

Sally: Yeah, we had a nice talk and I think he'll make a great first husband. (*After a moment.*) O.K., I guess it's on for tomorrow morning. Eight o'clock. Listen, you don't have to stay for the whole thing, just come at the end and take me back to your place. Dr. Gerstad says I'll be rocky for a coupla days . . .

Bum: Ain't no hands on this watch . . . What time is it? Anybody got the time here . . . ?

Sally: I don't know, nervous. And I've got this terrible, creepy sense of freedom.

Bum: It's like May or June or something, right?

Sally: Look, the . . . tomorrow, the procedure, how long does it take? . . . Gloria, "zappo" is, not my favorite surgical image . . . I *know* it's nothin' and I know it's legal, but it still ain't throwin' away a stale corn-muffin, right?

Bum: Anybody got the time, here? . . .

Sally: Listen, I'll see ya in a coupla hours, O.K.? Just leave the couch, Glo, I'll open it myself. Thought I'd sorta walk around for a coupla hours. Don't worry, I'll be fine— (*Indicates Street Lady.*) my mother is here. (*She laughs, Street Lady laughs with her.*) I'm fine. Really. I'm O.K. . . . (*Suddenly shaky.*) No, I don't want to speak to Barry . . . Because he's a *dog*, because he's a Goddamn dog! (*She hangs up sharply.*)

Nancy's Voice: (*A loud whisper.*) Watch it, Mister! (*Lights up on Martin playing his flute, his eyes closed, at edge of terrace. Nancy moving quickly into her terrace light as Sally exits with her suitcase at Right, Street Lady following her. Martin opens his eyes, stops playing flute.*) You keep your eyes closed you'll go right over.

MARTIN: Oh, yes . . . (*Turns to her.*) Thank you very much, Miss . . . appreciate that. (*He sits at his picnic-table. She starts to go inside . . . A loud whisper.*) Excuse me . . . Miss?

NANCY: (*Turns to him.*) Yes?

MARTIN: Hello.

NANCY: Hello.

MARTIN: How ya doin'?

NANCY: Fine. How *you* doin'?

MARTIN: Fine. I'm Martin Cramer.

NANCY: Nancy Gresham.

MARTIN: Hello, Nancy. (*Indicates the wide space between them.*) I'd shake your hand but I'd kill myself.

NANCY: Yes, you would. And I surely would miss your piccolo music.

MARTIN: Thank you. It's a flute, actually. (*They are silent for a moment. She becomes aware of her fading make-up; touches her cheek. He begins polishing his flute with the sleeve of his sweat shirt.*)

NANCY: You really must forgive me for appearin' before you in this fashion . . .

MARTIN: You look fine. Really.

NANCY: I was just about to do my arts and crafts . . . (*Points to huge make-up kit on her picnic table.*) Make-up. That tool chest there; that's my make-up kit.

MARTIN: All that? Hardly seems necessary.

NANCY: Kills the time . . . (*Smiles, touches her cheek.*) on my face. (*After a moment.*) Sure some hullabaloo last week.

MARTIN: Beg your pardon?

NANCY: Lord, you come runnin' out on that terrace, hollerin'. Thought you was hollerin' *at* somebody, but you were all alone, wavin' this piece of paper and hollerin' 'bout some Fishback fellah—

MARTIN: Pardon me—

NANCY: Then you was hollerin' 'bout Gristede Brothers—

MARTIN: No, Miss, that wasn't here—

NANCY: Then later, there was this cryin' sound—

MARTIN: (*Sharply.*) No, not possibly; you see I was alone here at that time and—

NANCY: That's why most people cry.

MARTIN: (*Raising his voice.*) It must have been another apartment, or perhaps a television set. (*They are silent for a moment.*)

NANCY: (*Nodding.*) Yeah; musta been the TV. . . . Sorry for making a personal remark.

MARTIN: That's quite all right, really. (*Silence. Martin searches his mind for the proper words and the courage to say them. He finds neither. Sound of distant Siren, rising, then fading away.*)

NANCY: Well, g'night now.

MARTIN: Yes, goodnight.

NANCY: You keep your eyes open, hear? I surely would miss that piccolo music.

MARTIN: Thank you. (*She goes to the other end of her terrace, sits at picnic-table, her back to Martin. He sits regretfully at his picnic-table; speaks quietly, to himself.*) It's a flute, actually.

  (*Carlton suddenly appears at the edge of the terrace just*

*above Martin's, holding the Doorman's pass-keys in his
hand. He glances about quickly, grabs an ice bucket and a
portable radio from the terrace and disappears quickly back
into the shadows. Nancy's lights dim, we can still see her as
she studies her reflection in the mirror on the lid of her
make-up kit and begins a very precise make-up ritual which
she will continue throughout this next scene. There is a sudden creaking noise from inside Martin's darkened apartment. A small, forbidding silhouette appears in the light of
the open front-doorway. Martin remains quite still at first,
his fingers tense on his flute. Then Martin enters quietly
through the terrace door, stands still in the darkened room,
his hand gripping his flute like a weapon at the ready. The
Silhouette holds quite still in the rectangle of light.)*

THE SILHOUETTE: (*Gravel voiced, tough.*) Come closer. (*Martin does not move.*) Identify yourself.

MARTIN: Who are you?

THE SILHOUETTE: Identify yourself, Goddamnit.

MARTIN: Who the hell—

THE SILHOUETTE: Are you Martin Cramer?

MARTIN: Why do you want to know?

THE SILHOUETTE: Because if you're Martin Cramer, then I'm
your father-in-law . . . and if you're not then you're a junky or
a darky or a spic with a club and I'm in a lot of trouble.

MARTIN: (*Turning the main light on.*) Joe . . . (*Joe Kaminsky
steps into the room. He is a small, tough, fast-moving old man
between seventy and eighty with a true New York street voice.
He wears an Air Force leather jacket, sun glasses, an old cap,
and a white silk scarf worn in World War One Air Ace style.*)

JOE: (*Clapping his hands.*) Okay, Stiffo, what's up?

MARTIN: Joe, it's three o'clock in the—

JOE: I drive a cab all night. For me it's lunch time. (*Gesturing at the room.*) What happened: Did I miss the auction? (*Goes into bedroom.*) Where's my daughter? Where's the furniture? Where's Barry? Not even the dog is here . . .

MARTIN: (*Following him.*) Joe, what're you—

JOE: Two months, Charlie. Nobody calls. New place, no invite. Something's wrong. (*Going out onto terrace.*) I'm driving, I see lights, I come up. Whatta they get for a place like this, five hundred, six? (*Sits at picnic-table.*)

MARTIN: (*Sits opposite him; quietly.*) Joe, what's happened is rather simple, really. Your daughter and I—

JOE: (*Jumps up from table.*) Wait a minute, I'm getting depressed here! (*Claps his hands, pacing.*) Whatta they get here, six hundred, seven? I love the protection. Downstairs they got a leprechaun sleepin' in a general's uniform. Upstairs the door is open—

MARTIN: I must've forgotten to—

JOE: Maybe that's how your wife got away. This here porch, ya got no view here . . .

MARTIN: You can see the river—

JOE: I got news for ya. That's a building with bricks. A river you get water with boats.

MARTIN: No, no, see— (*Leans over railing.*) Right down there, see, and around there—

JOE: You been gypped, fellah . . .

MARTIN: Look, it's—

JOE: Gypo, Charlie, gyperoonie . . .

MARTIN: Joe, it's right *there* . . .

JOE: Hey, wait a minute . . . you really believe you *can* see the

river, don't ya? . . . (*Touches his face, affectionately.*)
Schmuck, you been robbed. Goddamn porches . . .

MARTIN: Actually, it's a terrace—

JOE: Charlie, for seven hundred bucks you can call it a Lazy
Susan. Who's the tootsie? (*Indicating Nancy. She remains on
her terrace with her back to them, doing her makeup.*) I seen
ya lookin' at the tootsie.

MARTIN: That's a neighbor, we—

JOE: I love how dumb you think I am.

MARTIN: I think you've misunderstood the—

JOE: Wait a minute . . . (*Sits next to him; quietly.*) You think
I'm knockin' the tootsie? The tootsies, the bimbos, they are the
blood of life; they are hopefulness itself, without which I suggest you go sit in the closet and talk to your suits. (*Bangs on
the table.*) I am now seventy, seventy-five, maybe eighty; a
tootsie gets in the cab, no brassiere, the bouncing alone keeps
me alive another month. They wink at me and a young fellah
winks back at them from a million years ago; Kaminsky lives!
(*Pounding on the table.*) A nice tush moves tomorrow on the
avenue, I'll be there to see it! There's a lotta guys dead because they got nothin' better to do, dying is their *hobby*.
(*Stands, takes his cap off.*) *I* am a God damn dirty old man;
but a dirty old man beats a dead old man every time out.
(*Sits; pats Martin's hand.*) How's the marriage going?

MARTIN: Well, Joe, not splendidly. I'd like to talk to you about—

JOE: Sure, right . . .

MARTIN: See, I guess people change, and—

JOE: (*Jumps up.*) I'm getting depressed again! (*Pacing.*) I'm
seventy-five, maybe eighty, and I don't want any more bad
news!

MARTIN: I was hoping you could give me some insight into Sally's behavior—

JOE: (*Shoves Martin back in his chair.*) My daughter is crazy, always was. So is her mother, and the other two girls is total ding-dongs. There's nobody to talk to, that's why I come here . . . (*Sits next to him.*) Let's establish a little Goddamn *contact* here, Charlie . . . (*Quietly, confidentially.*) I will tell you at this time about a tootsie . . . from the old days, when there was *tootsies*. I had this act in vaudeville, perhaps I mentioned it to you . . .

MARTIN: Yes, you have, Joe, I—

JOE: You lookin' bored at me?

MARTIN: No, I'm just trying to talk to you about me and—

JOE: You was lookin' bored at me— (*Suddenly, fiercely, grabs Martin's arms; shaking him.*) You look bored at me one *second* I'll crack open your head! One shot and you got a porch fulla brains! Don't you *dare*—

MARTIN: (*Prying Joe's hands off.*) Stop shakin' me, will ya? Christ, what *is* that, a family tradition?

JOE: (*Shouting.*) We gotta *discuss!* (*Shoves him back down on bench, shouting.*) Let's have a Goddamn relationship here! (*Quietly, smiling, sitting next to him.*) We had this act, see. Dancing and jokes; me and Florabelle Newsome . . . Florabelle Newsome, to this day the name alone gives me a chill. Adorable Florabelle Newsome. Ginger hair and a face fulla secrets; terrific secrets, also the best tush in all of Newark, New Jersey . . . (*Suddenly depressed.*) Trouble is . . . Florabelle, on May fourth, nineteen twenty-one . . . I did this terrible thing to her . . . (*Joe lapses into silence, looking away. Martin leans close to him.*)

MARTIN: Joe . . . what did you do . . . ?

JOE: I married her . . . (*Banging on the table.*) I *married* her, Goddamnit! I loved her and I *married* her! *There,* I *told* you! I had to tell somebody . . .

MARTIN: Joe, I had no idea that you had a wife before Helen . . .

JOE: Dummy, *that's Helen!* (*Bangs his fist on the table, shouting.*) Florabelle Newsome, formerly the top tush in all of Newark! Helen Kaminsky! Can you believe it!? That crazy old lady who drives me up the Goddamn wall! That, *that* is adorable Florabelle Newsome . . . I mean, for Chrissakes, she must be what now, seventy, seventy-five . . . (*Whispers.*) My God, will ya look at that tootsie over there? She puts on her makeup and hope springs eternal . . . (*Stands, shouting.*) Hey, tootsie! Hey, tootsie on the porch! (*No reply. He speaks quietly, romantically.*) Don't she know she's a tootsie? Don't she know, right now, this minute, I would get in my cab and take her to the moon? (*Suddenly shouting, anguished.*) Love! Marriage! Children! I left show business! (*Outraged.*) Safe! Safe. Howd'ya-do, three daughters and a hundred miles of linoleum! I wake up every morning shocked! (*Pounding on the table.*) *Love,* Charlie, Goddamn love! Half the murders in New York, they say it's for love! (*Grips Martin's arm urgently.*) That's why I wanted to talk to ya tonight. What should I do, Marty?

MARTIN: About what exactly, Joe?

JOE: My marriage. I gotta get *outa* there; that crazy old dame . . . Been sleepin' in the hack five days runnin'. This is it, Charlie; over and out—

MARTIN: (*His hand on Joe's shoulder.*) Joe, Helen loves you, she—

JOE: (*Going to edge of terrace.*) Hey, tootsie! Hey, you . . . (*No reply; he shrugs.*) Maybe it's a fella . . . (*Goes to Martin, urgently.*) I want your frank opinion; how about a trial separation? Little place uptown, my own place, a little freedom; Goddamnit, a little time to think things out. Hey— (*Grabs*

Martin's arm inspired.) If you're gonna be alone, what about *here!* Perfect! You and me, Marty, terrific! (*Going to edge of terrace.*) Who knows, in a little while I'll see the river too! (*Joe is suddenly silent . . . exhausted, he leans against the terrace railing. He sits at the picnic-table, his energy gone; very quietly.*) Charlie, what the hell am I talkin' about . . . ? I ain't goin' *nowhere.* Fact of the matter is, I'm a crazy old man and I ain't goin' nowhere. (*Looks up at Martin.*) Christ, what *am* I, seventy, seventy-five . . . ?

MARTIN: You're seventy-eight, Joe.

JOE: (*After a moment, quietly.*) Already? (*Rising.*) Jesus, I better get outa here . . . (*Crossing into room.*) Ya leave a cab alone five minutes it turns into a taco stand . . . (*Stops, turns.*) How the hell do ya know Helen loves me? How do ya know that?

MARTIN: Because she—

JOE: I'll give the broad a call; *one* call. Been sleepin' in the Goddamn *cab* for five days; got robbed tonight. One quick nap and somebody clips my coin-changer! Reminds me— (*Goes to Martin.*) got ya a little somethin' for the new place, a household item— (*Takes a .38 caliber revolver from his pocket, hands it to Martin.*)

MARTIN: Joe, I can't—

JOE: Don't worry, I got six more— (*Pointing to street.*) There's a war down there, Charlie. Darkies, Puertos, junkies; war. (*Shaking Martin's hand.*) Marty, a pleasure; good night and God bless ya. (*To Nancy.*) Good night, tootsie . . . (*No reply; he shouts.*) Hey, tootsie with the towel! (*She turns to him; he whispers to Martin.*) See, she knows . . . the tootsies know . . . (*Goes to edge of terrace; grandly, removing his hat with a flourish.*) Dear girlie . . . tootsie of the night . . . I pause here to say good-bye . . . For future reference I can be reached by the Supreme Radio Cab Company, Taxi Number

Forty-One, Kaminsky. Wherever you want to go, love and Kaminsky will find a way . . . (*She smiles warmly. He whispers tenderly.*) Looka that . . . Oh sweet tootsie, you are good news . . . (*As he exits through terrace-doorway.*) Enough good news and a man could live forever . . . (*Martin goes quickly to doorway to give the gun back . . .*)

MARTIN: Joe . . . Joe . . . (*But Joe is gone. He hesitates; then goes out on terrace, looks up at Nancy. Nancy snaps shut the lid of the make-up kit; she has done well with her work, the edges are softened; she touches her hair delicately. Carlton appears in a slice of light on the floor above Martin; he is pulling a small dolly-platform, the caster wheels rolling audibly behind him; the dolly-platform carries the ice bucket and the portable radio, a lamp, a seventeen inch television set and two hi-fi speakers. He disappears into the shadows above, followed by his loot. Nancy and Martin's terrace lights are the only remaining illumination on stage now, other than the bit of night sky between them. The lights in the terraces and windows of the other apartments have long since gone out.*) Nancy, you look . . . fine.

NANCY: Thank you.

MARTIN: Your face; there was hardly any time for you to kill at all . . . A matter of minutes, I would say.

NANCY: Thank you.

MARTIN: Nancy, I would like to suggest . . .

NANCY: I'd feel a hell of a lot better if you put that gun down.

MARTIN: Oh, yes; of course . . . (*Puts gun down on picnic-table. Then, quietly.*) Nancy, I would like to suggest . . .

NANCY: (*Quietly.*) I live in apartment Seventeen N.

MARTIN: (*Leaning forward.*) I . . . I can't hear you . . .

MAN FROM ABOVE: (*In darkness.*) She lives in apartment Seventeen N.

MARTIN: Just mind your own damn—

MAN FROM ABOVE: (*Stepping into his terrace-light.*) I live in apartment Eighteen B . . . does anybody care?

MARTIN: Chrissake, will ya—

MAN FROM ABOVE: I've been listening to your voice, Martin, and I know now that you're *not* one of the short people . . .

MARTIN: Fine, fine; well—

MAN FROM ABOVE: No, you're the one who took a cab away from me last Monday . . .

MARTIN: I wasn't even—

MAN FROM ABOVE: I remember the voice; say "taxi" . . .

MARTIN: Now, look, mister—

MAN FROM ABOVE: Jumped in. Slammed the door in my face. "Taxi! Taxi!" and slam in the face. It was raining. Bet ya thought you'd never run into *me* again, Marty-baby . . .

NANCY: Mister, it wasn't him . . .

MAN FROM ABOVE: You, *you're* the one with the loud records. Why should I listen to *you?* Dancing, dancing, dancing—

NANCY: Look, mister, I—

MAN FROM ABOVE: (*Shouting.*) Be quiet, dancer! This is between me and the door slammer!

MARTIN: (*Leaning over the edge.*) Hey, fellah, I don't appreciate at *all* the way you're talking to the young lady!

MAN FROM ABOVE: (*Shouting.*) How about you come up *here* and not appreciate it! Eighteen *B;* as in *bone* crusher!

NANCY: (*Shouting.*) Go ahead, *holler* . . . and tomorrow night just try and find the *sunset!* (*Silence for a moment.*)

MAN FROM ABOVE: (*Quietly.*) What have you done with the sunset?

NANCY: We're *watchin'* it, baby; from where *you* can't see it! You're on the wrong side of the buildin'! (*Man From Above is silent. She smiles triumphantly.*)

MAN FROM ABOVE: (*Shattering the silence.*) *Great! Keep* the sunset! You want the Goddamn sunset; it's *yours!* I don't expect any better! I know this city! The door-slammers get the cabs and the dancers get the sunset!

NANCY: (*Quietly, to Martin.*) I live in apartment Seventeen N . . .

MARTIN: Seventeen N . . .

NANCY: As in neighborly . . .

MARTIN: I'll be by . . .
(*Nancy exits through terrace doorway to await him within. Lights dim on Martin as he sits at picnic-table contemplating his departure to join Nancy. The Man From Above continues, unaware that no one is listening.*)

MAN FROM ABOVE: (*Still shouting.*) I've got a rotten view of the rotten *parking* lot, but I'm a human *being* and my conscience is clear! *You,* you could have the Goddamn Grand *Canyon* out there and you'd still be miserable! I know alla you twitchy, screwed-up New York guys! You and your faggotty sunset! It's *yours!* (*After a moment.*) Think about that. (*Another moment.*) Nothing to say, Martin? . . . No smart talk, Seventeen N? (*Silence. Then, more quietly.*) Actually . . . I want you to feel free to discuss this with me. I'm willing to listen to your point of view . . . (*After a moment.*) Because, you see, there's a lot of this that I don't . . . understand . . .

(*A phone rings. Lights up on Gordon alone on his terrace, scanning the city with his binoculars. Phone on his picnic-table rings again. He will continue to look through binoculars during this scene.*)

CAMILLE'S VOICE: Aren't you going to answer that?

GORDON: Two in the morning. Must be a nut.
(*Phone stops in middle of third ring.*)

CAMILLE'S VOICE: Maybe it's the same nut who uses paper-clips in her hair. (*Silence.*) Anyway, I'm going home now. Because what I have asked for is a definition of this relationship. This relationship here, and if we're not going to have that discussion then I'm going home now. (*Sound of retreating foot steps, a door opening.*) Gordon, I'm going home now and don't expect to hear from me. Goodbye. (*Silence.*) If you should want to discuss this with me I will be at the office number during the day and from five to about seven-thirty I will be at the Russian Tea Room, they can page me. If there's any of this you want to discuss. Goodnight, Gordon.

GORDON: (*Turning from binoculars.*) Goodnight. (*Sound of door closing; the phone rings, he picks it up immediately.*) Hello. (*Silence.*) Hello . . . Hello . . . ?
(*Lights up on Sally at Far Right street phone; Street Lady on bench near her, listening intently to Sally's call.*)

SALLY: (*After a moment, tensely.*) Hello.

GORDON: Who is this? Who's calling?

SALLY: Hello, Gordon . . . ?

GORDON: Yes.

SALLY: Gordon, it's Sally, of all people.

GORDON: Sally?

SALLY: Did I wake you?

GORDON: No.

SALLY: You said to call anytime. And here it is, anytime.

GORDON: Right.

SALLY: Sally Cramer, from the park. I mean, the bench. You read some of my poems last week . . . said you published children's books, we—

GORDON: Sally Cramer, with the lovely poems. The lovely lady with the lovely poems.

SALLY: That's the one. The lovely one.

GORDON: I was hoping you'd call.

SALLY: I was hoping I wouldn't.

GORDON: Sally, where are you now? (*No reply.*) Sally, where are you?

SALLY: At the bench, I—

GORDON: Would you like me to come down there, Sally?

SALLY: No.

GORDON: Would you like to come up here?

SALLY: No.

GORDON: What would you like?

SALLY: I would like you to fall madly in love with me and think I'm wonderful and throw yourself at my feet; and I would like you to do it on the phone.

GORDON: (*Laughing.*) Sally, I'll be right over.

SALLY: No, I don't think—

GORDON: I'll be right over.

SALLY: Hold on now, let's— (*He hangs up. Lights out on Gordon's terrace as he exits. Sally stands still for a moment with the phone in her hand, realizing what she has just done. She hangs up, turns to Street Lady.*) Wait'll ya meet him, Ma; you're gonna love him. (*Lights dim on Sally. The three people are illuminated in their isolated positions on the stage—the Man From Above on his terrace; Martin at Center seated at his picnic-table, lighting a cigarette, about to leave for Nancy; Sally below at phone, waiting for Gordon. The three figures quite still, quite separate. The Street Lady goes to the phone-booth, delighted to find a few loose coins which have been left there; exits into the shadows at Right, chuckling over her treasure.*)

MAN FROM ABOVE: (*Quietly.*) I had this habachi stove out here; steaks, chops, frankfurters, you name it. I loved that habachi stove. Then, last month, I went to Camp Young-Fun for the weekend. I saw the ad, what the hell, I went. I drove sixty-eight miles upstate and when I got there everybody was old and there was no fun. And when I got back my habachi stove was gone. (*Glancing about.*) Who is taking all the things away? . . . Martin, do you know? . . . Seventeen N? . . . Any of you? . . . Feel free to answer please . . (*Quietly*) Miss Gerber, the receptionist with daisies on her blouse and sad, sad eyes; gone one day without a word and now there's a strange old woman answering the phone with a baby's voice. Who is taking all the things away? . . . Who are they? . . . Who are they? . . . (*Shouting.*) Who are they? (*The three people remain quite still, a siren wails distantly, the sound growing louder as . . .*)

Curtain

ACT TWO

Before the curtain rises there is the sound of the flute music and gentle, late night traffic.

At rise: It's about an hour later on this quiet summer night. Gordon lights a cigarette at Center, waiting. He wears carefully faded jeans and a sweater. The flute music fades as he moves into the light of the bench on the small balcony over the river at Right. He sits on the bench. Sound of a distant ferry-whistle from the invisible river below him. The Bum enters from the shadows at Far Left, wearing a baseball-cap; he shuffles towards Gordon. Gordon turns to him.

BUM: (*Cordially, tipping his cap.*) 'Evenin'. (*Sits next to Gordon on bench, crosses his legs, leans back comfortably, looks out at the river. He smiles sociably at Gordon. Gordon tries to ignore him. He looks at Gordon for a long moment.*) I'm in the goin' away business. You give me a dollar and I go away. (*Gordon sighs; give him a dollar. Bum remains seated, looking at him.*) I'm also in the stayin' away business. For another dollar I never come back. (*Gordon gives him another dollar. The Bum is very pleased; tips his cap, rises.*) It's a pleasure doin' business with you. (*Sally enters near phone, carrying a bag of Chinese take-out food and her suitcase; unnoticed by them, watching. The Bum is triumphant, inspired as he exits off into the shadows at Far Left.)* I found it. . . I found one . . . A specialty! I got me a specialty! (*Gordon watches him leave; turns, sees Sally standing near phone.*)

SALLY: Hello.

GORDON: (*He rises.*) Hello, Sally.

SALLY: That's not really a river, y'know.

GORDON: It isn't?

SALLY: No, it's an isthmus. It has no source, see. Just connects the Atlantic back up with the Atlantic. That makes it an isthmus.

GORDON: I see.

SALLY: That's what I came to tell you. (*He laughs warmly. She remains near phone, he remains several feet away at bench.*) Well, everybody showed up.

GORDON: Yes.

SALLY: Kind of a tension in the air, ya notice that? (*He smiles.*) Certainly is different from meeting here during the day.

GORDON: It's more exciting.

SALLY: Yes. It is.

GORDON: More possibilities.

SALLY: You bet.

GORDON: Also it's the beginning for us. That's the best part; hope, anticipation, the beginning.

SALLY: I figure you fool around a lot, right?

GORDON: I just try to arrange for as many beginnings as possible.

SALLY: "Fool around"; are they still saying that? I don't know what they're saying anymore. I've been away a long time. Fact is, there's a good chance I was never even there. (*He laughs warmly.*) Hey, I'm really goin' over pretty good here . . . (*She moves to the bench; sits, busily opening cartons and distributing food. He sits opposite her.*) I hope you like Chinese food. I always like Chinese food. It makes me feel optimistic somehow. There's this place on First that's open till three A.M. and I wanted to bring something besides myself. The spare-ribs are great. They put honey on them . . . God, there's nothing in my fortune cookie. Do you suppose that means anything? (*Follows his gaze to the suitcase.*) Oh, I'm crazy about big handbags. Actually, I just left my husband. I was gonna go to my girlfriend's place but she talks about abortions all night. Nothing's more boring than other people's abortions, right? I'm getting one tomorrow. At Bloomingdale's. There's a sale. You haven't touched your egg-roll. Did you really like my children's poetry? Do you remember the first line of "The Flying Festoon?" I mean, did you really like my poems or were you just trying to make out? . . . I bet they're not saying *that* anymore either . . . (*Softly, looking away.*) Well, what the hell *are* they saying . . . ? (*Puts down spare-rib, near tears.*) Damn it, what do people do? I don't know how to do this . . . (*She rises, picks up suitcase.*) I hate not knowing, I've always been the smartest one in my class. Especially now, they're all twelve. (*Starts to walk away.*)

GORDON: Sally, please stay—

SALLY: Look, I'm feeling crazy.

GORDON: That's O.K.—

SALLY: And I can't shut up—

GORDON: That's O.K.—

SALLY: And I'm not even going to sleep with you—

GORDON: Stay anyway—

SALLY: Christ, don't you have *any* standards? (*She walks briskly away, to Right.*)

GORDON: (*Softly.*) "Oh, I'm going to fly with the Flying Festoon, I'll jump on his back and I'll whistle a tune . . ." (*She stops, smiles.*) "Oh, I'm taking an apple, a ball and a prune, And we're leaving this evening, precisely at noon, 'cause I'm going to fly with the Flying Festoon . . . just as soon as he learns how to fly."

SALLY: Okay, let's go to bed. (*He laughs. She returns to the bench.*) Hey, I'm really very flattered . . .

GORDON: (*Sits on bench.*) Memorized it on my way over here. (*Takes pages from pocket.*) The stuff you gave me . . . you said it was your favorite so I figured I could score a coupla points with it.

SALLY: (*Sits opposite him.*) Oh.

GORDON: I also don't publish children's books. When I met you here you were writing children's poems, so that's what I was. If you'd been flying a kite I'd be an astronaut.

SALLY: Aren't you giving away a lot of trade secrets here?

GORDON: Part of my routine . . . when all else fails, I try honesty.

SALLY: You're amazing.

GORDON: Just dedicated.

SALLY: Tell me, do you . . . do you get alot of drop-in business like this?

GORDON: Some.

SALLY: What about somebody to care about, somebody there . . .

GORDON: You mean like marriage? Something always stops me.

SALLY: What?

GORDON: My wife. She's very much against it. And then there's the children . . . (*Rises, pacing in front of bench.*) You look surprised. Well, imagine how I feel; I thought I was twenty-six. Sitting here waiting for you, I thought I was twenty-six . . . Me and the kids, we have dinner together every other Sunday; they sit there, growing . . . calling me Daddy and other vicious names . . .

SALLY: Your wife won't give you a divorce?

GORDON: Not even for Christmas. (*He stops pacing.*) Truth is, Sally, I've stopped asking. Most of the ladies I see prefer it this way. It's like the fire law; all the exits are clearly marked. (*Gestures in the Bum's direction.*) I'm in the goin' away business. Give me a future, and I go away. (*He is silent for a moment. He turns to her, gently.*) Sally, you don't belong here.

SALLY: I've got a feeling this isn't part of your routine.

GORDON: It isn't. Sally, I like you.

SALLY: I sorta like you too. (*They are silent for a moment. She remains seated on bench, he remains standing several feet away.*) Well, that's it. That's the smallest small talk I've got . . . At least ya gotta give me credit for not telling you my life story . . . I think men like young girls because their stories are shorter . . . (*After a moment, softly.*) Look, am I too old for this?

GORDON: For what?

SALLY: (*Looking away.*) I mean, I figure you generally get a much younger crowd here.

GORDON: Sally, you're lovely . . . (*Moving to the bench.*) Funny and warm and straight and lovely . . . (*He leans forward, kisses her; perfunctorily at first, and then it becomes more tender, more involved. He holds her face in his hands; he is upset, speaks quietly.*) Sally, listen, I . . . see, I like you . . . I really like you.

SALLY: I know, that's why I didn't run away.

GORDON: (*Sits next to her.*) Sally, you don't belong here. Run, do not walk; this is for terminal cases.

SALLY: I know that too. Mister, I've got a rotten marriage on Eighty-First Street and a German shepherd on Seventieth . . . you look like my best bet tonight. (*Quietly, tensely.*) Be glad, will ya? I'm askin' ya to be glad to see me. (*He touches her hand gently. Silence for a moment. He rises, picks up her suit-case, turns in the direction of his building. She rises. They stand quite still for a moment.*) Look, I'm nervous.

GORDON: I'm nervous too.

SALLY: I can't help you.

GORDON: My hand is shaking . . . can you imagine that? (*Comes towards her.*) What happened is . . . I think what happened is, we talked . . . we became friends . . .

SALLY: And you never screw your friends, right? (*He laughs, hugs her warmly.*) Just keep laughing, Gordon, and we'll be O.K. (*He starts walking towards his building, carrying her suitcase. He stops, turns, holds out his hand to her. She hesi-tates a moment, then joins him. As they exit, hand in hand, into the shadows at Left.*) Jesus, it's hard to make this look like an accident . . .

(*The Street Lady scurries out from the shadows at Right, grabbing up the remains of the Chinese food and carrying her prize to the curb at Center where she sits portioning out the food into two paper-plates from her shopping-bag; care-fully giving equal amounts to her imaginary guest. During the Street Lady's picnic the lights cross-fade gradually to the colors of pre-dawn, indicating the passage of several*

*hours in about fifteen seconds, flute music rising and then
fading into the dawn light. Nancy comes out on her terrace
wearing Martin's red, N.Y.U. sweatshirt. She sips at a
glass of red wine, smiles at the gentle pre-dawn colors.
Although the light onstage has been altered enough to indicate the passage of time, there is still enough pre-morning
darkness to isolate the individual terrace areas with light,
and to fade in and out of these areas during the next few
scenes.)*

NANCY: (*Quietly, looking at the Man From Above's darkened
terrace.*) Poor ol' Eighteen B . . . Can't see the sunrise neither.
(*Silence for a moment.*)

MARTIN'S VOICE: (*Sleepily, from inside Nancy's terrace-doorway.*) Nancy . . . ?

NANCY: Yes, neighbor?

MARTIN'S VOICE: Did you . . . did you happen to see where I
put my shoes?

NANCY: (*Takes a sip of wine.*) What color are my eyes, neighbor?

MARTIN'S VOICE: (*After a moment.*) Green. With flecks of gray.

NANCY: (*Quietly.*) Son-of-a-gun . . . ain't had a winner in a
long time.

MARTIN: What?

NANCY: I said your stuff's out here. Your shirt too.

MARTIN'S VOICE: Oh. (*Comes to doorway wearing his jacket;
remains standing awkwardly in doorway, raises his hand.*) Hi.

NANCY: (*Turns to him.*) Kinda partial to your sweatshirt; d'ya
think I could—

MARTIN: Please, keep it. Glad for you to have it.

NANCY: Lord, we *slept* together . . . for hours. Regular ol' beddy-bye sleepin'. We made it till dawn . . . and that makes you the winner . . . (*Handing him his shoes as though presenting an award.*) the all-time, champeen, winner.

MARTIN: (*Accepting the shoes.*) Uh . . . perhaps some other time we could . . .

NANCY: (*Kindly, but not believing a word of it.*) Sure. (*Handing him a bottle of wine.*) We finished your red, here's some of my white.

MARTIN: Thank you . . . Unfortunately, I have to leave now. You see, I have some very valuable furniture downtown, that I have to check on, it's—

NANCY: (*Gently.*) Sure, honey.

MARTIN: No, really, it's a rather valuable collection of antiques; it's relatively unguarded at the moment and I was planning to—

NANCY: (*Smiling.*) Good night, honey.

MARTIN: Good night . . . (*His hands full with the shoes and wine, gesturing to flute on her picnic-table.*) Uh . . . my . . . piccolo . . .

NANCY: (*She hands it to him; smiling gently.*) It's a flute, actually.
> (*Martin exits; light remains on Nancy, alone again on her terrace. She sips her wine. Lights up on Street Lady below on the curb continuing her picnic, deeply engaged in a very animated though mute conversation with her imaginary guest.*)

MAN FROM ABOVE'S VOICE: (*Quietly.*) Hello? . . . Hello . . . ?
> (*Lights up on his terrace, he is talking into the phone. Lights gradually fading on Nancy and Street Lady while he contin-*)

ues.) Good morning, Speedy's All Night Pizza? Good. I tell ya, I'm the kinda guy I feel like a pizza at five-thirty in the morning, I order a pizza; because that's the kinda guy I am. I go with the moment . . . Oh, I'm sorry; of course, what kind of pizza. I musn't keep you . . . uh . . . I imagine you're handling the phones and the pizza all by yourself at this hour; of course, forgive me. I'll be brief. May I ask who I'm speaking to . . . ? (*Smiling broadly.*) Speedy? Speedy himself? My goodness. Well, Speedy, let me tell you, your ad in the Yellow Pages is really quite an eye-catcher. Wonderful design; A smiling pizza with wings! Y'know, I really . . . Hello? . . . Hello, Speedy? . . . Speedy? . . . (*Lights up on Gordon's terrace; Sally alone at railing, wearing Gordon's bathrobe, looking out at us and the city through his binoculars. Her hands begin to tremble, she puts the binoculars down; she is crying.*) Hello? . . . Hello, Speedy? . . . Hello? . . . Hello . . . ? (*Lights fade on Man From Above. Sally grips the terrace-railing tensely, still crying softly. A piece of the railing comes off in her hand; she grips the small piece of railing in anguish and surprise, drops it on the terrace-floor, covers her eyes with her hand.*)

BUM'S VOICE: My own specialty! . . . (*Lights up on Bum entering at Left and Street Lady on curb at Center eating spare-rib, as lights fade on Sally. Bum approaches Street Lady.*) See, lady, I used to work Third and Fourteenth . . . hustlin' cars at the light; wipe the windshield, get a quarter, somethin' . . . (*Sits next to her on curb, takes a spare-rib.*) Down there, see, they *expect* to see ya there; that's Bum-turf, that's Wino-land for sure . . . but up here, uptown, they want you out and gone; up here they will shell out to see me go . . . a dollar, maybe two, *disappearin'* money! They don't want to see them bad faces, lady, no sir; gets 'em thinkin' on hard times, gets 'em thinkin' on time comin' and time gone . . . gets 'em to lay out that beautiful go-away money. Sweet Jesus, I got me a specialty! (*Looks at her a moment.*) Give ya a tip . . . (*Leans towards her confidentially.*) Ladies up here, face like yours, I bet you could get five dollars to go away, easy.

(*Sally enters at Left with suitcase, crossing to entrance of Riverview East. The Street Lady watches as Sally places her suitcase inside the entrance doorway and comes back out to the still sleeping Doorman.*)

SALLY: Devlin, I'm leaving my suitcase in the lobby for a coupla minutes. I'll be right back, keep an eye on it for me, will ya . . . ? Devlin . . . ? (*Leans closer to him.*) Devlin . . . ? (*Shrugs.*) Sleep tight, Devlin, darling. (*Sally exits into the building. The Street Lady rises from the curb carrying her shopping bags, carefully passing behind Devlin and going into the building. She has left behind the umbrella she stole earlier; it rests on the curb next to the Bum. The Bum grabs up the umbrella and scurries off into the shadows, Far Left. The Street Lady comes out of the building carrying Sally's suitcase, walking slowly at first and then racing off into the shadows at Right.*)

MAN FROM ABOVE: My TV is gone . . . (*As lights come up on his terrace.*) I was right, it is the midgets! Stood here and watched one of them. A small, dark midget with a little truck . . . came right into the living room and took the Late Show away.

SALLY: Marty . . . (*Light fades on Man From Above, as Sally appears in the doorway of the darkened Cramer apartment; a silhouette in the rectangle of light. The shape of the blankets on the bed give her the impression that Martin is lying there. She remains in the doorway.*) Marty, it's me . . . Sally Jane Cramer; moving and storage . . . Well, how's the separation going so far? (*No reply.*) Look, there's something I didn't think we should talk about on the phone. There's something I'm gonna do tomorrow and all of a sudden it seemed sorta unconstitutional that you never got to vote on it or anything—

CARLTON: (*From the darkness.*) Mrs. Cramer . . .

SALLY: (*Startled, whispering.*) Who's that . . . ?

CARLTON: Man, you been cleaned out. Somebody clean you out good here.

SALLY: (*Going toward light-switch.*) Carlton—

CARLTON: (*Rushing to her.*) Hold it—don't turn on the light yet—

SALLY: What the hell're you—

CARLTON: Been comin' around here a week now. Where you been?

SALLY: Where have *I* been? You haven't been in *school* for two months, I haven't been able to find you *any*where—

CARLTON: Got a deal for ya—

SALLY: No more deals, Carlton. Look, I've got a lot on my mind tonight; my own troubles— (*Crossing through darkened room to lighted terrace, reaches for phone on picnic-table.*) I'll call your father, he'll take you home—

CARLTON: Wait a minute— (*Coming quickly toward her.*) Here's the deal. I been in grade six three years now. Long time in grade six. Now all you gotta do is move me smooth into grade seven . . . (*Crossing back into room.*) And this here's yours . . . (*Carlton turns on the light. Placed about the room are three T.V. sets, two hi-fi speakers, several lamps, an ice-bucket, some portable radios, an electric broiler, a gold-leaf mirror, an oriental vase, a set of bongo-drums, the rest of Carlton's loot and the dolly-platform he brought them on. Carlton gestures grandly.*) Well, how do ya like the deal?

SALLY: I don't.

CARLTON: What's wrong?

SALLY: Everything. (*Her hand on his arm.*) Carlton, all this stuff, we gotta—

CARLTON: (*Ducking away from her hand.*) Why you always *do* that?

SALLY: What?

CARLTON: That *touchin'*.

SALLY: O.K., Carlton, get this straight. I am your teacher, I am not your fence. On my birthday the other kids bring an apple, you bring a color television set. (*Urgently, close to him, needing him to understand.*) Oh, Carlton; this is not the way outa grade six. I put a lot of time in on you, three hours a week trying to teach you to read, trying to—

CARLTON: (*Picks up one of his books.*) How'm I gonna read this here? "The Wizard Of Oz." Three years now I been with that stoned chick, dumbass dog, an' all them freaks.

SALLY: Carlton, I just can't deal with this tonight (*Goes to phone.*) I'll call your father, he'll come and—

CARLTON: He dead. Somebody blow him away.

SALLY: Oh, God . . . Carlton, I'm sorry, I . . .

CARLTON: Seven years ago.

SALLY: Seven *years* ago . . . who've I been speaking to on the—

CARLTON: Friend James. Old wino cat. Live in the basement there.

SALLY: But how do ya live . . . ? Where do ya—

CARLTON: My daddy's on the Welfare. Wasn't doin' me no good dead, so I put him on the Welfare. Daddy's been on the Welfare 'bout two years now. James pick up the check, me an' him split it.

SALLY: (*Sits, exhausted, at picnic-table.*) Carlton, what am I gonna do with you?

CARLTON: You're gonna move me into grade seven . . . (*Gesturing about the room.*) And I'm gonna get you a couch, coupla chairs, coffee-table . . .

SALLY: Carlton, I'm not in shape for this tonight, I'm—

CARLTON: Four years in grade six; that's pushin' it. They gon' start checkin' up on ol' Carlton here, gon' find out 'bout my Welfare scam, gon' re'bilitate my ass. Livin' loose now, lady, livin' good; city livin' is the best—

SALLY: (*A sudden burst of anger, gripping his arm.*) Carlton, stop it! You *can't live* like this, ya—

CARLTON: No touchin'!

SALLY: Okay! (*Continues forcefully.*) Carlton, here's the score. You can't just come waltzing back into school after two months; they're looking for you, they're gonna slam you right into one of those correctional schools . . .

CARLTON: (*Taken aback, frightened.*) Now that's bad . . . that's the lock-up . . . (*Sits on bed; silent, upset.*)

SALLY: (*Quietly.*) Okay, okay . . . (*Sits next to him, comforting.*) What I could do, see, is get them to place you in my custody. They'd give you a year's probation; means I'd be responsible for you. But if you're gonna hang around with me there's gotta be some rules, see; like about stealing—

CARLTON: (*Indignantly.*) There ya go with that *stealin'* talk. This custody scam, maybe I try it a while, but you got to get things straight. Lady, maybe *you* the one can't read. Check out the Daily News, look what it say there—*every*body takin'. Cops takin', Welfare takin', school takin', whole city takin'. All kinda scam goin', but Carlton the best . . . because he is scammin' the *scammers*. (*Leans back on bed.*) No sir, ain't gon' end up no ol' guy bummin' dimes on the street, no James in the basement . . . (*Nancy comes out on her terrace, sipping wine, still wearing Martin's sweatshirt. Sally sees Nancy and sweatshirt, rises from bed, moves toward terrace; Nancy sees Sally, retreats quickly into her apartment. Sally remains frozen at terrace-railing, more sad than shocked. Carlton closes his eyes, his voice drifting into sleep.*) Sign say "Irving Trust; Save For A Rainy Day" . . . Yeah, ain't no rainy day gon' blow me away . . . no storm neither, no cyclone gon' blow me to Oz . . .

(*There is a blackout and then the sound of someone playing "Streets Of Laredo" on a flute from the back of the theatre as a huge, tattered old motion picture screen drops down in "one" covering the entire set; a glaring work-light goes on at the downstage edge of the apron, above the screen a faded banner reads "Loew's Delancy—Home Of The Stars." Martin comes down the aisle from the back of the theatre, playing his flute, moves up On Stage and then to Center, stops playing, bows gracefully. Martin puts flute in one pocket of jacket, takes wine-bottle out of the other. Drunk, unshaven, punchy, he looks about at the orchestra, the balcony, the ceiling with fondness, even love. His face reflects that beneath the peeling paint, the torn plush seats, the ghostly angels on the ceiling, he still sees the glories of this once grand movie palace. He raises his wine bottle, a celebration and a salute.*)

MARTIN: Here's to ya . . . here's to ya, Loew's Delancy; better known as Low-wees Dee-lancy . . . Home of the stars, home of the galaxies, home of the moon, home of the good guys and the bad guys, a hundred years of Saturday, home sweet home . . . (*Sips the wine; turns, touches the old screen tenderly.*) Hey, baby . . . hey, Dodge City . . . Iwo Jima . . . Casablanca, Shangri-La, Transylvania . . . hey . . . (*Sees his enormous shadow thrown on the screen by the work-light*) Hey, big guy, how's the big guy? (*Watching his shadow, Franken-*

stein's walk, Karloff's voice.) "I don't remember . . . only the flames . . . the flames . . ." (*His jacket a cape, Lugosi's voice.*) "Good evening . . . I don't drink . . . wine, my dear . . ."

MAN'S VOICE: (*Puerto Rican accent; from pit below.*) Hey, what you do here, mister? Hey . . .

MARTIN: (*Looks down in direction of voice; cordially.*) Any requests . . . ?

MAN: (*His head and shoulders appearing from pit.*) Hey, you break in here, I call the cop, they come soon; I'm tellin' you, mister.

MARTIN: (*Takes flute from pocket.*) Could I interest you in the theme from "Spellbound"?

MAN: I'm tellin' you, the cop come soon; I call them, mister.

MARTIN: May I ask your name, sir?

MAN: My name Perez, I call the cop, you better go now.

MARTIN: And in what way are you employed here, Mr. Perez?

PEREZ: I'm the Ni' watchman here, I think you better go now. I see you break in here.

MARTIN: You bet your ass I broke in here—zap, up the fire ladder—wam, through the fire door—zing, down my aisle—

PEREZ: The cop come, I tell the true, mister.

MARTIN: Mr. Perez . . . (*Peering out over glaring light to back rows of theatre; gently.*) Please go up to the second balcony and tell Ruthie Kaplan . . . Ruthie, I appreciate all favors done me at a time of desperate need . . . she will be wearing this powder blue, sorta fuzzy sweater—

PEREZ: Mister—

MARTIN: (*Gently.*) And while you're up there, tell Brucie

Cohen . . . Brucie— (*Shouting.*) you don't lay off I beat the shit outa you!

PEREZ: Is a sin; you talk like that in a house of God, a sin . . .

MARTIN: Huh?

PEREZ: This here Reverend Elija Lincoln's Universal Church Of The Lord. You talk bad on holy ground here.

MARTIN: Jesus . . .

Perez: That's right, Mister. This a blessed place.

MARTIN: What happened to Loew's Delancy?

PEREZ: Gone. Long time now. This here Eglesa now. Religion place. You go now; okay, mister?

MARTIN: It was always a religious place . . . (*Holds bottle down towards Perez.*) Come have some wine with me, Perez . . . let's talk a little . . . (*Perez exits, frightened, into the darkness below.*) Come on, join me . . . wait . . . a little wine . . . (*Martin stands silently for a moment, looking out at the old theatre, alone, confused, homeless; he speaks quietly*) It's gone, Sally; don't ya see? Long, long gone . . . Loew's Delancy is closed, Bogart is dead, and Robinson is dead, and Bendix and Lou Costello, and Gail Russell and Betty Grable . . . Peter Lorre is gone, and Harpo and Sidney Greenstreet, and Whitey Arkish became an accountant and lives in Forest Hills . . . We don't belong here. Everybody went away and it's too late . . .

COP'S VOICE: (*Calmly, from back of theatre.*) Good morning . . . (*Martin looks out in the direction of the voice.*) Good morning, I'm Officer Miranda and this is Officer Simmons, and what we'd like very much is for you to put down your club and—

MARTIN: This is a flute . . .

COP'S VOICE: Good. We got flutes, too. Officer Simmons and me, we've both got flutes.

MARTIN: Jesus, this is silly . . . (*Laughing shakily.*) See, I came for a little visit here, I—

COP'S VOICE: That's called breaking and entering, fellah. Now, if you'll just—

MARTIN: (*Laughing, suddenly aware of his rumpled pants, his jacket over his bare skin.*) Look, I know what this looks like . . . whole thing's really misleading . . . you see, I'm the Principal of the Little Bluebell School . . .

COP'S VOICE: That's good. I'm Robin Hood and this is one of my Merry Men. (*Coming closer.*) And since you won't come down here, we're gonna have to—

MARTIN: I used to live in the neighborhood, see, and I was—

COP'S VOICE: Good. Give us all the details when we book ya . . .

MARTIN: Oh, no . . . no, that would be very unfortunate . . . at this time . . . (*Takes Joe's gun out of his pocket.*) I'm terribly sorry about this . . . but you really must not come down here . . . (*Points gun.*) I would rather you didn't move at all (*Looks at his enormous shadow on the screen, twirls the gun with his trigger-finger; smiles at his shadow; whispers.*) Jesus, Miranda, you got no idea how many times I saw myself on this screen holding a gun . . . no idea . . .

COP'S VOICE: (*Quietly.*) Don't fool with this one, Ralph . . . wait him out . . . (*Louder, carefully, as to a madman.*) See, what you don't know is that all the little bluebells miss you . . . they're havin' this party, they want to see ya and—

MARTIN: (*Trying to be pleasant, dignified.*) I can see that there's no point in attempting to explain these circumstances to you . . . at this time . . . (*Moving towards wings at Right, carefully; holding the gun on them.*) I'm sorry, there would be an incalculable amount of awkwardness involved in my coming with you . . . Forgive me, I have to go now, goodbye . . . goodbye, I don't live here anymore . . .

(*Sudden sound of a wailing siren . . . Martin exits, racing into wings as siren grows louder and screen goes up . . . revealing the set at the beginning of dawn. The Bum is asleep on the bench, Far Right, his baseball cap pulled low over his eyes. The DeSoto is parked at left on the street. Joe is busily involved in a chrome-polishing ritual, an open can of Noxon metal polish rests on the hood; the grill and hubcaps have already been buffed to a glistening shine. Sally follows Joe about the DeSoto as he fondly, delicately buffs the bumpers and doors. Carlton is asleep on the back seat, we see him through the open back seat door as Joe polishes the handle. The sound of the pursuing siren from the preceding scene fades down as the dialogue from this scene begins.*)

JOE: (*As lights come up, pointing to Bum.*) Now *that's* an old man. You want to talk about *old; that's* old.

SALLY: Pop, do you have to polish the cab at this very moment?

JOE: (*Continues polishing.*) This is Wednesday. Wednesday is cab polishing, Tuesday is washing. You know how many DeSoto Skyview Cabs they got left in the world? It's like eagles. You gotta save 'em from extinction. What's the emergency? Where'd you want me to take you?

SALLY: Look, I really appreciate this . . .

JOE: Used to talk to me, you don't talk to me anymore . . .

SALLY: Tell ya the truth, Pop, last coupla years I get the feeling you don't really hear most of what I—

JOE: (*Turns to her.*) What's up? Cash? You need cash?

SALLY: Just company, really. Got an hour before I have to be there.

JOE: Why ya goin' to the doctor?

SALLY: Guess you'd call it female trouble . . .

JOE: My female trouble, I got no doctor for.

SALLY: (*Smiling.*) Everything's about the same at home then.

JOE: Except I'm gonna be a great grandfather.

SALLY: Hey, terrific. Who . . . ?

JOE: The one who hums to herself; y'know, what's her name; with the sweater says "Peace" on it . . .

SALLY: Beth? Jesus, is she married?

JOE: Nobody knows. You ask her and she just hums to herself. Frankly, I don't worry about dying, I only worry that the world will come to an end before I do. (*Comes over to her, points back to cab.*) What're ya doin' with the jungle darky?

SALLY: Damn it, Pop, you're—

JOE: Don't worry, he's asleep. Asleep and dreaming about moving into my neighborhood. You and your Goddamn strays, even when you was a kid; dogs, cats, Italians—

SALLY: Fact is, Pop, I'm thinking about adopting him.

JOE: Adorable. That's adorable. What's Marty say?

SALLY: That's another piece of news. Looks like we're . . . y'know, splitting up.

JOE: Oh, adorable. This is an adorable morning.

SALLY: See, me and Marty—

JOE: Shoulda had children. How come no children?

SALLY: Children?

JOE: Yeah, you see them in the park a lot; they're the small ones in the carriages.

SALLY: Way things worked out, it's damn lucky I—

JOE: Lucky, lucky; it's a winning streak. (*Turns away from her, goes back to his cab.*)

SALLY: (*Comes over to him.*) Pop, I called you this morning . . . I called you because I'm going to get an abortion and I don't want to be alone.

JOE: Uh-huh. (*Continues polishing the front fender.*) What else is new?

SALLY: See, Pop, we—

JOE: You're getting a divorce, a darky, and an abortion. That's some full morning we got here.

SALLY: And I thought afterwards you could take me and Carlton over to my friend's place.

JOE: Sure; what father would want to miss such an experience? (*Picks up rag and polish can.*) *This* one! (*Sits in front seat of cab.*) This one's gonna miss out on all the fun.

SALLY: Pop, *listen* to me—

JOE: (*Slams the cab door.*) Get the darky out. You and the darky, *out!*

SALLY: Even if you're against the—

JOE: I'm not for, I'm against, I just don't want the fare, lady! (*Takes car keys from pocket, puts them in ignition.*)

SALLY: Pop, *listen*—

JOE: (*Shouting.*) Since you been a minute old ya could hustle me into *any*thing! Not this, I'm not partners with this venture, I'm—

SALLY: (*Hits a short burst on the horn.*) Hold it, will ya?!

(*Shouting.*) I need your help! How about a little father action here!?

JOE: That's how ya talk to an old man?

SALLY: Christ, you're not gonna pull *that* one on me, are ya?

JOE: Okay, forget that one. (*Shouting.*) But I remain firm on all other points covered! Understood? (*Folds his arms, sits back.*) All right. Proceed. I'm listening. (*She is silent. There are tears in her eyes. He gets out of the cab; quietly.*) Look. It's okay, say anything you want.

SALLY: Well, about the abortion . . .

JOE: Except that!

SALLY: I'm not sure I'm right, but I—

JOE: I'll save you a lot of trouble. You're wrong.

SALLY: Pop, ya know who I've been thinking about all night? . . . Uncle Abe. Uncle Abe, with the stomach trouble. There was that year he slept in the same room with me, I musta been about five at the time . . . he'd wake up in the middle of the night and he'd sit at the edge of his bed and he'd holler . . . (*With a Russian accent.*) "Sally, Sally, what's it all *for?*" Just like that, Pop, "Sally, Sally, what's it all *for?*" (*Shrugs.*) What the hell did I know, I was five at the time . . . I thought maybe it was all for Saturday afternoons . . . chocolate chip cookies was another strong possibility . . . Pop, it's thirty years later, and he's been askin' me all night . . . "What's it all *for?*" . . . (*Turns to him.*) Look, don't be offended . . . but I'm sure you haven't heard much of what I said . . .

JOE: I'm not offended. I'm deaf.

SALLY: What?

JOE: Four years ago the left ear went, one year ago the right. I receive only the picture portion of the program. (*Goes back to cab.*) Looks to me like I'm not missing a thing.

SALLY: Pop, you never told anybody.

JOE: Deaf means old; people stay away from what's old.

SALLY: But how do ya—?

JOE: Lips. I read the lips and the faces. Nobody knows. (*Points to huge, rear view mirror.*) Triple-size, with a magnifier, I see what they say to me. (*Picks up tiny transistor earphone attached to radio-intercom.*) This goes in the ear; sounds like a mouse being raped, but I don't miss any calls. The Company catches on, I'm out on my ass. With your mother it's easy, all I gotta do is nod a lot and say "they don't appreciate you" every ten minutes. (*Opens door, steps out.*)

SALLY: Pop, I'm really sorry.

JOE: (*Crossing towards bench, at Right.*) Dummy, I'm into my sixth life and you're still sitting in a pickle barrel! Listening was always in my way anyway. (*Goes to balcony over the river.*) What's anybody got to tell me I ain't heard already? (*He leans on the balcony railing. The dawn light is gentle, the street is quiet and empty; they are alone except for the Bum asleep on the bench.*) The quiet is good. Sometimes even beautiful. At night, all night it's like driving through new snow. (*Closes his eyes.*) Listen. Listen to the quiet . . . quiet on quiet . . . in an hour the rush hour starts. (*Opens his eyes; smiling.*) Beautiful . . . Sally, I love it. The traffic starts, the rush hour starts and I love it. Turning, hollering, moving, tells you you're around. Alive ain't enough, you gotta have ways to know it. Traffic, some kinda traffic— (*The Bum rises from bench—Joe shouts.*) Un paso mas, estas muertos, Carlos! (*The Bum lies down again.*) Good.

SALLY: What did you say to him?

JOE: I said "one more step and you're dead, Charlie!" I know just enough Spanish to get me around the city.

SALLY: Pop, he was just—

JOE: I don't gamble! Only the horses. Got a thirty-eight under the dashboard and a billy-club on the seat— (*Turns to her, shouting.*) What keeps *you* alive? I got a great grandchild comin'; don't know where it's comin' *from*, but it's comin'! Whatta *you* got to remember yourself by? How do ya know you're not an ashtray? What's it all *for?* It's for staying alive! Ya heard it here first, girlie! That's the trick, that's the ball game. Get outta the traffic and you're dead, Charlie! (*Grabs her arm; shaking her.*) Am I talkin' loud enough? Estas muertos, Carlos? (*Quietly.*) I see your face . . .

SALLY: Pop . . .

JOE: You're still goin' to the doctor, right?

SALLY: Pop, you don't understand, it's—

JOE: Okay, that's it! You're . . . you're *fired!* (*He walks briskly away towards the cab.*)

SALLY: (*Following.*) You can't fire a daughter.

JOE: I got *plenty* o'daughters! *All* kinds! (*The Bum starts toward them from the bench; Joe shouts at him.*) No money! I got no money! No tango dinero! (*The Bum is frightened away, exits to the Right. Joe opens door, gets into cab.*) Hey, he's gone. Your darky skipped! He's gone, and so's my new coin-changer! Adopt him? *Adopt him? Arrest* him! (*Sally goes quickly to the cab, looks in at the empty back seat, upset.*)

SALLY: Jesus . . . (*Shouting to the empty street.*) Hey, Carlton . . . ?! Carlton . . . ? (*But he is gone. She opens the cab door sadly, about to get in next to Joe.*)

JOE: Where the hell ya think *you're* goin'? Out, out!

SALLY: All I'm askin' ya to do is—

JOE: Ain't no door to door abortion service. Out.

SALLY: (*Points to lobby.*) Wait a second, I'll just get my suit-case, and we'll—

JOE: You'll *walk*. You'll *think!* (*Puts key in ignition.*) Only booked fifteen on the clock all night. I'm in the transportation field here. (*She doesn't move; still holding door open. He shouts.*) I'm seventy-eight! My time is limited! Out!

SALLY: Damn you . . . (*She slams the door.*) *Damn* you. (*She walks sharply away down the street to the Right.*)

JOE: (*Shouting after her.*) Years from now, Sally, believe me . . . you're gonna thank me for this!

SALLY: (*Stops, turns sharply.*) The hell I will— (*Fiercely, bit-terly.*) I won't be thanking you for this. Not now, and not later. You missed a big chance here, Kaminsky. You had a chance to hug me, to understand me, to know me a little, but you were off duty and you missed it . . . (*He turns away.*) Don't you *dare* turn away from me! Watch the lips, Joe! You were deaf to me twenty years before your ears went. Daugh-ters who love ya, Joe; do ya know how many there are left in the world? They're like eagles; you gotta save them from ex-tinction. Keep your billy club and keep your thirty-eight; but you still won't be safe. Turn your clock on, Pop, feel it tick; *that's* the thief. That's the biggest thief in town. (*She turns and walks away, about to exit at Left.*)

JOE: (*Shouting.*) Hold it! (*She stops.*) You want help, I got something for ya— (*Gets out of cab.*) How old are you?

SALLY: You know damn well how—

JOE: How old?

SALLY: Thirty-three.

JOE: Wrong. When you was four, the house was crowded; Abe, Benny, the cousins, all the girls to look after. Helen says to me we gotta get you into school a year early. Okay, Benny gets a blank certificate from his friend works for the city. We make you a year older. You're a kid, we're afraid you'll spill the beans at school, we don't tell you the truth . . . Coupla years go by, keep meanin' to tell ya but I start to notice I'm not rich . . . and I think, what would I ever give you? Money; forget it. Property; unlikely. I figure I'll give you time, when you need it. You got married, I figured it for a dowry; but you were happy and you didn't need it yet . . . Finally, I put it in my will; three grand for each girl and a year for Sally. But today I figure you need it. So there it is; you're thirty-two. (*Going back to cab.*) You got a year. Don't blow it.

SALLY: (*Smiling, gently.*) Thanks, Pop . . . Thanks for the extra year.

JOE: (*Shouting.*) Dummy, don't ya know? . . . they're *all* extra years. (*Turns on ignition; puts his foot on the gas.*) Listen to that, quietest damn motor in town. (*Lights out on DeSoto Far Left, as Joe backs the cab Up Stage and into the shadows.*)

HARRY'S VOICE: Taxi! Taxi! Goddamnit! . . . Taxi! (*Lights up on entrance to Riverview East as Harry steps out onto the street, waving wildly in the direction of Joe's departed cab.*) Goddamnit, *wait!* Don't you *see* me! What *am* I, the Goddamn Invisible Man?! (*Goes back to lobby to sleeping Doorman.*) Goddamn you, Devlin . . . wake up and blow your Goddamn *whistle*, for Chrissakes! . . . (*Sally comes towards entrance.*) What the hell am I *paying* for? (*He shakes Devlin's shoulder.*) Missed four *cabs;* four, Devlin . . . I've got to get to *work.*

SALLY: Leave him alone, mister, he's just sleeping, he—

HARRY: Oh, he's *sleeping*, is he? Well, thank you very much for the information— (*She has gone into the lobby for her suitcase; finds that it is gone.*)

SALLY: Hey . . . Devlin, my suitcase. (*She shakes his shoulder gently.*) I'm late for a very important appointment—where'd ya put my— (*Slowly, quietly, Devlin's very old and very dead body falls off the chair and onto the street, the braided cap rolling . . . Sally kneels next to him, touching his ice cold hand . . . Harry begins to back away involuntarily towards the door, his briefcase held close like a teddy bear.*)

HARRY: Oh, my God . . . oh, my God . . .

SALLY: (*Quietly.*) Poor dear man . . .

HARRY: Oh, my God.

SALLY: (*Kneeling close to him, touching his hand gently.*) So cold . . . All this time, all night he's been . . .

HARRY: (*Still backing away.*) Oh, God, he's . . . he's . . . (*Gilbey, another harried businessman with a briefcase, comes briskly out of the building and onto the street, glancing briefly at the group behind him, then scanning the street for a cab.*)

GILBEY: (*Shaking his head.*) Devlin loves his bourbon. (*Shouting up the street.*) Taxi! Hey, taxi! (*Shakes his head at the loss of his cab; turns to Devlin's chair, takes whistle tied to thin strap around the chair, wipes off the mouthpiece, blows the whistle at an Off Stage cab . . . turns back to the group, Sally kneeling next to Devlin, Harry frozen several feet away.*) Hey, what's wrong with him? (*No reply.*) He . . . he looks . . . uh . . .

SALLY: (*Not looking up.*) Dead. I think the word we're all looking for is "dead." (*Silence for a few moments; nobody moves. She looks up at them.*) Well, what've ya got in mind, fellahs?

HARRY: (*Whispering.*) I'll . . . I'll get the superintendent . . .

SALLY: This isn't maintenance. (*She rises, commanding.*) Pick him up, both of you; gently. Put down your briefcases and

pick him up . . . put him on the couch in the lobby . . . gently
. . . and give back his whistle . . . give him his whistle back!
(*Backing away slowly toward the street-phone, at Right.*) I'll
call the police . . . Stay with him till they come . . . (*The two
men approach the body awkwardly; they avoid looking at
each other. Gilbey reaches forward, holding Devlin's shoulders. Harry reaches for Devlin's feet. Gilbey nods and they lift
the body up slowly, carefully. Sally reaches phone, deposits
coin, dialing as Harry and Gilbey exit into the building carrying the body.*)

GILBEY: (*Politely.*) My name's Gilbey, I'm in Fourteen C . . .

HARRY: Harry Soames, Seventeen J . . .

SALLY: (*Into phone.*) Look, somebody died. His name is Devlin.
He's in the lobby of Two-Sixteen East End Avenue. My name
is Sally Cramer, same address. Okay. (*Hangs up, deposits another coin, dialing; speaks into phone as the Street Lady appears on the street Up Right, approaches Devlin's body, studying Devlin's cap.*) Hello, would you page Doctor Gerstad,
please? Thank you. (*She waits; the Street Lady leans over,
picks up Devlin's cap, looking it over. Sally shouts.*) Drop the
hat, creep! (*The Street Lady drops the cap, startled, very
hurt.*) I'm sorry, lady . . . I . . . (*Sally points to the briefcases
left by Harry and Gilbey.*) Take one of those. Take them both.
They're yours. A present. (*The Street Lady looks over at the
two suitcases, studying them with interest. Sally speaks into
the phone.*) Hello, Doctor Gerstad? Sally Cramer. Little transportation problem; but I'm calling a cab, I'll be there in ten
minutes, okay? Did you get a good night's sleep? . . . No, I'm
fine, really. Lenox Hill, Fourth Floor Admissions, okay. Wash
up. 'Bye. (*She hangs up, deposits another coin, dialing. The
Street Lady puts down her two shopping bags, picks up the
two briefcases, holds one in each hand like the shopping bags,
and scurries off at Right. Martin appears on the street, Up
Left. He is a wreck; unshaven, exhausted, hung over, his jacket*

*open against bare smudged skin, black smudges everywhere
from climbing, sweat stains from hard running, his sleeve
ripped, his pants leg torn up to the knee, the material flapping
as he stumbles along, glancing back furtively as though still
pursued. Into phone.*) Hello, Supreme Radio Cabs? Send a
cab to Two-Sixteen East End Avenue; anybody but Kaminsky.
No, he didn't say anything obscene to me. Two-Sixteen East
End and hurry, I'll be waiting in front of the building. (*She
hangs up. Martin stands at Far Left on street, unnoticed by
her. Sally walks sleepily to the curb in front of the building,
picks up Devlin's cap, sits on curb, hunched up, her arms
around her knees like a tired street-kid. It is still very early,
very quiet, no sound of traffic; the sun is not bright yet but it
is there, warming and soft. Sally closes her eyes, feels the sun
on her face. Martin, still unnoticed by her, is trying to figure
out what attitude to take. He decides on controlled dignity,
buttons his torn jacket, sits at the edge of the curb some distance from her, puts his flute down, crosses his legs casually,
holding his torn pantsleg together with one hand. Sound of a
single, distant car driving by. Silence again.*)

MARTIN: (*Calmly, looking away from her at the river.*) Forget
something?

SALLY: (*Not looking at him.*) I've got a cab coming in five minutes.

MARTIN: Right.

SALLY: I came back for something. I thought I'd left something.
But there was nothing here. (*After a moment.*) Congratulations, Cramer. We did it. We joined the losers.

MARTIN: Sally, I . . .

SALLY: (*Turns to him.*) Dead is dead, Mister. (*Suddenly aware
of his appearance.*) What the hell happened to *you?*

MARTIN: (*Calmly.*) Interesting. You can still get from Loew's

Delancy to the subway without being caught by the cops. Eight alleys, six basements. It still works.

SALLY: What were you doing on Delancy Street?

MARTIN: (*He shrugs.*) Lookin' around.

SALLY: For what?

MARTIN: Us, I guess; or me, or . . . Anyway we weren't there . . . Neither was our furniture. That nice old guy you had watching the stuff . . .

SALLY: Yes . . . ?

MARTIN: He sold it. (*She smiles.*) He gave me the money, though . . .

SALLY: Well at least he gave you the—

MARTIN: Forty dollars . . . (*She laughs.*) He said he was lucky to get that much for old junk. (*She continues laughing.*) I didn't find it very amusing . . .

SALLY: No, you wouldn't . . . (*She suddenly cracks, burying her face in her hands, shaking with sobs, the emotions of the night flooding in.*)

MARTIN: (*Rising.*) Sally . . .

SALLY: (*Rising, moving away from him.*) This isn't crying . . . this isn't really crying here . . . This is just crankiness; a cranky kid who's been up too late, or at the zoo too long . . . (*Starting towards the bench, Far Right.*) I'll wait for my cab across the street. You go up to the apartment and look for your river . . .

MARTIN: Sally, wait . . .

SALLY: (*Sharply, with finality.*) Marty, the odds are against the house.

MARTIN: (*Calmly, controlled, his hand in his pocket.*) Sally, I

think we should take this opportunity to examine several of
the issues . . . to discuss and examine several of the options
available to us . . .

SALLY: (*Shouting, bitterly.*) Christ, *listen* to you! Save it for the
bluebells, Marty! (*She walks briskly away toward the bench.
The Man From Above comes out of the building carrying a
briefcase, wearing a snappy business-suit and ready for the
new day. Martin takes the gun quietly from his pocket, points
it at the sky. A deafening shot shatters the still morning air.
The Man From Above freezes, his mouth open, his eyes wide
with shock. Sally turns sharply. Martin stands quite still, the
thirty-eight pointed at the sky.*)

SALLY: (*After a moment, to the Man From Above.*) We're trying to get a cab . . .

MAN FROM ABOVE: (*Quietly, nodding.*) They've got guns now
. . . They've got guns . . . of course . . . (*Walking quickly
back into building.*) The police, I'm calling the police . . .
(*Sally and Martin remain quite still, a distance from each
other.*)

MARTIN: (*Trying to remain under control.*) As . . . as I began
to say . . . We can't break up till we know whose fault it was.
We have to decide who was wrong . . . (*Pointing.*) You!
You're wrong. I'm the right one, you're the wrong one. Please
remember that . . . look, look at me, look what you did to me!
. . . I went back to the past and it beat the crap outa me! Oh,
God, I'm outa breath and I can't wear sneakers anymore . . .
Look, look what you did . . . guns, *cops*, cops chasin' me . . .
I broke my watch . . . I went up to a guy on First Avenue to
ask him for the time. He gave me a quarter . . . I *kept* it! . . .
Total for the night, forty dollars and twenty-five cents! . . .
(*Suddenly, moving towards her.*) Don't go, don't go . . . I'm
married to you. God help me, I'm married to your Goddamn
dumb jokes . . . I ran, I ran . . . (*Holding her, crying softly.*)

Running home, running to you, running, shouting, find her, find her . . . find her . . .

FLO'S VOICE: (*Shouting, from above.*) What's happening down there? I heard a gun! . . . Who is that? What's he *doing?* What's *wrong* with him?!

SALLY: (*Holding Martin close; with love, delight, relief; looks up in the direction of Flo's voice.*) He's crazy . . . my husband is crazy . . . Crazy Marty . . . (*They kiss each other tenderly. Silence for a few moments as they embrace . . . a police siren wails distantly, Off Right, coming closer . . . Sally turns towards the sound.*) Marty, I think we better start walking now . . . that guy called the police . . . (*Martin starts towards the entrance, but Sally leads him away Down Center.*) Better not go in there, that guy'll identify us . . . and we've got an apartment fulla hot furniture . . . (*The siren grows louder, at Right . . . Martin gets rid of the gun on curb at Center, picks up his flute; she grabs his hand, they start up the street to the Left.*)

SALLY: Better start walking quickly . . .

MARTIN: Actually, running . . . running would be wise . . . (*Hand in hand they run to the Left up the street . . . Another siren starts to wail, Off Left, coming closer . . . they run to the Right, but that siren is wailing even closer now . . . they run back to the Center, not knowing how to escape. They finally race towards the ramp at Left, running down the ramp into the pit . . .*)

SALLY: (*Pausing on the ramp, delighted.*) Marty . . . sirens . . . sirens and everything . . . (*They disappear down the ramp . . . The sirens grow louder . . . and then the gradually building sound of heavy morning traffic as the city comes alive again. The following action and dialogue blend together; no distinct lines of dialogue, all movements happening at once with the growing sounds of traffic.*)

GORDON: (*On terrace, with phone.*) I thought maybe a little breakfast here at my place—eggs, sausage, a Bloody Mary just the way you like it— (*Street Lady coming Down Center to pick up gun. Gilbey exits from building on his way to work. New, young Doorman comes out of building, blowing whistle. Bum enters, following Gilbey. Harry and Flo come out on their terrace. Man From Above comes out on his terrace, dressed in his bathrobe again.*)

HARRY: Shoulda seen how I handled it, Flo; the guy keels over, see—everybody panics—

FLO: You're all heart, Harry—

NANCY: (*On terrace, with phone.*) A *party?* At eight o'clock in the *mornin'?* You gotta be funnin', Chuck. Well now, I'll have to think on that; get m'self together here—

BUM: (*Following Gilbey.*) I'm in the goin' away business—

GILBEY: Great, I'm late, Mac—

BUM: You give me a dollar and I—

MAN FROM ABOVE: (*Shouting; his voice heard above the others.*) . . . I'm having all my food sent up! Never! I'm never going out there again! (*The rising sound of city traffic filling the stage as . . .*)

Curtain

The Goodbye People

The Goodbye People opened at the Ethel Barrymore Theatre, New York City, on December 3, 1968. It was produced by Feuer and Martin and directed by Herb Gardner, with sets and lighting by David Hays and costumes by Alvin Colt. The case was as follows:

Arthur Korman	Bob Dishy
Max Silverman	Milton Berle
Nancy Scott	Brenda Vaccaro
Eddie Bergson	Jess Osuna
Michael Silverman	Tony Lo Bianco
Marcus Soloway	Sammy Smith

The Goodbye People was presented at the Solari Theatre in Los Angeles, opening January 2, 1979. It was directed by Jeff Bleckner. Sets were designed by James Freiburger, lighting by John Beilock. The cast was as follows:

Arthur Korman	Peter Bonerz
Max Silverman	Herschel Bernardi
Nancy Scott	Patty Duke Astin
Eddie Bergson	Bruce Weitz
Michael Silverman	Michael Tucker
Marcus Soloway	Sammy Smith

The Goodbye People, produced by Joseph Kipness and Maurice Rosenfield at the Belasco Theatre in New York City, opened May 1, 1979. It was directed by Jeff Bleckner, with sets, lighting and costumes by Santo Loquasto, Jennifer Tipton and Elizabeth Palmer. The cast was as follows:

Arthur Korman	Ron Rifkin
Max Silverman	Herschel Bernardi
Nancy Scott	Melanie Mayron
Eddie Bergson	Marvin Lichterman
Michael Silverman	Michael Tucker
Marcus Soloway	Sammy Smith

ACT ONE

Before the curtain goes up, we hear about twenty seconds of an old Al Jolson recording of "TOOT, TOOT, TOOTSIE! (GOOD-BYE)." The sound is loud and clear, but it is obviously a scratchy old record.

JOLSON'S VOICE:
TOOT, TOOT, TOOTSIE! GOOD-BYE.
TOOT, TOOT, TOOTSIE, DON'T CRY.
THE CHOO-CHOO TRAIN THAT TAKES ME
AWAY FROM YOU,
NO WORDS CAN TELL HOW SAD IT MAKES ME.
KISS ME, TOOTSIE, AND THEN,
DO IT OVER AGAIN.
WATCH FOR THE MAIL,
I'LL NEVER FAIL,
IF YOU DON'T GET A LETTER THEN YOU'LL KNOW I'M IN
    JAIL. . . .

The music is joined by the sound of rolling surf, gulls, a winter wind, a distant buoy bell, and then the curtain goes up . . .

Scene: The beach at Coney Island. It is late February, a few minutes before dawn. The boardwalk lamps are lit, the surf crashes, the winter wind whistles. The audience is where the ocean would be and the beach angles down toward us. Upstage is a section of boardwalk; a wide wooden stairway leads down from it to the beach at right, disappearing into drifts of sand. Far left are two battered phone booths, back to back under the boardwalk, with sand banked against them like gray snow. Above the boardwalk we can see the open sky, and below it the boardwalk planks drop striped shadows on the sand. Under the boardwalk, to the left of the stairs, is a boarded-up refreshment stand, obviously closed for the winter but old and faded enough to indicate that it has been closed for an even longer time. The front of the stand is about fifteen feet wide; it shows years of being battered by wind and water. Above the stand is an old, faded sign; originally silver letters against a blue background, it is now a mixture of the many colors of age, wear, rust, and strong sun. We can just about make out that the sign says "Max's Hawaiian Ecstasies." At center, a weather-beaten pier extends about four rows into the audience.

At rise: The Jolson song continues for a few moments . . .

JOLSON'S VOICE:
TOOT, TOOT, TOOTSIE, DON'T CRY,
TOOT, TOOT, TOOTSIE, GOOD-BYE,
GOOD-BYE, TOOTSIE, GOOD-BYE . . .

The music fades into the sound of wind and ocean; the stage is empty for a few moments and then Arthur Korman enters, running breathlessly along the boardwalk and down the steps. Arthur is about forty, wears a Mackinaw with the hood up and a pair of dark glasses, and is carrying a banjo case and a folded newspaper. He is in a great hurry as though late for an important appointment. He goes quickly into the shadows under the boardwalk, emerging in a moment with a folded beach chair, striped with the colors of summer. Moving quickly down center, he drops everything in the sand, unfolds the beach chair, and sits on the edge of it expectantly, looking anxiously out at the offstage horizon where the audience is. A moment; then he checks his watch; then he looks at a page in the newspaper as though to verify something, nods to himself, and returns to his vigilant pose, leaning forward, his eyes squinting with concentration on the horizon. Another moment and then he jumps up, moves down to the edge of the pier for a closer look at the horizon. He is getting annoyed.

ARTHUR: (*Quietly*) Goddamn *New York Times* . . . (*Going quickly to phone booths.*) Who ya supposed to believe any more? Who ya supposed to trust? (*Deposits coin, dials angrily, glancing over his shoulder from time to time as though something might suddenly happen on the horizon. Speaks into phone.*) Hello, *New York Times?* I think we got a problem. We got a definite problem here. Your Late City Edition says here, page 70, column 3: "February 22; sunrise: 6:41." O.K., well, it's six forty-*eight* right now, and I don't know what's happening in *your* neighborhood, lady, but down here we got darkness . . . Well, if you're just the operator, then who's responsible, who's on top of the sunrise situation over there? . . . City Desk? Fine. Lemme speak to them . . . Who's this? Mr. Mallory? Mr. Mallory, look out your window. What do ya see? That's called darkness, Mr. Mallory. That's nighttime you got goin' on out there. My name is Arthur Korman, a regular subscriber to your publication, come at great inconvenience to myself to witness the birth of a new day, come on the B.M.T. in quest of beauty and gettin' my ass froze off in total blackness down here! What the hell're you guys usin' for weather information up there? What're ya, a buncha *gypsies* up there!

  (*During these last few lines, Max Silverman has entered from under the boardwalk. A short man, about seventy years old, he wears an overcoat, a fishing hat, and an unlit cigar that appears to be part of his face. He carries a shopping bag from which he takes a folding ruler and begins to meas-*

ure the front of the old refreshment stand; nodding and murmuring in total agreement with everything Arthur is saying. Max speaks in a rich, full-bodied, tasty Russian-Jewish accent.)

MAX: Sure . . . sure . . .

ARTHUR: Great. Beautiful. You're sorry. Meanwhile I'm down here at Coney Island, alone in the dark, and you guys're up there in leather chairs, drinkin' hot coffee and makin' the news up outa your head!

MAX: Sure, that's the story . . .

ARTHUR: Of *course* you wanna hang up on me now. What difference do *I* make, right? You don't need *me* . . .

MAX: (*Measuring.*) Sure . . . sure . . . they don't need you . . .

ARTHUR: I'm just a victim of your imaginary weather reports, the hell with *me*, right?

MAX: (*Nodding.*) Sure, the hell with you . . . the hell with *all* of us . . .

ARTHUR: The sunrise, the sunset; that's a responsi*bility*, fella . . .

MAX: A big organization . . . who cares? . . .

ARTHUR: Hello? Hello? Hello, Mallory? . . . They hung up.

MAX: (*Folding his ruler.*) Sure they hung up. A Mallory will hang up on you.

ARTHUR: (*Seeing this stranger for the first time, but continuing his anger.*) Goddamn it, goddamn gypsies . . .

MAX: You called them at the wrong time, buddy. (*Looks at pocket watch.*) I'll tell you the right time to call them. Never.

ARTHUR: (*Shouting, pointing to horizon.*) I mean, look at that, will ya!

MAX: (*Shouting.*) Disgraceful!

ARTHUR: What the hell is *that?*

MAX: Blackness! Blackness and darkness!

ARTHUR: I mean, am I being un*reason*able?

MAX: You're being reasonable! Reasonable and cold and lied to!

ARTHUR: What about the front page here? What about "President Buoyed by Senate Support of Asia Policy"? I don't believe *that either* now!

MAX: He could be sitting around at this moment, not buoyed! What do *we* know? We know what they *tell* us!

ARTHUR: Far as I'm concerned they've thrown a doubt on their entire Late City Edition!

MAX: The *Daily News* too! You can forget *them* also!

ARTHUR: I mean, really, who ya supposed to *trust* any more?

MAX: This city, forget it! It's a miracle even that the telephone worked!

ARTHUR: The goddamn B.M.T., we sat stalled thirty minutes in the tunnel this morning!

MAX: Garbage in the river, smoke in the lungs, and everywhere the Mallorys are hanging up!

ARTHUR: And who do ya *talk* to? What do ya—

MAX: They don't care, they cover up! It's a scientific *fact* that every minute the entire island is gradually sinking into the ocean! Do they *mention* it? Do they *do* anything? Next week we'll all be on Sixth Avenue breathing through *straws;* and nobody *mentions!*

ARTHUR: (*Quieting down; becoming more aware of the stranger he's been talking to.*) Funny, I'm usually the only one around here at this hour; do you—

MAX: (*Still angry.*) A big organization, they don't *care!* (*Close to Arthur, confidentially*) I'm last night at Katz's Delicatessen; forty-six tables, what they take in there, one night, unbelievable. It's 1 A.M., two frankfurters, I'm a happy man. Suddenly they're closing up, they say go finish your hot dogs outside; in a flash of an eye I'm on the street. A big store, who needs you? A little store, they let you finish. But do you know who owns a little store these days? I'll tell you who. Nobody. And that's the whole story today. Yessir, that's what you got in your world today. How-do-you-do-sir, Max Silverman right here!

(*Suddenly shoots out his hand.*)

ARTHUR: (*Shaking his hand.*) Arthur Korman.

MAX: What're ya hangin' around here?

ARTHUR: Well, actually, I've come to see the sunrise . . .

MAX: Sure. Why not? A sunrise is nice. What line are you in? I'll bet you're in the art line. (*Arthur nods.*) Sure, I figured the art line. Where are you located? (*Arthur hands him a card; Max holds it up close to his eyes.*) "The Jingle Bell Display Company. Bill Fairchild, President. Arthur Korman, Designer." I'll tell you right now, I like the sound of the whole organization. (*Arthur sits in beach chair, looks off at horizon.*) Right, you better get ready. Because a sunrise out here'll run you, tops, ten, fifteen minutes. (*Sits next to him on chunk of driftwood.*) A whole week now I see you here, who knew we could be such terrific pals? With your odd behavior; what is that to sleep here in February?

ARTHUR: I don't *sleep* here, Mr. Silverman; sometimes while I'm waiting for the sunrise I—

MAX: A whole half hour I spoke to you yesterday. With them

dopey glasses, who knew the eyes were closed? I'm having a gorgeous and terrific conversation, right in the middle you say, "Goodbye, Bill . . ."

ARTHUR: (*Rises, begins to fold beach chair as though to move on; politely*) Talked in my sleep, eh? Well, that's—

MAX: A fella comes in February to dream about Bill. Funny glasses. Goodbye, Bill. Jingle Bells. Arthur, you'll pardon me, but maybe you're a fairy?

ARTHUR: Mr. Silverman, Bill is my employer's name, I—

MAX: Arthur, you'll be what you want to be, I'm still your pal! (*Rises, a sympathetic hand on his arm.*) Listen, you'll make a life for yourself. I'll tell you somebody who doesn't have problems. Nobody. (*His arm around Arthur, leading him up center; Arthur carrying the chair.*) O.K., O.K., you're being straight with me, I'll be from the shoulder with you . . . it's time I revealed to you my true identity . . . (*Points to boarded-up stand.*) You see that sign? That place? "Max's Hawaiian Ecstasies"? Well, that Max from there . . . and this Max . . . are one in the same Max . . . (*Turns to him, quietly*) I am that Max, of Max's Hawaiian Ecstasies . . . Yessir.

(*Max steps back, waiting for a big reaction to this revelation.*)

ARTHUR: (*Politely*) Oh . . .

MAX: Of course, we been closed now awhile for various alterations, remodeling, renovations, and modernization . . .

ARTHUR: Uh-huh. How long?

MAX: Twenty-two years. A special place, you gotta wait for the right moment.

ARTHUR: (*Attempting, politely, to disengage himself.*) Mr. Silverman, I think the sunrise is about to—

MAX: We had here a class operation . . .

ARTHUR: I see a bit of light on the—

MAX: *Al Jolson.* Yessir, Jolson himself comes once for a frank-furter—*two* frankfurters and a large coconut drink; July 10, 1943, he's here on the boardwalk for a War Bond Rally. Gives you an idea the type clientele. (*He slaps the side of the stand; the small building shudders with age.*) We had 'em all here; your various show-business greats, your various underworld personalities, a couple artists, tenors from the opera, some of your top politicos, they come running from all walks of life. You're asking "Why" and the question will be answered. Be-cause we had here . . . ecstasy. Grass on the walls, lush; hang-ing from the ceiling, jungle novelties; tropical foliage; had a record playing with your various exotic-bird noises. A coconut drink costs a dollar. Can you imagine what that was in 1943, a dollar for a soda? Musta been some terrific soda, right? And frankfurters—ground special, my own meat—frankfurters that you could soar to the sky, one bite and you need a pilot's li-cense! Hamburgers I wouldn't even discuss, *tears* would come to your eyes . . . (*Arthur has put down his beach chair, listen-ing.*) And crowds, crowds all the way back to Tenth Street, on Saturday nights back to Neptune Avenue . . . They ate on the beach here, pineapple paradise under the moonlight, summer nights that last forever . . . and up above the store, with soft blue lights, put a shiver in your neck, my sign, my credo, with silver letters for Silverman, it said, "Without a Little Ecstasy, What's Life? Don't Worry about the Prices!"

ARTHUR: Well, that must've been—

MAX: Unfortunately, they started worrying about the prices . . . (*Goes to stairway, taking in the whole neighborhood with a sweep of his hand.*) And the big places started to open on the boardwalk . . . aluminum nightmares! Fifteen cents for a frankfurter! Coney changes under my feet; comes in garbage, goes out style. Who needs ecstasy? My place becomes here a ghost and haunts itself . . . (*Moves up the stairs, points lovingly to an area of boardwalk above his store.*) Was once, right there, Soloway's Bath, Beach, and Sports Club. Guided by the hand of Marcus Soloway, a gentleman and a genius; with columns, pillars, almost marble, rising up. On top, a roof built like a pagoda would make even a Chinaman happy . . . and, oh, oh, on this roof a sea lion, buddy . . . almost marble, with green eyes that looked out at the sea . . . (*A sweep of his hand; shouting.*) And now gone! The only Roman Jewish Oriental bathhouse the world will ever know! (*He sits on the top step of the stairway, for the first time like an old man. Arthur is at bottom of steps, listening.*) You want to know who ends up twenty-two years with a job manager of the Burger Circus, cheap food on Lexington Avenue? Me. Max. The same Max. And Marcus Soloway is today a salesman sports goods in Jersey. You want to know God's job? To give every great man a squash! (*He stands, angrily*) Yessir, I got *that* boy's number! He's a joker, a fooler, a whimsical fella, and a rascal altogether! (*Moving down the steps to Arthur.*) What kinda monkey business that without Max to give it a spin, the world turns anyway? How come the ocean is still there without Soloway's sea lion watching it? (*Poking Arthur's chest.*) I'll tell ya what, mister; the difference between me and God is that I know how to run a class operation.

ARTHUR: Mr. Silverman—

MAX: Would you let me talk, please? I have only recently recovered from a serious and delicate operation on my only heart—(*Gives Arthur a slight shove; Arthur, off-balance, sits back down on the beach chair.*) I'm buddies with the angel of death, I'm operating on a very tight schedule, so close-'em-up-the-mouth—

ARTHUR: I'm sorry, I—

MAX: You came here to see the sunrise; but today, mister, Max Silverman *also* rises! (*Leans close to him.*) I notice that don't take your breath away . . . but they almost took *mine* away altogether. Two months in Mount Sinai Hospital—all day my family sits around the bed watching me with funerals in their eyes. Every lively move I make is to them a miracle and a wonder. I lift a cup of tea, I get an ovation. Suddenly I'm a talented man and my talent is that I'm not dead. What I got to look forward is in ten years I'll be my brother Harry whose big accomplishment is that he's eighty years old and he gets outa bed every morning! Look at Harry, they say, will you look at him how he eats his *soup,* look how *cute,* look how he hears almost ten percent of what you say to him—(*Suddenly, rushing to Arthur.*) And they almost had *me!* (*Grips Arthur's arm urgently.*) I'm lying in the bed there and I'm starting to think I'm terrific just because I'm *breath*ing! (*As though in the hospital room*) I look around at them . . . my wife, God bless her, a silly person . . . Joey the Bum and Michael the Bore . . . Rhoda and Barbara . . . or Barbara and Rhoda . . . married to Harold and Arnold . . . or Arnold and Harold . . . A *gross* of grandchildren: Sean, Adam, Kate, Mary-Jane, Mindy, Mandy, Molly; it's an Irish lullaby! "Dad," says Rhodabarbara, "not a *bunch* people—a bunch *of* people—you can hear that, can't you, Dad?" From the whole crowd one person who ain't ashamed—*likes* even how I sound, and that's Shirley, Crazy Shirley. I used to think the whole family isn't a total loss there's one Crazy Shirley in there . . . (*Shouting.*) The hell with *her also!* A whole year I don't hear from her! She run away from her husband—O.K., her used husband with his used-car lot, *him* you run away from—but why from Max? Max who is adorable! (*Exhausted, leans back against the dune.*) She wasn't there . . . and in the bed I look around at the rest of them, with their blank faces you could write a message on their foreheads like on a sheet of paper . . . and I'm thinkin', if I die, when I die, this here is all I leave, this is all the world will know of me, this bunch American beauties here . . . so *then,* right *there*— (*Shoves himself upright off the dune; shouting.*) —buddy, I make-'em-up my mind—right there in Mount Sinai Hospital, Room 423, semiprivate—I decided *not* to die! Halt! Stop the horses! Rip it from the schedule! Max has got business to do! First I gotta leave something you should know I been around; somethin' says I was alive, somethin' terrific, somethin' classy . . . somethin' beautiful; can't just leave behind this crowd of Silvermans . . . (*The lights have gone out along the boardwalk; and now the sun begins to rise, throwing a pink glow on the sand and the edges of the boardwalk.*) . . . and what's it gonna be?! Yessir— (*He points to the boarded-up stand.*) —rising up from the ashes— fresh, thanks God, like a daisy—awakened like a sleepin' princess—here ya go, whatta ya say—the grand and gala reopening of—the *Original Max's Hawaiian Ecstasies!* (*Arthur murmurs something.*) I'll tell ya who's not gonna die! *Me;* the original Max! (*Arthur murmurs, shifts in his chair.*) I'll tell ya—

ARTHUR: (*Murmuring.*) Goodbye . . . goodbye, Bill . . .

MAX: (*Goes to chair, looks at Arthur; then lifts up Arthur's sunglasses. Arthur is sound asleep.*) Out like a light. You rotten kid. Well, it's your misfortune, buddy; you missed a lot of terrific conversation. (*Max notices the sunrise, now a rich, redorange glow filling the stage.*) Stupid, you're missing the sunrise! A spectacle, what you came here to see: (*Shakes Arthur, shouting urgently.*) Wake up! *You're missing it!* Beautiful view, beautiful words . . . you're missing it . . . (*Sadly; lets go of Arthur's arm.*) Oh, you people are always missing it . . . (*Max is silent for a moment, quite still; then he shrugs.*) What the hell; sleep. I can't bother you. I got business. (*Picks up the shopping bag, starts up the boardwalk steps.*) Contacts to make. Money to raise. Business. (*A girl steps forward from the striped shadows under the boardwalk; she is wheeling a brightly painted bicycle, a foreign-made racer called a Peugeot. The girl is a thirty-three-year-old who dresses like sixteen: jeans, serape-sweater, beads, little white boots, everything out of place with her adulthood and the February weather. Max reaches the top of the steps; looks down, sees her.*) What is it, girlie? What can I do for you? (*She shakes her head.*) You're lost? (*She hesitates; shakes her head again.*) The bicycle path is over by Ocean Parkway. Now you'll excuse me, I got business . . . (*He hoists his shopping bag up under his arm, walks left down the boardwalk . . . stops, looks out at the horizon. The sunrise fills the stage with a red-golden glow. He looks up at the sky, angrily*) A joker, a fooler, a rascal. Also a show-off!

    (*Max exits to the left of the boardwalk, singing as he disappears from sight.*)
TOOT, TOOT, TOOTSIE, GOOD-BYE,
TOOT, TOOT, TOOTSIE, DON'T CRY . . .

GIRL: (*Singing softly.*)
THE CHOO-CHOO TRAIN THAT TAKES ME
AWAY FROM YOU . . .

ARTHUR: (*In his sleep*)
NO WORDS CAN SAY HOW SAD IT MAKES ME . . .

GIRL: (*Smiles; wheels her bike toward Arthur*)
KISS ME, TOOTSIE, AND THEN . . .

ARTHUR: (*After a moment*)
DO IT OVER AGAIN . . .

GIRL:
WATCH FOR THE MAIL . . . I'LL NEVER FAIL . . .
(*Silence. She moves closer, testing the depth of his sleep.*)
WATCH FOR THE MAIL . . . I'LL NEVER FAIL . . .
(*Silence. She rings her bicycle bell. Silence; he is deeply asleep. She feels the sunrise on her face; looks out at it; awed, whispering.*) What'd he call ya—Arthur? Arthur, you're missing a beauty . . . (*Glancing up and down the deserted beach.*) Oughtta be a bigger crowd for a show like this . . .

ARTHUR: (*Singing.*)
IF YOU DON'T GET A LETTER THEN YOU'LL KNOW I'M IN JAIL . . .

(*She laughs. He murmurs.*) Quitting, Bill . . . leaving organization . . . goodbye, Bill . . . (*He moves restlessly in his sleep.*) Light, light . . . shade is up . . .
(*She holds her hand in front of his eyes. He relaxes peacefully.*)

GIRL: (*She lays her bike down near him, sits next to him in the sand; leans against his chair, continuing to hold her hand in front of his eyes.*) Tell ya what, Arthur . . . altogether, so far, it's the best relationship I've had with a man this year. (*He murmurs.*) Nancy. Nancy Scott. (*He murmurs.*) Yes, I'm married; but maybe we can work something out.

ARTHUR: Bill . . .

NANCY: Bill will just have to understand. That was never a very healthy relationship, anyway. (*Leans more comfortably against his chair.*) Oh, beach buddy, we have got something very valuable here. Dr. Berman says I've got trouble relating to people. Well, he's wrong. I relate terrific. It's when they all start relating *back* at me, *that's* when the—

ARTHUR: Leaving organization, Bill . . .

NANCY: Nobody blames you . . .

ARTHUR: Quitting, Bill. *Had* it . . . Quitting . . .

NANCY: You took as much as you could . . .

ARTHUR: Up to here, Bill. Quitting now . . . no more, good-bye . . .

NANCY: (*Indicates banjo case.*) I think it's time you concentrated on your music anyway— (*A phone rings. She glances about.*) Phone. Where?
(*The phone rings again.*)

ARTHUR: (*Cordially, in his sleep*) Hello. How are ya?

(*A third ring; she spots the two booths under the board-walk, runs for them.*)

NANCY: Jesus, who calls up the beach? (*Opens the door to first booth; grabs phone.*) Hello, Atlantic Ocean. (*Sits down in booth.*) Huh? Well, who is *this?* . . . Sounds like rolling surf because it *is* rolling surf. Arthur Korman; yeah, just a second— (*Leans out of booth.*) Arthur! For you on "one"! Arthur! Phone! Hey, Arthur! (*He remains motionless.*) Sorry, he's asleep. That's right, on the beach. Who shall I say called? Oh . . . Bill. Look, Bill, hate to break it to ya like this, but he's quitting. Yeah, leaving the organization. Well, what can I tell ya, Bill, he seems very definite about it. Yeah, O.K., 'bye.
(*She hangs up.*)

ARTHUR: Leaving, Bill . . . leaving . . .

NANCY: You left. (*She leaves the booth, unaware that Eddie Bergson has just entered at the top of the boardwalk steps. A tall man, about forty, he wears an overcoat and carries two containers of coffee. Nancy looks back at the phone booth, suddenly regretful about what she's done. She moves toward Arthur.*) Mr. Korman . . . I think you better wake up now, I—

EDDIE: Shirl . . . ? (*She freezes; her back to him.*) Shirley . . . ? (*After a moment, she turns to him.*) Oh. Oh, excuse me, miss, I was . . . (*He is about to leave; he stops, looks at her for a long moment.*) Hey . . . (*He takes a step down the stairs.*) Hey, is that you, Shirl?

NANCY: Can you start with an easier question?

EDDIE: Jesus . . . the nose . . .

NANCY: Yeah; how about that?

EDDIE: And you musta lost . . .

NANCY: Twenty pounds. Five in the nose alone.

EDDIE: Your . . . your hair, it's . . .

NANCY: Mr. Gaston calls it "Dazzling Midnight."

EDDIE: Jesus . . . (*Coming slowly down the steps.*) I mean, you warned me on the phone, but . . . I was still lookin' for, y'know, Shirley.

NANCY: That makes two of us.

EDDIE: (*At bottom of steps.*) Well, hello.

NANCY: Hello, Eddie.

ARTHUR: (*Cordially, in his sleep*) Hello. How are ya?

NANCY: (*Shrugs.*) I think he's a friend of my father's. (*Going to dune, far from Arthur.*) Appreciate your coming down here, Eddie. I thought, y'know, a divorce isn't something we should talk about on the phone, right? (*He nods, following her to dune.*) I mean, we owe each other a better goodbye than that, don't we?

EDDIE: Yeah. Kinda cold here, though, isn't it?

NANCY: Been coming here a lot this winter . . . (*Points to Peugeot.*) The bike keeps me in shape, but I need destinations, see. And the mornings are lovely here . . .

EDDIE: Yeah. It's very nice. Very cold here, though. Maybe we could—

NANCY: That was Pop's store there. When I was a kid I used to come here at this hour to help him cut the French fries . . . (*With Max's accent*) "Crispy, curly edges, please!" (*Looking at the store.*) Funny, it gets smaller every time I—

EDDIE: Cold. You want my coat?

NANCY: No thanks. (*Sits.*) Here; pull up a dune, Eddie.

EDDIE: (*He sits opposite her. They are silent for a moment.*)

Long time, Shirl. (*She nods.*) Here. Coffee. I think it's still warm. (*She accepts one of the containers; nods thank-you.*) Fact is, I got over here pretty fast. Took a '71 Chevy hard-top off my lot, come over on the Belt Parkway. You take your East Side Drive down to your Brooklyn-Battery Tunnel; then—zing —you shoot right out on the Belt till you hit the Coney Island exit. (*Silence; they sip their coffee.*) So what ya been doin' with yourself, Shirl?

NANCY: Been working on television, Eddie. Acting.

EDDIE: No foolin'.

NANCY: Yeah. Me and my new nose. I do that commercial for Wonder Suds where they say, "Did you know washday could be paradise?" I play the girl who didn't know.

EDDIE: Hey, no foolin'.

NANCY: Here, I'll show ya—(*Flashes a blank, wide-eyed stare.*) That was me, not knowing.

EDDIE: Great eyes.

NANCY: What?

EDDIE: You still got the same eyes. Great eyes. (*Silence; they sip their coffee.*) Does it hurt a lot when they do it—fix up your nose? (*She shrugs.*) Yeah, I figured it must hurt a lot. Look, how about you come back with me, stay married and everything—

NANCY: Eddie—

EDDIE: I got the car right out on Neptune, we could—

NANCY: No, Eddie— (*Then gently*) Eddie, we decided; we agreed—

EDDIE: Right.

NANCY: I'm sorry, I—

EDDIE: Right. Right.
   (*He sips his coffee.*)

NANCY: Believe me, Eddie, I've thought about it a lot; even been to an analyst, I—

EDDIE: What does he say?

NANCY: I do most of the talking, he just listens—

EDDIE: Then come home, Shirl, I can do that for ya at home—

NANCY: Eddie—

EDDIE: Jesus, Dazzling Midnight, a new nose, what do ya—

NANCY: "What do ya need it for?" Your favorite question, Eddie; they're gonna put it on your tombstone: "Here Lies Eddie Bergson; What Did He Need It For?"

EDDIE: Fact is, I love you, Shirl . . . and I loved you just the way you were, too . . .

NANCY: Dear, sweet Eddie . . . you were in love with a midget. I'm what I'm asked to be, see, and you were asking for a little toy lady. Eddie, I had to get outa there before I got too short to reach the doorknob . . . (*Grips his hand urgently.*) Oh, Eddie, there's so much maybe I can be, so much I want to . . . (*She looks at him for a moment.*) Gettin' any of this, Eddie?

EDDIE: Gettin' the sound of it. Sounds like leaving.

NANCY: Oh, Eddie . . . dear, sweet—

EDDIE: (*He stands.*) That's enough "dear, sweet Eddie" for today. I'm startin' to take offense at it. (*Crushes his coffee container, drops it in the sand.*) Look, Shirl; it's what people do: being married. It's what there is. Not fantastic, but what there is. Six years we had no chairs in the dining room because you were waiting for fantastic ones. You're lookin' for fantastic, Shirl, and there isn't any. But there *is* the Bergsons, and that knocks me out. Just seein' it on your driver's license, "Shirley Bergson," just knocks me out. (*Walking to the stairs.*) You still got the same eyes but they look frightened to me. Out in the cold with frightened eyes; you'll forgive the expression, kid— (*Turns.*) —but what do ya need it for? (*Checks watch.*) Gotta open the lot by eight . . . (*Going quickly up the stairs.*) Probably make it in forty, forty-five minutes. No traffic comin' out, but goin' back you get your rush traffic building up on the parkway. Course, I could always just shoot straight out on the— (*Stops at top of stairs; turns, looks down at her.*) This doctor you go to; he just listens, huh? (*She nods.*) Uh-huh. (*He puts his coat collar up.*) Well, I think you better go to one who talks to you; because, fact is, Shirley, it's really very cold out here.

(*He shoves his hands deep into his coat pockets, turns left down the boardwalk, and exits quickly.*

Silence. There is the sound of a lone and distant buoy bell. A gust of wind; she hugs herself against the cold.)

NANCY: Well; looks like you and me, Art.

ARTHUR: Goodbye . . .

NANCY: These seaside things never last . . . (*Going to her bike.*) Listen, Arthur, we tried, we hoped . . . but let's be sensible; it's over. I think the best thing is a simple "goodbye" . . .

ARTHUR: Goodbye . . .

NANCY: Never really felt like a woman with you, anyway. I think it had a lot to do with your calling me Bill all the time . . . (*She suddenly lets go of her bike, buries her face in her hands, trembling. The bike falls over in the sand. After a moment she looks up, frightened, surprised by her own behavior.*) Goddamn it . . . (*She marches angrily to the two phone booths, enters one of them, deposits coin, dialing fiercely. A gust of wind: she shivers; speaks into phone.*) Hello, Dr. Ber-

man? Nancy Scott. Look, I'm sorry to bother you at this hour,
but I want my money back. It's not working out, Berman; I
asked you for happy and fulfilled and you gave me lonely and
frightened. (*Sits in booth, shivering.*) Listen, I . . . I think
Nancy Shirley Silverman Scott has gone and flunked the freedom test. The alone thing . . . I can't seem to handle the alone
thing. It's not the dark I'm afraid of; it's the light, it's the
mornings, it's the goddamn mornings. I wake up next to lovers
with noses as strange to me as my own. I know they must be
lovers because they never look like friends. Maybe I should go
back to Eddie, huh? I mean, he's still got the same face . . .
(*Quietly; hugging herself against the cold.*) Listen, keep the
money; just give me an estimate—I'm thirty-three, how many
years are gonna be left by the time I figure out how to live
them? Make me happy, Wizard; make me happy and we still
got a deal . . . a happy above happy that guilty can't reach; a
happy so high that the guilties'll die on their way up after me
. . . Hello? Hello? . . . God damn you, *wake up!* Everybody
up! (*She stands, shouting into the phone.*) I don't care *how*
early it is! Don't you know a crazy lady when you hear one?
O.K., Berman, that's it. We've *had* it. We're finished! You *bet*
I'm serious. Goodbye; I don't need you any more. I don't need
you . . . So I'll see you at two o'clock, O.K.? Boy, are you
lucky I can't make a decision. (*Hangs up sharply. Quietly, to
Arthur*) Problem now is what to do till two o'clock. (*Going to
her bike, which lies in the sand next to Arthur's chair.*) This is
the difficult period, see: between doctor's appointments. (*Set-
tles herself down in the sand between the chair and the bike.*)
Pop'll be back. I'll wait for Pop . . . (*Rests her head against
the bike.*) No sleep all night . . . (*Closes her eyes. Arthur suddenly moves in his sleep—she whispers urgently.*) No, no,
don't go . . . (*He relaxes again, murmuring peacefully.*)
Good. Tell ya the truth, I hate to sleep alone . . . (*Closes her
eyes, drowsily*) Just don't wake up, see . . . As long as you
don't wake up, m'friend, you are the best there is . . . (*Her*

voice trailing off.) Hey, don't feel the wind down here . . . no wind, the best . . . the best . . .

(*She is asleep. Silence.*

Arthur awakens; he stares out at the horizon for a few moments, trying to remember where he is. He looks down sleepily, sees the bicycle wheel; he studies it curiously for a few moments—suddenly startled to see a pair of feet next to the wheel and an entire girl connected to them.)

ARTHUR: Oh . . .

NANCY: (*Opens her eyes, also startled.*) Oh . . .

ARTHUR: Hello. Hello there . . .

NANCY: Arthur, you're awake.

ARTHUR: Yes. Yes, I am. Yes.

NANCY: (*Rising.*) Hello.

Arthur: Hello. How are ya? (*Rising.*) Good morning. (*Stumbling over the bicycle.*) Your bike?

NANCY: Yes.

ARTHUR: Nice bike.

NANCY: Ten-speed Peugeot with handle brakes.

ARTHUR: Hey, the old guy . . . the old guy, Silverman; where's—?

NANCY: It's a curse. All night long I'm an old Jewish man and in the morning I turn into the beautiful girl you see before you.

ARTHUR: (*To horizon*) Oh, God. Oh, my God—

NANCY: What—

ARTHUR: The sun! Looka that! It's up! It's up already! Goddamn sunrise, they slipped another one right past me . . . (*Slumps defeated in beach chair.*) Looka that. Six mornings in a row . . . (*Jumps out of his chair.*) Excuse me. You wanna sit down? Forget it, stranger on the beach; who knows, right? I don't blame you. I'm Arthur Korman, I'm harmless, how-are-ya? (*Holds out his hand—withdraws it before she can respond.*) Right. Watch out, I could be anybody. A nut. This city; I know how you feel. (*She sits down on the beach chair.*) Beautiful. Look, you sat down. I'm Arthur Korman; I'm completely, completely harmless. (*Shakes her hand vigorously.*) Don't worry about it. You're free to leave any time. You're a very pretty girl. Exceptional.

NANCY: Thank you, I—

ARTHUR: Don't worry about it. (*Sits opposite her, on sand dune.*) I'm just going to sit here and you sit there and everything'll be beautiful. You want some coffee?

NANCY: Great; yes.

ARTHUR: Oh; I don't have any. How did you know my name? You must be freezing. Hey, I'll give you my coat.

NANCY: Truth is, I am cold, if it isn't—

ARTHUR: Beautiful. Beautiful. (*Taking off his coat.*) Situation like this, believe me; you know how to handle yourself. May I ask your name?

NANCY: Nancy Scott.

ARTHUR: Beautiful. I like the way you handle yourself.
    (*He has forgotten to give her the coat.*)

NANCY: Excuse me . . .

ARTHUR: Right, baby.

NANCY: Your coat, I—

ARTHUR: Oh, my God, of course—
    (*Rolls it up, tosses it to her like a basketball.*)

NANCY: Thank you.

ARTHUR: So what're ya doin' around here? I come to see the sunrise, but I fall asleep.

NANCY: Don't worry; great thing about the sun is that it comes
back every morning.

ARTHUR: Even fell asleep on this crazy old guy today . . .

NANCY: He's my father.

ARTHUR: Weather like this, how come you don't wear a coat or
something?

NANCY: That crazy old guy, he's my—

ARTHUR: I mean, it's February.

NANCY: Well, when I go to buy coats I think I'm very tall. I've
got six tall coats and they all look terrible on me.

ARTHUR: Beautiful.

NANCY: So if I was tall I'd be warm. Meanwhile I'm short and
cold.

ARTHUR: Beautiful. Beautiful. See what we're doing? We're talking. Opening up. This is terrific. (*After a moment*) You got to
let it happen. Letting it happen is what it's all about. (*Silence;
he picks up his banjo case, opens it, takes out banjo.*) This is
called a Whyte Lady, this banjo. Great sound. Haven't made
'em for thirty, thirty-five years. (*Sits next to her on chunk of
driftwood, holding the banjo with great affection.*) See this
here; carved bone pegs . . . pearl inlay on the frets . . .

NANCY: Would you play something for me?
(*He holds the banjo in playing position; plucks one of the
strings, listens to it critically, tightens it. Silence for a moment. He puts it back in the case.*)

ARTHUR: Tell ya what, it wouldn't be a good idea.

NANCY: Why not?

ARTHUR: Because I don't play the banjo.

NANCY: What are you doing with it?

ARTHUR: Carrying it. I carry it.

NANCY: Oh.

ARTHUR: I carry things. Idea is you carry something around long enough you become obligated to it, see; to learn what to do with it. Got the instruction book in there too. And my sculpture tools. Used to do sculpture and I'd like to get back to it, so I carry my tools in there and it reminds me. Of my obligation. (*He snaps the case shut. He looks off at the horizon for a few moments; sings softly to himself.*)
IF YOU DON'T GET A LETTER THEN YOU'LL KNOW I'M IN JAIL . . . (*Silence.*) Well; 'bye now. (*Rises; picks up banjo case.*) Yessir, that ol' clock really ticks away, doesn't it? (*Shaking her hand vigorously.*) This was great. Talking to you. Beautiful to meet you. Beautiful experience here. (*Walking briskly to the stairs.*) Right; but now it's time to start the ol' day goin', huh?

NANCY: Your . . . your coat, I . . .

ARTHUR: (*Going up the stairs.*) Keep the coat. It's your coat. I want you to have it; it's February.

NANCY: (*Unbuttoning the Mackinaw.*) Take your coat. I don't want it . . .

ARTHUR: (*At the top of the stairs; he turns to her.*) Please. Please keep it . . .

NANCY: (*Holding the coat out to him.*) I really don't want it. Here . . .

ARTHUR: (*A casual wave of his hand.*) Hey, keep the coat . . . (*Suddenly, desperately, clutching the banjo case.*) Please . . . Keep it . . . Keep the goddamn coat, will ya? Lady, I gotta leave now. The gaps. The gaps in the conversation. The gaps

are coming! Get out while you can! Believe me, you're in for a
losing experience. That's it, lady; that's all I do. You've just
seen everything I do. That was it. I don't follow up with anything. I'd like to play you a song on my banjo or invite you for
a swim but I don't play I just carry and it's too cold. Forgive
me, I'm sorry; goodbye—
  (*He starts to exit left down the boardwalk.*)

NANCY: (*Shouting.*) This is a four-thousand-dollar nose! (*Throws
  his coat down on the sand.*) You're walkin' out on a four-
  thousand-dollar nose here, dummy! (*He turns, startled by her
  outburst.*) Don't stand there! Go away! Alla you! I don't need
  any of you! This is Dr. Graham's nose! A top nose! This is Mr.
  Gaston's hair! Mr. Gaston of Lexington Avenue! This is my
  agent's name and this is Dr. Berman's attitude and this voice
  I'm talking to you with is from Madame Grenier, the vocal
  coach! I'm not just a pretty girl, I'm a *crowd* of pretty girl! A
  convention . . . a parade . . . a . . . (*There are tears in her
  eyes. She turns away from him, sits down on the beach chair.*)
  So who needs you; I got company . . . (*She hugs herself
  against the cold, trembling.*) Go away, goodbye; we're goin'
  over great here . . . Graham, Gaston, Berman, my agent, the
  madame and me . . .
    (*Silence. A gust of wind.*)

ARTHUR: (*Gently*) Lady, I . . .

NANCY: You still here?
    (*She remains seated with her back to him.*)

ARTHUR: Listen, all those people . . . I want you to know something, they did a terrific job on ya. (*Silence.*) You really look
  . . . fine. Just fine. (*Silence; he comes down the stairs, picks
  up his coat, stands behind her.*) Here. You're shivering. Please
  take this . . . (*She does not respond; he drapes the coat very
  delicately over her shoulders.*) When it gets windy you can

put the hood up, O.K.? (*She reaches behind her head, letting her longish hair fall outside the coat. He assists her carefully with a strand or two.*) Very real; the hair . . . (*She continues to look the other way. He touches her shoulder gently.*) I'm sorry that I upset you. You mustn't take it personally . . . Believe me, you're a pretty girl. You must be a pretty girl because I can't talk to you. I can't talk to you people . . . There's a special code. Some guys know the code. I don't know the code . . . (*Silence.*) Please, give me your number. I'll call you. I'm terrific on the telephone. (*No reply. He shrugs sadly, turns to leave.*) I know I could have a great life if there was just some way to phone it all in.
(*Starts to walk slowly away.*)

NANCY: (*Quietly*) The hair, y'know . . . the hair *is* real.
(*He stops, delighted to hear her voice.*)

ARTHUR: I thought so. It had to be.

NANCY: It's just the color that was changed, see.

ARTHUR: Well, it's very suitable.

NANCY: (*After a moment*) Thank you.

ARTHUR: I think it's *all* very suitable.

NANCY: Thank you. (*After a moment*) It's just the nose, actually, that's not mine.

ARTHUR: Really? It certainly *looks* like—

NANCY: I know it's not mine because yesterday at Bloomingdale's I saw another girl with it. Dr. Graham, he does a certain style of nose and it turns out there's a goddamn *army* of us walking around New York with it. (*They both laugh at this for a moment. She turns toward him.*) Yukon five, six, one, four, one.

ARTHUR: What?

NANCY: That's my number. For when you're feeling terrific.

ARTHUR: Thank you.

NANCY: Or if you ever want to visit your coat.

ARTHUR: Coats . . . (*Looks up at the sky.*) Tall coats, you've got six of them . . .

NANCY: Yes, I—

ARTHUR: The old guy . . . the old guy, you said he was your father . . .

NANCY: I thought you didn't hear that.

ARTHUR: I didn't. I just heard it now. It takes about twenty minutes for sound to reach me . . . (*She laughs, enjoying him.*) See what you're doing? You're listening. How do ya do that? You even look like you're listening. That's the hard part. I gotta work so hard on that part I can't hear a thing . . . there's one now . . .

NANCY: What?

ARTHUR: A gap. And that's just the beginning, that was just a little one—

NANCY: Hey, Arthur—

ARTHUR: Wait'll the big ones come, they can kill ya—

NANCY: Take it easy, we've got plenty to talk about—

ARTHUR: Seems like we've covered everything—

NANCY: About me being pretty, we could talk about that some more. That's always good for a coupla minutes . . . (*He smiles, relaxing a bit.*) What's really fascinating, see, is that nobody seems to know me any more . . . (*He sits opposite her, nodding attentively.*) My own father, for example . . . Truth is, I was afraid to introduce myself to him. Sees my new nose, hears my new name—I'll wake up at the bottom of the

Atlantic with fifty pounds of frankfurter tied to my foot. (*He continues nodding.*) You hear any of that, Art?

ARTHUR: Parts. Parts of it . . .
  (*Silence. He glances about anxiously.*)

NANCY: Chrissake, that was a *pause*. Pauses are O.K. . . . (*Another silence. They both glance about anxiously.*) Uh . . . work—our work, let's talk about our work—

ARTHUR: O.K.—

ARTHUR and NANCY: What kind of—

NANCY: You're first, Arthur . . .

ARTHUR: Well, I've got this sorta silly job . . . I'm with the Jingle Bell Display Company, see; I run this department there called Santa's Workshop . . .

NANCY: (*Suddenly, remembering.*) Jesus, your *job*—

ARTHUR: I *told* you it was silly—

NANCY: Arthur, do you . . . how do you like it there?

ARTHUR: Eighteen years of Christmas? It's a nightmare. I'm slowly turning into an elf . . . (*Pacing in the sand.*) Pixie, pixies. I'm a fella lives with pixies. You hang around with pixies too long, something happens to your head . . . Planning to quit any day now.

NANCY: How about today?

ARTHUR: Today?

NANCY: (*A bit of strained laughter.*) Arthur, this funny thing happened . . . (*After a moment*) A nutty, impulsive, funny sorta . . . (*Turning away, quietly*) Arthur, forgive me . . . I had no right, I . . .

ARTHUR: (*Gently*) What is it? Tell me . . .

NANCY: See, this guy Bill called . . .

ARTHUR: Bill, right . . .

NANCY: And you seemed so definite there . . . in your sleep . . .

ARTHUR: Definite in my sleep, right . . .

NANCY: So I told him you were quitting . . .

ARTHUR: Quitting, right . . .

NANCY: Arthur, I'm sorry . . . I was in a crazy mood, I—

ARTHUR: Is *that* what's worrying you? Is *that* what you're worried about? Quitting my *job?* That dumb, silly *job?* I was going to quit *any*way! I was *going* to quit! Not right *now* maybe, not this very *minute;* but I was going to quit! *I was going to quit!* He thought you were kidding, he thought you were crazy, right? Some nut making a joke, right?

NANCY: He *must* have, Arthur, he—

ARTHUR: Eighteen years of my *life,* he couldn't've just—

NANCY: Arthur, he said he'd call *back*, he—

ARTHUR: When? When?

NANCY: In a little while, he—
    (*Arthur collapses into his beach chair.*)

ARTHUR: (*After a moment, quietly*) Good. Good. That's nice . . . (*Recovering, with a grand sweep of his hand.*) Style, see . . . it's just that I meant to leave with a little style. Eighteen years, you don't just walk out and slam the door, right?

NANCY: Of course not.

ARTHUR: (*Opens banjo case, takes out stack of letters.*) Wrote him twenty-six really fine letters of resignation this year; it's just a matter of selection . . . (*Looks fondly through letters.*) Been working on my style. Even got one here in sonnet form

. . . listen; ends with— (*Reading, lyrically*) "The blossom is fruitless for he who seeks the lotus And I, Arthur Korman, give you two weeks' notice." (*Rises, points to horizon.*) Said in the *Times*, "Sunrise: 6:41," so I sent Bill a telegram with the number here to call me twenty minutes later. I figured all that beauty comin' up . . . and I would quit so great. The world being born again; the world and me . . . (*Smacks his fist into the side of the dune.*) Damn it, lady you want a great life, you gotta have like that book, *Great Whattayacallits*, first!

NANCY: *Expectations.*

ARTHUR: Right! That's why I started coming here, I got up last Wednesday and I noticed I didn't have any. It was my birthday, forty-one years old and I wasn't even expecting *that* . . .

NANCY: Come on, forty-one's not old . . .

ARTHUR: I know; but it happened the day after I was twenty-three, so naturally I was a little shocked. Wednesday morning —zappo—forty-one. I felt like I'd left a wake-up call for thirty and I musta slept right through it . . . (*Turns to her, urgently*) Something terrific was supposed to happen by now, see—some terrific reason for shaving and buying shoes and keeping the clocks wound—something terrific, a dazzler, a show of lights, a— (*Grips her arm.*) I had this whole other fella in mind once, lady. You woulda been crazy about him. I was gonna be a sculptor, I had in my mind once . . .

(*His voice trails off; he turns away.*)

NANCY: What, Arthur? Tell me . . .

ARTHUR: Monuments . . . I had in my mind once, monuments. How do ya like that?

NANCY: Sounds wonderful . . .

ARTHUR: (*His spirits soar.*) I wanted to sculpt those heroes like you see in the park, guys on horses with swords, terrific guys

outa bronze and metal and they stay there in the park forever
. . . forever, lady . . . (*Running to the top of the dune.*) They
got bronze eyes looking outa their heads and bronze fingers
pointing somewhere in particular, and if it's a good statue, a
really great one, you can see five hundred people in the air
behind the guy, looking where his eyes are looking and ready
to go where his finger is pointing . . .

NANCY: Wonderful . . .

ARTHUR: So I went to this school to study sculpture . . . Trouble
is, I was in that school for five years and by the time I came
out they were all outa them.

NANCY: All outa what?

ARTHUR: Heroes and parks. They were all outa them. Seems like
the world run outa heroes and the parks run outa space and I
come outa school all at the same time . . . (*Slides to bottom
of dune.*) I mean, there just didn't seem to be any call for
what I did. Truth is, there's not a helluva lot of action in the
monument field . . . (*Picks up the letters of resignation.*) So I
took this job meanwhile . . . eighteen years of meanwhile and
every year they give you a birthday party . . . (*Going to end
of pier, carrying the letters.*) Except Wednesday it was special; besides the beer there was champagne in paper cups because I been there longer than anybody . . . Everybody singing "Happy Birthday" . . . Bill, the fellas, the secretaries,
everybody around me in a circle singing, and all of a sudden I
couldn't remember what I'd meant to do with it . . . my,
y'know, life. Stood there trying to remember and they went on
singing like a machine I couldn't stop, "Happy birthday,"
they're singing, "happy birthday, dear Arthur," and I wanted
to rip the building down, *hit* something, *crush* something, and
then I thought I was crying but it turned out I'd squirted
champagne in my face from squeezing the paper cup. (*Suddenly, violently, he crushes the letters in his hands. He whispers.*) What am I waiting for? (*Turns to her, shouting.*) Hey,

lady, what am I waiting for? (*Points to phone booth.*) Today
. . . today I get out! When he calls back, I get out! When he
calls back, I *quit!* Not another day dying alive! Arthur says
goodbye! (*He tosses the letters high up over his head.*) Santa's
little helper says goodbye! (*The letters spin in the air like confetti; Nancy bursts into applause.*) A week late, but here's my
birthday and you're at the party!

NANCY: Happy birthday!

ARTHUR: Thank you, thank you—

NANCY: And many happy returns—

ARTHUR: And how about *that*—?

NANCY: What—?

ARTHUR: No gaps! (*He races across the beach to her, grips her
hands in delight. She laughs, kisses him spontaneously on the
cheek.*) My God, things are going well here . . .
   (*The phone rings. A moment; then he lets go of her hands
. . . starts across the beach to the phone booth. She picks up
the banjo, roughly plucking the notes for "Happy Birthday"
as he marches to the booth, opens the door . . . He puts his
hand on the phone, she smiles expectantly . . . he does not
pick up the phone; he stands in the booth with his hand on
the phone while it continues to ring . . .*)

NANCY: (*Quietly, putting down the banjo.*) Arthur . . . (*The
phone continues to ring; she shouts urgently.*) Arthur! *Arthur!*

ARTHUR: (*He sits in the booth; very quietly*) Damn cold here,
isn't it . . . ?

NANCY: (*Coming toward him.*) Arthur—answer it—

ARTHUR: (*Turning away.*) The sunrise—I missed the sunrise . . .

NANCY: I saw it, it was gorgeous, now answer the goddamn

phone— (*Shouting above the phone.*) Arthur, you're using the sunrise as a *crutch*—

ARTHUR: (*Shouting.*) I know, but I'm a cripple, so it's O.K.—

NANCY: Arthur, you said not another *day*— (*She grips his arm.*) You said you were dying alive—

ARTHUR: (*Leaves booth, moving away from her.*) That listening you do, it has some terrible disadvantages—

NANCY: O.K., go ahead, run away from the truth—

ARTHUR: The truth! The goddamn *truth!* They keep tellin' ya how beautiful it is and they never tell ya what the hell to *do* with it— (*Shouts at the ringing phone.*) Stop! Stop! My God, will ya please *stop*— (*He runs to the booth, slams the door, stands with his back against it; shouts to her above the muffled but insistent ringing.*) Here's the truth, lady! Ain't it gorgeous? It's eight o'clock. At eight o'clock I go to work. At seven thirty I dream, and at eight o'clock I go to work . . . (*The ringing stops. His back against the booth, he slides down, sitting in the sand; bows his head.*) You see the truth comin', take my advice—run home, lock your doors, paint your mirrors black. The son of a bitch'll kill ya . . .

NANCY: (*Moving toward him.*) Oh, baby, you're a wailer . . .

ARTHUR: Right. Also a coward and a—

NANCY: (*She kneels next to him in the sand.*) Arthur, people can change their whole lives; I believe that . . . their whole lives if they want to . . .

ARTHUR: Don't you get it, lady? I blew my time. I used up my turn. My cool talk and my kid's clothes, it doesn't work. Only young is young and they don't let you do it again . . .

NANCY: Arthur it's—

ARTHUR: (*Nodding sympathetically.*) I see you got the same kinda problem . . .

NANCY: Huh?

ARTHUR: Excuse me, but I couldn't help noticing the funny clothes . . .

NANCY: What funny clothes?

ARTHUR: The funny clothes you got on . . . the kid's clothes . . .

NANCY: Wait a second, buster—

ARTHUR: I mean, you must be what now: thirty-one, thirty-two?

NANCY: Arthur, you're a charmer . . .

ARTHUR: Forgive me, Nancy . . . it's just I've been the route, I can save you some pain . . . (*Gently, touching her arm.*) There's things we can't change. Believe me, they ain't lettin' either of us into the world at half-fare any more. Keep telling yourself you're a kid and— (*She rises; starts to take his coat off.*) Hey, what're ya doin' . . . ?

NANCY: Giving your coat back.

ARTHUR: Hey, what're ya doin'?

NANCY: It's called "leaving." You will recognize it by how I won't be here any more.
   (*She drops his coat in the sand.*)

ARTHUR: Hey, where ya goin'?

NANCY: (*Lifting up her bicycle.*) I'm taking my funny clothes and getting the hell outa here.

ARTHUR: (*Scrambling to his feet.*) Hey, I . . . I alienated you, right?

NANCY: *Alienated?* I came here a cute girl and I'm leaving a nervous old lady!

ARTHUR: See, it's just . . . I thought we had this problem in common, I—

NANCY: The only thing we got in common is sand in our shoes! (*Wheeling her bike to the left under the boardwalk.*) I'm not climbing into any cookie jars with you, buster! Too late, years passing, that's all you talk about! It's like hangin' around with the Hunchback of Notre Dame—he doesn't have much to say, but you always know what time it is! (*Gets onto her bike, turns to him.*) Mister, I'm sorry; but I have looked inside your head this morning and it's fulla bluebirds. Unfortunately, not one of them is the bluebird of happiness . . . (*Starts to ride to the left under the boardwalk.*) And for your information, I happen to be twenty-six . . .

MAX'S VOICE: (*Approaching, off left; singing.*)
IS IT TRUE, WHAT DEY SAY ABOUT DIXIE,
DOES DE SUN REALLY SHINE ALL DE TIME . . . ?
(*She immediately stops, gets off her bike, starts wheeling it in the opposite direction.*)

ARTHUR: Nancy, you've come back—

NANCY: I haven't come back, you idiot! My God, I'm surrounded by crazy old men!
(*She starts to drag her bicycle up the boardwalk steps.*)

MAX'S VOICE: (*Coming closer, at left on boardwalk.*)
DO DE SWEET MAGNOLIAS BLOSSOM
AT EVER'BODY'S DOOR . . .

NANCY: Where the hell is he *coming* from—?
(*Turns around, dragging her bike back down the steps, wheeling it to the right under the boardwalk, away from the voice.*)

MAX'S VOICE: (*Coming closer.*)
AND DO DE FOLKS KEEP EATIN' POSSUM,
TILL DEY CAIN'T EAT NO MO' . . . ?
IS IT TRUE, WHAT DEY SAY ABOUT SWANEE,
IS A DREAM, BY DAT STREAM, SO SUBLIME . . . ?

(She stops; deciding to face him, wheels her bike back to the bottom of the stairs, stands there with it proudly as though with her gallant steed, awaiting Max.)

DO DEY LAUGH, DO DEY LOVE,

LIKE DEY SAY IN EVERY SONG . . . ?

(She abruptly lets go of the bike; grabs up Arthur's coat from the sand, puts it on, zipping the hood up over her head so that only her eyes are exposed; returns to her proud position at the bottom of the stairs.)

WELL, IF DEY DO, THEN YESSIR,

DAT'S WHERE I BELONG . . .

ARTHUR: The old guy . . . *(Looks up at the sky.)* . . . your father, he doesn't recognize you . . . you didn't introduce yourself . . .

NANCY: *(Introducing Arthur to an unseen audience.)* Here he is, ladies and gentlemen; Mister Memory . . . *(Shouting from inside the hood.)* Chrissakes, go away! Please go away!

(Max appears on the boardwalk, singing with great gusto. Caught up in the finish of the song, he proceeds down the steps like a vaudeville performer, one at a time; and once, for effect, moving back up a few steps before proceeding down for the finish of the song. This performance is not necessarily for anyone's benefit; it's something he would do even if the beach were empty.)

MAX: *(Singing.)*

DO DEY LAUGH, DO DEY LOVE,

LIKE DEY SAY IN EVERY SONG?

WELL, IF DEY DO, THEN YESSIR . . .

(Going for a big finish.)

DAT'S WHERE I BELOOOOOONG . . .

(He takes off his hat and bows to no one in particular.)

ARTHUR: *(After a moment)* Uh . . . very nice.

MAX: Nice? Nice? What's wrong with wonderful? That's a song,

sir. With a melody. Who since Jolson? Who? Nobody is who.
Since Jolson, a wasteland of pipsqueaks. (*Max breaks into a
warm smile, comes down the steps toward Arthur, his arms
outstretched. Nancy turns to him as he approaches, takes the
hood off. Max passes Nancy without any sign of recognition;
goes to Arthur, grips his shoulders in greeting.*) Arthur, my
sleeper, my darling, you're awake; terrific! I see you and my
heart, what's left of it, skips a beat. (*Indicating Nancy.*) Good.
Good. You got yourself a girl friend. (*Moving down to pier,
his arm around Arthur, confidentially*) What happened, it's all
finished with Bill? Good. (*Nancy sits on the bottom step of the
stairway, zips up her hood.*) You got yourself a shy one. Do
me a favor, you got a match? (*Indicates his cigar; Arthur
lights it.*) Good. Now one more thing I need from you. Ten
thousand dollars.

ARTHUR: Huh?

MAX: I'm lookin' for who's gonna get in on the ground floor, get
a nice percentage of Max's Hawaiian Ecstasies. Who's gonna
be the lucky fella? Two days now, I been on the telephone
calling; turns out there's not a lot of lucky fellas around.
Arthur, ten thousand dollars.

ARTHUR: I—

MAX: I'm on the telephone calling up some of my former business associates; any one of them would jump at the opportunity. Unfortunately, they're all dead. (*Outraged.*) It's only
twenty-two years; everybody died! (*Sits at edge of pier, takes
list of names from shopping bag.*) Al Glickman, my meat sup-
plier, *gone*—I'm speakin' to Al Glickman *Junior*. Kramer's
Kitchen Supplies, I'm speakin' to Kramer Junior. Cantor and
Sons, the contractor, I'm on the phone with "and Sons." How
long I been gone? All of a sudden I'm living in New York Junior! And these Juniors, these winners, senior voices on the
phone with junior guts, wouldn't advance you credit for a
Hershey bar. Gotta know first, for *sure, everything*— (*Imitat-*

ing their voices.) "Max *who?*" they say, "Hawaiian what? We'll see first how you do—after you open—maybe then . . ." Cold voices, people born for telephones . . . (*Nancy approaches him at the pier, removing her hood. He looks at her, then at Arthur, suddenly laughing.*) The joke is, what's payin' the phone bills for these darlings is a business they got from their fathers who wouldn't *trust* a voice on a telephone! Billy Gallino, Gallino Rolls and Buns—I'm talking yesterday to William . . . Gallino . . . Junior—a hundred receptionists answer the phone he shouldn't catch cancer from my voice—I ask him for credit, two months' goods, he gives me a cute maybe on the telephone. (*Nancy, assuming that Max doesn't recognize her, moves closer to him, becoming involved in what he is saying.*) His father, I'll tell you frankly, was a thief. Overcharged me, sometimes delivered me stale merchandise; I'm sure he's not resting easy right now because he didn't steal the ground he's buried in. But Monday I'm on the phone with Junior and I'm sorry Billy isn't still alive to sell me yesterday's bread . . . (*Suddenly standing, shouting; using the pier tie as support.*) I'm sorry *none* of them are alive, those hondlers, those hustlers, those *faces!* Now I got the Maybe Babies! A dozen numbers I dialed and each place the *same fella* answered! You couldn't tell who, what, which one! Could be they all got together, hired a fella to make a record? O.K., their fathers had accents, but *they* got no sound at *all!* Billy Gallino, he read a bread order aloud, you could *tango* to it! We had a fight once on Canal Street. I hit him, he hit me— (*Points to a mark over his eye.*) Here's a scar from Gallino. We did business! Junior with his micey voice, he nibbles, he nibbles, he noshes on my soul. Billy, I knew what he was— Junior, he could be anything, a sea captain, a potato chip, a corn muffin, what? (*A sudden burst of energy brings him to the end of the pier.*) Ah-hah! But at the end of the conversation, these sweethearts'll do a "Goodbye" for you—oh *boy, it's beautiful!* "Hello," they don't do so good; and after "Hello," nervous and rotten . . . but "Goodbye," will *they* do a job for you on "Goodbye"! (*He blows a goodbye kiss into the air.*) "Goodbye . . keep in touch . . . so long . . ." All of a sudden warm and personal and terrific . . . (*Waving goodbye.*) "Goodbye to ya . . . alla best to ya . . . we'll have lunch . . . see ya around . . ." All of a sudden it's happiness, it's sweetness, it's their best number, it's the goodbye people and they're feelin' terrific; they got through a whole phone call without promising anything, without owing, they lived another day without getting into trouble . . . (*He takes off his hat and waves it toward the ocean.*) "Goodbye . . . goodbye . . . we're rootin' for ya . . goodbye . . ." (*He puts his hat back on; turns to them.*) I'll tell ya the truth, buddy . . . the old days wasn't so terrific, but God help me from the new ones. (*He picks up his shopping bag as if to leave; suddenly turns to Arthur.*) Arthur, ten thousand dollars, I could open the store in two weeks; whaddya say?

ARTHUR: Ten thousand dollars, Jesus, I—

MAX: Eight then; seven . . .

ARTHUR: So suddenly, I—

MAX: Five. O.K., *five.* A full partnership for five . . .

ARTHUR: You see, it's—

MAX: Three! My final offer is three!

ARTHUR: Mr. Silverman, I'm—

MAX: Forget it! You lost it! It's finished!

ARTHUR: A sum like that, you can't expect a perfect stranger—

MAX: How perfect should a stranger be? Please, Mr. Sunrise, forget it. (*Squeezing Arthur's face gently, as though he were an infant.*) Arthur, darling, relax . . . sleep, my child. (*Hoists the shopping bag up under his arm, turns to leave.*) You just missed an opportunity, pure gold. (*Walking briskly to the stairs.*) I just figured you were in a generous mood. I mean,

since you gave my daughter your coat, I figured maybe you'd give *me* a little something too . . .
(*He starts quickly up the steps.*)

NANCY: (*Startled, whispering.*) Pop . . .

MAX: (*He continues up the steps, singing.*)
DO DE SWEET MAGNOLIAS BLOSSOM
AT EVER'BODY'S DOOR?
AND DO DE FOLKS KEEP EATIN' POSSUM,
TILL DEY CAIN'T EAT NO MO' . . . ?
(*He turns left on the boardwalk, about to exit, still singing . . .*)

NANCY: (*Shouting up at him.*) No guilt, Silverman! Forget it! I'm booked ahead solid! I'm not free to feel guilty about you till the first Saturday in August! So forget it!
(*He continues walking, ignoring her, about to leave. She turns angrily, wheeling her bike under the boardwalk, about to leave.*)

ARTHUR: Hey, wait . . . Nancy . . . Mr. Silverman . . .

MAX: Nancy? Nancy? (*He turns.*) Who's Nancy? Where's Nancy?

NANCY: (*Stepping out from under the boardwalk.*) Me. I changed my name to Nancy Scott.

MAX: Terrific.

NANCY: I kept the S.

MAX: Wonderful.
(*He turns to leave.*)

NANCY: Pop, wait . . . hey, Silverman . . .

MAX: Silverman? Who's Silverman? There's no Silverman here

... (*He turns to them.*) Allow me to introduce myself. Ricky Rogers. How do you do?

NANCY: O.K., Pop—

MAX: I kept the *R*.

NANCY: O.K., Pop, get it all out; now tell me about my new nose. Go ahead—

MAX: What nose? I don't see a nose. Arthur, do you see a nose?

NANCY: It's not that small—

MAX: First try and hold up a pair of glasses with it, then we'll talk. Whatsa matter, they couldn't leave you with something? They took away a nose and left a message. Listen, Mary-Lou, I'll tell ya—

NANCY: It's *Nancy*—

MAX: Excuse me, it's hard to remember a name when you don't know the face.

NANCY: It happens to be a damn good job, Pop—

MAX: Sure it's a good job. For a pixie. For a person it's ridiculous.

ARTHUR: Actually, Mr. Silverman, a pixie's nose is quite—

MAX: Ah, the daredevil speaks! What's with you and Captain Courageous here; funny business on the beach?

NANCY: Pop, *Jesus*—

MAX: Right, that's the name; Jesus. Used to be Max, but I changed it to reach a bigger crowd. (*Standing firm at the top of the stairs, he stares off at the horizon now, refusing to look down at her.*) Some people are in the hospital for three months. Some people don't come to visit them. That's some people.

NANCY: Pop, I didn't even *know*, I—

MAX: Some people didn't even know. So out of touch, certain parties are. That's certain parties.

NANCY: O.K., Pop . . . you got all the aces . . . (*Sits, defeated, on bottom step.*) The hospital, I didn't know; I never think of you as being sick. Pop, I listen to you talking about the guys you spoke to on the phone . . . and I realize how much I need you to be alive. (*He remains looking the other way; makes an elaborate business of shifting his shopping bag from one hand to the other.*) Silverman; you gonna keep standing up there like that?

MAX: You; you gonna keep sittin' down there like that?

NANCY: (*Taking a deep breath.*) The air; you can taste it out here . . . damp and salty and full of Silverman pride.

MAX: Silverman? I see only one Silverman! One Silverman and one runaway nose-fixer in a stranger's coat! The victim of a recent massive coronary stands here waiting for an explanation.

NANCY: (*She suddenly stands, shouting.*) O.K., Silverman, I have seen your vengeful moods before! Your ears close, your accent gets thicker, and Zorro rides again! You don't *want* an explanation; you just want me to stand here and keep feeding you straight lines! Either you warm up a little and *talk* to me or I'm on my way . . .

MAX: Threats, ultimatums . . .

NANCY: Well, what's it gonna be, Silverman?

MAX: Deals, negotiations . . .
   (*He remains silently looking the other way, straightening his hat. Arthur looks tensely from one to the other.*)

NANCY: Well . . . I tried . . .
   (*She turns sharply, wheeling her bike quickly off left under the boardwalk.*)

MAX: Sally-Ann . . . (*She stops.*) You see that stairway there? (*Still not looking at her, he gestures toward the stairs.*) It has got, by actual count, twenty-two steps. You show up on step number eleven, and maybe I'll meet you there shortly. (*She looks up at him.*) I heard a weather report on the radio this morning. Says cold air masses are coming down from Canada. (*He turns, smiles, holds out his arms to her.*) Quickly, quickly . . . before they get here . . . (*She laughs, drops her bike, and races up the steps into his arms.*) Devochka, devochka . . . welcome to the top of the stairs.

NANCY: "Devochka," doesn't that mean—

MAX: It means you fixed your nose but I love you anyway.
(*They sit on the top step; she holds his hands in hers. Arthur, unnoticed by them, has been moved almost to tears by their reconciliation; sits on dune, watching with pleasure and fascination.*)

NANCY: O.K. now, Pop, admit it; I don't look so bad.

MAX: Certainly you are a pretty person. But once you were a novelty item; now regular merchandise.

NANCY: Pop, I just wanted things to be new . . .

MAX: Must be a good attitude because I got the exact same attitude; that's why I'm opening the store again—

NANCY: Pop, the store—

MAX: I'll tell you what chance you got to talk me out of it. No chance.

NANCY: But you're not well—

MAX: Not well is twenty-two years workin' for somebody else, that's a disease you can die from—

NANCY: How ya gonna do it alone?

MAX: What's alone? Comes back with me, once a partner, still a gentleman and a genius, Marcus Soloway!

NANCY: You spoke to him . . .

MAX: Not for a couple years . . . but I'll fix the store like it was, he'll see it, he'll join right up! I know what's in that classy Soloway head! He owns still fifty percent of the property, it's valuable, it's beach-front. Like me, a hundred times Marcus coulda sold his share. But he keeps it twenty-two years. Why? Because, like me, he's got the same idea! Because, like me, he waits for our turn to come again . . . (*He stands.*) You're thinking I'm crazy, why open? Who'll come in the winter? People come; for the best, people come . . . for ecstasy they show up . . .

NANCY: But, to fix up the store, where will you get the money from?

MAX: Where will I get the money from? I'll . . . I'll *tell* you where I'll get the money from!

ARTHUR: From me . . .

MAX: From *him!* I'll get the money from him! (*Turns, looks down at Arthur.*) From him . . . ?
   (*Nancy, also surprised, looks down at Arthur. Arthur stands on top of the dune, a little surprised himself.*)

ARTHUR: (*Quietly*) I've been thinking about it . . . and I've decided to invest in this . . . (*Gestures to store.*) . . . this project here, yes . . . (*Slides to bottom of dune.*) Property, yes . . . property at the beach . . .
   (*He touches the store; the little building shudders with age.*)

MAX: (*Coming quickly down the stairs to him.*) Congratulations, Mr. Sunrise, you just made a first-class investment—

NANCY: Arthur, why the hell're you—

MAX: Close-'em-up-the-mouth, Mary Jane—

ARTHUR: Actually, I *would* like to tell you why. You see, Mr. Silverman, I've—

MAX: For ten thousand dollars you can call me Max—

ARTHUR: O.K., Max, I—

MAX: I said for ten thousand dollars. Until I get the check keep calling me Mr. Silverman—

NANCY: Let him finish what he's *saying*, I wanna know why the hell he's—

MAX: (*Sharply, aside*) No-sir, this kinda fella you let him open his mouth he'll talk himself right out of it—

ARTHUR: (*A slight tremor in his voice.*) You see, a time comes when one must—

NANCY: (*Coming urgently down the steps.*) Arthur, its *February*, he's not *well*; what do ya think you're *doing?* Being nice? Doing us a *favor?*

MAX: (*Offended; gesturing grandly.*) What nice? What favor? He's waltzing into a gold mine!

ARTHUR: (*With genuine admiration*) Jesus, Mr. Silverman, how do ya do it? You just *believe* that everything's gonna work out for ya, you just—

MAX: *Crap!* I don't believe in *noth*ing or *no*body! (*Pokes Arthur's chest.*) Including *you* till I get my check. (*As he busily takes shopping bag from stairs, begins removing items from it: blueprints, deeds, sandwiches, pens, contracts, a thermos bottle, zoning maps, etc.*) I believe in *me, Max*; and why's that? Because I'm terrific? No-sir. Because I'm what's left. Hello and goodbye; I look around, what's left is

me. Willy and nilly, what's left is me. I believe in Max Silverman, and when the weather is nice I believe in God; a couple
days in the spring and that's *that* . . . (*Takes two new pam-
phlets from bag.*) Meanwhile, darling; if God don't work out
. . . there's contracts. Sign this and a check and then we'll *all*
believe . . . (*Smooths out a plateau of sand on the side of the
dune, lays out the contracts on it, hands Arthur a pen.*) The
signed contracts you'll take to Michael David Silverman, a
lawyer and a son . . .

NANCY: (*Approaching them.*) Pop, wait . . .

MAX: His address is on the top there . . .

NANCY: Both of you, please . . . look; the Alamo with pine-
apples, look . . .

MAX: (*Ignores her, reading contract softly to Arthur.*) "Joint
Venture Agreement . . ." Beautiful, all poetry . . . "The
party of the second part, hereinafter referred to as Joint
Venturer . . ." That's you, darling; yesterday a sleeper, today
a party and a venturer! Says here also, "Right of Survivor-
ship"; means one of us dies, the other one gets the entire
kaboodle. Arthur, if you don't drop dead, you got a terrific
deal here . . .

NANCY: Snow, it's gonna snow next week . . .

MAX: Now the best part . . . paragraph 7 . . . (*Softly: a hymn.*)
"The party of the first part does hereby grant joint ownership
of the property to the party of the second part . . . and to
all his heirs and successors forever . . ." Ah, such words . . .
a contract like this you don't need a lawyer, you get a mixed
chorus to sing it to you . . . (*Arthur's pen is poised over the
contract.*) Your name is Arthur Korman . . .

    (*Arthur suddenly signs. Max snaps it away and flashes a
    second copy under Arthur's pen. Arthur signs the second
    one.*)

NANCY: (*Sits helplessly on the stairs.*) Oh, God . . .

ARTHUR: (*Quietly*) A short name . . . what a short name I've got . . .

MAX: (*Softly*) Arthur . . . you know what this means . . . ? (*They have been seated at the dune; Max rises now and extends his hand to Arthur.*) It means shake the hand . . . (*Arthur rises unsteadily, takes Max's hand.*) Shake the hand and you own a piece of the world forever . . .

    (*There is a gust of whistling wind; it rattles the papers on the beach. The men stand with their hands joined, the lights dim; Nancy shivers, looking up at the winter sky as . . .*

Curtain

ACT TWO

Before the curtain goes up we hear a scratchy old record of Al Jolson singing a Hawaiian love song . . .

JOLSON'S VOICE:
DOWN HAWAII WAY
WHERE I CHANCED TO STRAY
ON AN EVENIN' I HEARD
A HULA MAIDEN SAY . . .
    (*Arthur's voice joins in softly.*)

ARTHUR and JOLSON'S VOICE:
YAAKA HULA HICKEY DULA
YAAKA HULA HICKEY DU . . .
    (*As the curtain rises*)
DOWN HAWAII WAY
BY THE MOONLIT BAY
WHERE I LINGERED AWHILE, SHE
STOLE M'HEART AWAY . . .
    (*It is early evening; the boardwalk lamps are lit, there is moonlight and a gentle glow on the sand. Everything else is as it was, with one extraordinary exception—to the left of the store is a rather well sculpted seven-foot palm tree; it is arched gracefully over the store and over Arthur, who sits*

beneath it holding his banjo and singing quietly in the moonlight.

To his right, tacked onto one of the boardwalk pillars, is his designer's "rendering" of the projected Hawaiian Ecstasies, in which the store is seen in all its imagined glory— many palm trees, tables and chairs spread along the beach; the store itself is pictured as a multicolored grass hut, the roof features a glowing Hawaiian volcano, and towering above that is a neon frankfurter. The actual steps toward realizing the rendering are small at this point, but promising; there is the tree that Arthur is building, and just downstage of it a wicker table and two small wicker chairs; an open carton marked "Colby's Outdoor Products—Everything under the Sun" stands nearby. Several of the boards have been removed from the front of the store, partially revealing the old counter; an ancient portable Victrola rests on the counter, from which the music continues . . .)

YAAKA HULA HICKEY DULA

YAAKA HULA HICKEY DU . . .

(He hits two chords on his banjo; chuckles with satisfaction, goes on with the song.)

OH, I DON'T CARE IF YOU'VE LOVED THE LADIES

FAR AND NEAR . . .

(Rises, continues work on the tree, molding swirls of bark around the trunk.)

YOU'LL FORGET ABOUT 'EM ALL IF

YOU COULD HEAR

YAAKA HULA HICKEY DULA

YAAKA HULA HICKEY DU . . .

(There is a gust of wind; the tree begins to sway. He hugs the tree to steady it. The phone rings. He continues to hold on to the tree, singing softly.)

YAAKA HULA HICKEY DULA

YAAKA HICKEY DU . . .

(The phone continues to ring, piercing the gentle moonlit setting and the soft music. Arthur finally lets go of the tree,

turns the music off, walks decisively to the phone booth, humming a bit more of the song . . . shifting unconsciously to "Jingle Bells" as he reaches the booth. Grabs phone; speaks briskly.)

ARTHUR: Arthur Korman here! Right, Bill; how the hell are ya, fella? Well now, where were we? We haven't talked so we couldn't be anywhere, right? O.K., here's the situation, Bill; here's how it shapes up . . . That's because it *is* rolling surf, Bill . . . Right, but this is a very nice time of year also. Picturesque . . . Glad that amuses you, Bill; but the fact is . . . (*Looks at horizon for inspiration. There is only the moon.*) The fact is I'm involved in a very interesting project here at the beach, Bill . . . a design project of my own, and I might well continue to . . . A restaurant, I guess you might call it a sort of an outdoor restaurant, a sort of an outdoor-restaurant-beach-design project is what I'm involved in here, Bill . . . I wish you wouldn't do that . . . Bill, I'd really rather you didn't laugh at this . . . (*Sits in booth; quietly*) Don't laugh, please . . . (*Nancy enters on boardwalk, at right, wearing his Mackinaw and carrying a portable electric heater. She stands at the top of the stairs, unnoticed by him, listening.*) Quitting? Quitting? Who said that? Oh; well, she's an associate of mine here at the project, poor kid's been under a lot of pressure; fact is, we're all under a lot of pressure here at the project right now, so I'd appreciate your calling me back in ten minutes because there's something important I have to discuss with you, Bill, a whole area of discussion. Beautiful; finish your dinner and call me back. That'll be beautiful. I really appreciate your cooperation on this, Bill. Later, man. Beautiful. 'Bye. (*Hangs up quickly; slumps in booth, exhausted. Sees Nancy at the top of the stairs.*) Oh . . . (*Leaves booth.*) Good evening. I'm glad to see you . . . (*She remains at the top of the stairs, looking the other way.*) I was just discussing the quitting area with Bill. (*Silence. He gestures about.*) Well, Max and I . . . we've be-

gun. How do you like the tree? The tree here . . . (*Silence. No
reply.*) It's just Celanese strips over aluminum armature, but
I think you still get this graceful-tree feeling . . . (*Touching
the tree.*) Used all of my old tools . . . (*He bounds over to
the wicker table.*) Hey, first table sample in from Colby's—
(*Takes umbrella from under table; fits it into center of table,
opens it. It is in the shape of a small palm tree.*) Sort of a
follow-through here on the graceful-tree feeling see, it's—

NANCY: (*Quietly, calmly*) You've gone mad.

ARTHUR: I'm sorry you feel that way . . .

NANCY: You have set sail on the banana boat.

ARTHUR: I really wish you'd consider the—

NANCY: (*Shouting.*) Crazy! The word is "crazy"! A man who
can't play the banjo and an old man who can't lift one are
gonna sell frankfurters on the beach in the dead of winter!

ARTHUR: Well, it's a unique enterprise, that's true, but—

NANCY: Graceful-tree feeling! Oh, my God—

ARTHUR: And you're wrong; I can play the banjo—
    (*Picks it up, strums two chords.*)

NANCY: Oh, Jesus—

ARTHUR: Well, I'm still learning—

NANCY: Dead of winter! Dead as in dying! As in dying old man!
I saw you with my own eyes, I saw you give him a check for
ten thousand dollars! That's not a *business* investment, that's
funeral expenses, that's—

ARTHUR: How much did you give him?

NANCY: Two thousand. (*Sits on top step; quietly*) How could
I do that? I don't understand; I went with him to deposit your
check, to talk him out of it, and the next thing I knew . . .

How could I do that? I asked Dr. Berman about it this afternoon . . .

ARTHUR: What did he say?

NANCY: He said the best he could do was three hundred.

MAX'S VOICE: (*Approaching, at left, singing.*)
MOONLIGHT BECOMES YOU,
IT GOES WITH YOUR FACE,
YOU CERTAINLY KNOW HOW
TO FIX YOURSELF UP TERRIFIC . . .

NANCY: I'm trapped, mister. I can't stop him, and I can't leave
him either, I . . .

MAX: (*Enters on boardwalk, carrying two large toolboxes; sing-
ing.*)
MOONLIGHT BECOMES YOU,
I'LL TELL YOU RIGHT NOW . . .
    (*Sees Arthur's tree; stops, deeply impressed. He takes a step
    down the stairs, looks at the tree in the moonlight; whisper-
    ing.*)
Oh . . . oh, boy . . .

NANCY: Pop, you shouldn't be carrying all those—

MAX: (*Quietly, to Arthur*) What can be said? O.K., a partner
. . . a friend even, I figured. But an artist, a great artist, I was
not prepared . . . (*Coming quickly down the stairs.*) *The Last
Supper*? Forget it! A comic strip! The *Mona Lisa* is a bimbo!
Move over, God, we got another fella here makes trees!
(*Squeezes Arthur's face.*) Your check goes today into Irving
Trust, smooth . . . smooth like an egg into a cake, and all day
my ear is filled with "yes" . . . "yes" from Auerbach Refrig-
eration, "yes" from Holiday Juice Machine, "yes" from—

NANCY: (*Trying to take one of the toolboxes.*) Here, let me—

MAX: Same nose from this morning? Good. I'm getting used to

it. (*Goes to counter with toolboxes, sets them down.*) Partner, up the street by Shatzkin's Famous Knishes, is James Carlos Velásquez—a Spanish gentleman, a cab-driver, and a visionary. A small percentage, deferred, he does our deliveries here — (*Points to street.*) Go; look for a young fella, sixty-eight, with a Dodge, '73—inside is a new sign for the store, unpainted. Bring it and paint it!

ARTHUR: (*Indicates rendering.*) Max, I'd like to discuss—

MAX: At my earliest possible convenience— (*Points, under boardwalk.*) Shirley, two blocks down Stillwell, a Pittsburgh Paint Outlet. They're open ten more minutes; establish credit and bring me a rainbow. (*He looks at them both.*) What I got here? Sand castles? (*Claps his hands.*) Move . . . Move . . . Time. Time. A couple weeks we open here! (*Nancy exits reluctantly under the boardwalk. Arthur hesitates on the stairs.*) O.K., I'll look at the picture . . . (*Goes to rendering; studies it for several moments. Turns solemnly to Arthur.*) I'll tell ya what you're talkin' here, mister . . . you're talkin' ecstasy.

ARTHUR: I think we need some really big palm trees, Max—

MAX: No others would be acceptable!

ARTHUR: The volcano on the roof, I—

MAX: Guaranteed, a volcano!

ARTHUR: (*Going quickly up the stairs.*) Grass huts!

MAX: I love it!

ARTHUR: (*Exits to right, on boardwalk.*) Tribal masks!

MAX: A must! Whatever they are! (*Alone now; looks at rendering.*) A little dull; but he'll learn.
   (*Takes crowbar from toolbox, begins prying loose the first of the boards covering the front of the store; singing.*)
MOONLIGHT BECOMES YOU,
I'M NOT KIDDING AROUND . . .

(*The phone rings. He grabs it, instinctively distrusting the instrument.*)

What is it, who is it? I'm busy here! . . . The what? The beach project? Correct, yessir, this is the beach project. I'm the chairman. State your business . . . He's not here. Later, call later. Sunrise is a good time . . .

(*During these last few moments, a man has entered on the boardwalk at left. He stands in the spill of light from one of the boardwalk lamps, a silhouette carrying a briefcase, looking down at the proceedings . . . During the next few lines he comes down the stairs, looking solemnly about at the palm tree, the wicker table, the rendering. A rather neatly dressed man in his late thirties, his air of efficiency and organization is immediately at odds with the beach and the open sky. His attitude and his clothes belong to closed rooms. He will be constantly brushing sand off his shoes and his well-pressed overcoat.*

He very carefully places his briefcase out of sight under the wicker table, then watches Max finish his conversation.)

Who may I say rang? Who? Bill? Bill, from "Goodbye, Bill"? Listen, he's got a girl friend now, leave him alone. Palm trees, girls, a healthy life by the sea; it's not too late for *you*, either. (*Sits in booth.*) Tell me something, what line are you in? . . . Jingle Bells? Sounds risky. Seasonal and risky. Listen to me, you want to get involved with something sturdy, with a foundation? Do yourself a favor, Billy; come down, give a glance here; Tenth Street and the boardwalk. Look for the volcano!

(*Hangs up.*)

MAN: My God . . . what's this?

MAX: (*Turns to him.*) What's this? What does it look like? It's paradise. Who are you? (*Leaves booth, studying the Man's face.*) Wait . . . I know you from some place . . .

MAN: (*Sits on wicker chair.*) Take a second, Max. It'll come back to you.

MAX: Atlantic City, nineteen fifty-eight . . .

MAN: No.

MAX: Sure; business. I know you from business . . .

MAN: No.

MAX: Wait, wait, a *relative* . . .

MAN: Right.

MAX: A cousin, a nephew, a . . .

MAN: A son. I'm your son.

MAX: Which one?

MAN: Michael.

MAX: (*Snaps his fingers.*) Of course, my son Michael. Must be him. Looks just like him. (*Shakes his hand, cordially*) How-do-you-do-sir.

MICHAEL: Max, there are some urgent legal matters—

MAX: Sure, now I remember. My lawyer, the son. See, at first I couldn't recognize; because a son, you make a simple cash request—(*Points to store.*)—an investment in paradise, he doesn't tell you to go to hell—

MICHAEL: Max, I refuse to finance your suicide—

MAX: Even a lawyer, what's the good? I give you something to handle, a simple divorce—

MICHAEL: A simple divorce? My mother and father; a simple divorce? Max, I told you, this insane divorce, you have no right to ask me. You'll have to get a stranger—

MAX: With a son like you, who needs a stranger?

MICHAEL: Max, get another lawyer—

MAX: What do I pay you?

MICHAEL: Nothing.

MAX: Then I'll wait till I get a better buy.

MICHAEL: Max, there is another, quite imperative matter which I have attempted, unsuccessfully, to bring to your attention—

MAX: Who stops you?

MICHAEL: Max, I came to the house last week and you threw me out. I came in, you hollered, "Yich! Briefcase-carrier!" And shoved me out the door.

MAX: You shouldn't bring a briefcase to dinner. It's not nice.

MICHAEL: And now the matter has increased in urgency. (*Taking Arthur's contract from his overcoat pocket.*) Max, some fellow named Korman left this on my secretary's desk this morning—

MAX: (*Glancing about*) Hey, where you got it?

MICHAEL: What?

MAX: The briefcase, where you got it?

MICHAEL: Out of sight, don't be concerned . . .

MAX: (*Pleasantly*) Where you got it? Let me see . . .

MICHAEL: (*Lifts it out from under table.*) Here, I've—

MAX: (*Shouting.*) Yich! Briefcase-carrier! Old man! Go away!

MICHAEL: (*Quickly putting case back under table.*) It's gone, Max, its gone—

MAX: In a briefcase comes always bad news. Now you got worse anyway; that suit. A suit for old people. A suit to be buried in. Or to bury somebody. (*Sits opposite him; quietly*) Tell me: you came here to bury somebody . . . ?

MICHAEL: Max, if we're finished with my briefcase and my suit, there is an urgent legal matter—

MAX: The tone, the voice, I don't like it—

MICHAEL: What *do* you like about me?

MAX: Since eighteen: nothing. You went into the boredom business, became a pioneer in the field— (*Bangs on the table.*) The *looks* of you. Old. Old. Go eat a hamburger, get a *stain* on yourself, wear the wrong *tie, something*. What happened to sloppy kids?

MICHAEL: I'm not a kid, Max—

MAX: Sure, a kid—

MICHAEL: Max, I have a profession, a wife, two sons—

MAX: Two? How nice for you; I don't have *any*. (*Rising.*) Now you'll excuse me, I open here soon, there are touches to finish—

MICHAEL: Max, wait, we've got to talk— (*Quietly*) Max, have you spoken to Soloway . . . ?

MAX: What's to speak? When I finish the store, I'll call him, he'll join right up—

MICHAEL: Max, to begin with . . . believe me, I never expected you to be able to get *any*body to invest in—

MAX: What's to tell me?

MICHAEL: It seemed reasonable to assume—

MAX: (*Coming toward the table.*) What's to tell me, Michael?

MICHAEL: Please remember, you were in the hospital, you were not expected to survive—

MAX: What, the cemetery is suing me for breach of promise?

MICHAEL: The store had just been sitting here for years . . . of no use to anybody . . . there was Mother to consider, an income to consider . . .

MAX: What, what . . . ?

MICHAEL: Max . . .

MAX: What, what, what—?

MICHAEL: Max, the property was sold. A month ago, when you were in the hospital . . . (*Max is quite calm; he sits opposite Michael at the table.*) Max, please understand, it's just this week you've talked about reopening . . . after all these years . . .

MAX: (*Quietly, calmly*) Sold. To who, sold?

MICHAEL: The Mister Hot Dog stores. It's a chain of—

MAX: I have seen them.

MICHAEL: They're always interested in beach-front locations, they—

MAX: You have received a check? You have cash in the hand?

MICHAEL: Not yet.

MAX: And Marcus. He agreed? He is selling his share?

MICHAEL: Yes.

MAX: (*Lights his cigar; leans back calmly in his chair.*) Uh-huh.

MICHAEL: Max, I hope you understand; I acted in what appeared to be the best interests of . . .

MAX: Certainly.

MICHAEL: You see, we all thought . . .

MAX: Certainly; you all thought I was passing away . . . (*Without rising, Max suddenly grabs the lapels of Michael's overcoat and pulls him across the table.*) Well, I passed back in again, Sonny Boy . . . (*Pulling him closer.*) Tell Mister Hot Dog the deal is off! Tell him Max had a change of heart; it's still beating!

MICHAEL: Max, listen to me—

MAX: There's no conversation— (*Lets go of him.*) Refuse the money—

MICHAEL: Max, you don't have to *take* the money, they're quite willing to offer you a percentage of the profits instead. They'll put one of their stores here this summer, you'll share in all the—

MAX: Here? In paradise? (*Rises from table.*) They'll put up a Mister Hot Dog in paradise?

MICHAEL: Please, Max . . . don't you see, you won't have to knock yourself out. And you'll still be in *business*, you'll be a *partner*, you'll drop around from time to time . . . like your brother Harry and the hardware store . . .

MAX: I don't want to do business like my brother Harry, and I don't wanna shimmy like my sister Kate neither! Partners with *them*? Garbage merchants! The answer is out of the question.
    (*Goes to front of store, continues prying board loose with crowbar.*)

MICHAEL: (*Follows Max to store.*) Max, I *told* you, they're getting Soloway's share, they'll *be* your partners whether you sell or not. They're going to want one of their chain stores here by June 15, for the summer season—

MAX: (*Turns to him with crowbar.*) My regrets to Mister Hot Dog, also *Mrs.* Hot Dog—

MICHAEL: Max, unless you can prove you're running a profitable business here by June, they've got the legal right to put up one of their own—

MAX: Profits; there'll *be* profits!

MICHAEL: How, Max? From what?

MAX: From business! From customers! It's almost springtime!

MICHAEL: Max, they'll take you to *court*, it's—

MAX: Gorgeous! Court is gorgeous! (*Delighted, he grips Michael's arm.*) Everybody sues everybody! Meanwhile the store is open, meanwhile profits! They'll take you to court, you'll *keep* them there. Delays and stalling, legal monkey business. You'll do it, Michael; you and the magic briefcase. Get me time, get me the summer, and I'll show you profits . . .

MICHAEL: Max, there won't *be* any profits . . . not here . . . there never were . . .

MAX: Take a sniff that breeze, there's gold in the air . . .

MICHAEL: Max, no . . . we can't . . .

MAX: Why no? Why *can't?* (*Holding Michael's arm, shaking him.*) *Do* it, Michael! Do this thing! Do a silly thing! Get a wrinkle in your suit! Give me a sign I'll know you're alive . . .

MICHAEL: (*Quietly*) Max, please . . . this place won't last a month. And if *it* does, *you* won't. It's foolish, it's impossible . . . it'll kill you, Max.

MAX: (*Lets go of his arm.*) When you were a baby, you were smart. At three months you knew to wave bye-bye . . . (*Walks away from him to counter*) It's still the thing you do best.

MICHAEL: Max, I'm trying to—

MAX: Soloway, he made a contract?

MICHAEL: Not yet, they're negotiating; but by the end of the week they—

MAX: (*Delighted*) He's negotiating. Perfect. (*Returns to work, prying board with crowbar.*) Now you may leave the premises.

MICHAEL: Max, I'm—

MAX: (*Shouts.*) Kindly leave the premises!

MICHAEL: It never varies, Max. Whenever I see you, you say the same three things to me: "Hello," "Who are you?" and "Leave the premises." (*Going to table.*) Actually, Max, since eighteen I haven't been too crazy about *you* either. (*Picks up briefcase.*) You keep telling me I'm ashamed of your accent. I never was. Only mystified. I just can't figure out why it's thicker now than it was twenty years ago . . . (*Turns to him.*) The anger too. Thicker and thicker. Today I'm trying to talk you into staying alive, and you're angry. You were angry last year, and year before that, and three years ago you came to my house for dinner . . . and asked me to leave the premises. My own home, Max; y'know, the one with the two sons . . . ? (*Max ignores him, busily prying board with crowbar. Arthur enters at right on boardwalk carrying large wooden sign. Stops, listens, unnoticed by them.*) Tell me, Max; what is it? Solve the mystery. What makes you perpetually angry with me? (*Max continues his work. Michael raises his voice, almost shouting.*) Come *on*, Max! I'm *asking you*—my client, the father! *What the hell is*— (*Checks himself; regains control; speaks quietly again.*) Well, it's certainly not going to accomplish anything for *both* of us to get angry— (*Picks up his briefcase, about to exit.*) No point in . . .

MAX: (*Quietly*) Wait a minute . . . (*Points with crowbar.*) What you were just doing here . . . *that* was angry? What kinda angry is that, I don't know till you tell me? Here, I'll show you angry . . . (*Max suddenly smashes one of the boards with his crowbar, shouting.*) *This is angry!* (*Quietly, smiling.*) You see that? There's no mix-up. (*Coming toward Michael.*) *There's* the mystery, *that's* why I'm angry—because I never know when *you* are. I look in your face: what's up? If that's angry, it's not enough. I look in your face, I don't see anybody. I look for Max, I don't see him either . . . that's why I got a store. The accent? Was a time, there were neigh-

borhoods in this city I could cash checks with it. Whatta *you*
got tells you you're not somebody else? An American Express
card? The store is foolish, the store is silly, but the store is
mine. Whatta you got belongs to *you?* A briefcase fulla bad
news and an old man's suit. Go away from me, you're breaking
my eyes. Wave bye-bye, sonny, I'll see you in a million
years . . .

>(*Max takes ledger pad from overcoat pocket, sits at table
>with his back to Michael, checking figures with a pencil
>stub. Michael turns to leave, stops.*)

MICHAEL: Max, you're going to open the store . . .

MAX: Of course.

MICHAEL: Then I'm quite certain I won't see you alive again.

MAX: Get a Polaroid. Take a picture.

MICHAEL: I don't understand . . . (*Shouts.*) God damn you,
Max . . . why do you want to die here with a bunch of palm
trees! (*Covers his eyes with his hand.*) Damn you, damn you,
old man; I'm crying . . .

MAX: You feel so bad, help me to open the store.

MICHAEL: I can't help you to kill yourself, Max.

MAX: (*Turns to him.*) Yessir, you're crying . . . but not enough!
(*Turns abruptly back to the ledger, immediately absorbed.*)
"Six counter grills, double weight, two hundred eighty, in-
stalled . . ." (*Michael steps forward violently, about to smash
his fist into the table—checks himself, composes himself; turns
to leave.*) "Malt mixers, eight-speed, gallon size, with filter
. . ." (*Michael remembers that he has left his briefcase, picks
it up, exits quickly under the boardwalk at right, brushing the
sand off his briefcase.*) "Quart-size, twenty-two eighty, repairs
up to one year . . ."

NANCY'S VOICE: Pop . . .

(*She steps solemnly out of the shadows under the board-walk, at left, carrying carton of paints. She has apparently been standing there for some time.*)

NANCY: Pop, I was . . .

MAX: (*Rises, goes toward her.*) Ah, the colors . . .

NANCY: Pop, I heard . . .

MAX: All?

NANCY: Enough.

MAX: Good. Then you know there's nothing to worry— (*Smiling, takes carton of paints from her.*)

NANCY: (*To Arthur, who is carrying the sign down the stairs.*) Arthur, Soloway's selling his share to the Mister Hot Dog chain . . .

ARTHUR: Oh, God—

MAX: I don't need "Oh, God" from you, I can get "Oh, God" from her. (*Happily opening the carton of paints.*) Nothing to worry, plenty time. He's not *selling*, he's *negotiating*. Like people *breathe*, Soloway negotiates. In a subway he negotiates the carfare—

ARTHUR: Max, if he sells—

MAX: Darling, darling, if he knew we were opening he wouldn't enter*tain* such an offer, wouldn't even give it a cookie. Be advised, sir; we are talking here of Marcus Soloway . . . a man built temples in the sand, sea lions, pillars toward the sky . . . (*His arm around Arthur.*) Arthur, wait'll he sees your volcano . . . your trees . . . (*Points to rendering.*) How much can we do in three days?

ARTHUR: Well . . . some, I—

Max: "Some" is exactly enough! (*Shakes Arthur's hand.*) It's settled; we open in three days!

Nancy: Oh, God . . .

Max: See how good she does it? (*His hand on Arthur's shoulder.*) Arthur, all we gotta do is show Marcus we're in business, show him we're alive . . . I promise you, he'll join right up. (*Quietly*) Partner . . . do you trust me on this?

Arthur: Well, yes, I—

Max: Then what're ya hangin' around for! (*Points to sign.*) The colors like the sunrise! (*Hands crowbar to Nancy.*) Quickly, the boards come off the store; tomorrow equipment arrives! Installations! (*Walking briskly to stairs.*) Some words in English are beautiful. "Installations" is beautiful. "Deliveries" is beautiful. (*Going up the stairs.*) "Goods," "equipment," "counter," "register" . . .

Nancy: Where are you going?

Max: The première has been advanced, I must go now to Margolis on the corner—formerly tailor of Florenz Ziegfeld, "Flo" to him—makes me an outfit for the opening, stripes; stripes to dazzle the eye . . .

Nancy: Pop, wait . . .

Max: "Wait" is not a beautiful word . . . (*As he exits*) "Wholesale" is a beautiful word. "Contract" is another beauty . . . (*Disappearing to the left down the boardwalk.*) "Percentage," "price," "bargain," "customer," "sale" . . .

Nancy: (*Quietly*) I can't do it. (*To Arthur*) Nope. Sorry. Can't. (*Shakes her head.*) Uh-uh. (*He approaches her.*) I can't. I can't watch this. I thought I could; but I can't . . . (*She hands him the crowbar.*) I have to leave now. (*Points to heater she brought earlier.*) That's portable; make sure he uses it to keep warm . . . (*Going left, under boardwalk.*) Promise me . . .

ARTHUR: Nancy, I think we should try to—

NANCY: Arthur, you're a nice man, a gentle man; but you're quite crazy. You're both crazy and I have to leave now.

ARTHUR: (*Gestures to store.*) The three of us together, maybe we could—

NANCY: It's a wonderful group. I don't know who I am, he's dying, and you can't quit your job.
(*She starts to exit left under the boardwalk. Arthur suddenly hauls back and smashes the crowbar against the stairway railing; the sound rings in the air—she turns, startled.*)

ARTHUR: All right, goddamn it, that's it! (*He flings open the phone booth door.*) Gotta be done, the time has come! (*Deposits coin, dialing fiercely.*) No more foolin' around here . . . damn it . . .
(*The phone in the second booth starts to ring.*)

NANCY: Arthur, he's calling you back! Arthur, the other phone! (*He ignores her, bent on his mission.*) Arthur! (*She races to the second booth, grabs the phone.*) Bill, listen; Arthur's calling you on the other—

ARTHUR: Hello.

NANCY: Hello. Listen, he's—

ARTHUR: Hello, Nancy?

NANCY: Who is this?

ARTHUR: It's me, Arthur.

NANCY: Arthur . . .

ARTHUR: Look, I tell ya why I called . . .

NANCY: Arthur, I'm hanging up now . . . (*Leans around corner of booth; speaking directly to his back.*) Arthur, I'm hanging up now, O.K.?

ARTHUR: Nancy, don't go— (*He grips the phone tensely.*) Nancy, I'm twenty minutes late for *everything*; conversations, trains, sunrises, people . . . Being alive; I'm twenty *years* late on that one. So don't go, Nancy, not now . . . not now, I just got here. (*Touched by what he has said, she delicately, soundlessly hangs up her phone, leaves her booth, stands behind him. Unaware, he continues on the phone.*) Hello? Hello, Nancy . . . ?

NANCY: (*Quietly*) Hello. (*He turns to her.*) I came as soon as I got your call . . . (*Sadly*) Arthur, forgive me, I can't do it. You and me, the store; it's too late. It got too late . . .

ARTHUR: People can change their whole lives if they want to—

NANCY: You just heard that—

ARTHUR: I've been hearing it all day—

NANCY: Arthur, I'm married—

ARTHUR: Oh.

NANCY: I was getting a divorce, that's why I came to the beach today . . .

ARTHUR: Wherever you get it, I'm delighted—

NANCY: Arthur, I want to go back . . . (*Crossing to dune.*) My old buddy, Shirley, I want her back. She didn't expect a helluva lot, but she didn't shake like this either . . . My husband's got a used-car lot on Fourteenth Street; nothing'll ever be new there, but I know I'll never be scared . . . I . . .

ARTHUR: No.

NANCY: Huh?

ARTHUR: (*Quietly, shaking his head.*) No. You can't go back

... (*Comes toward her, at dune.*) We've gone too far. I built a tree, you built a nose, and we can't go back now ... (*He takes her hand.*) I built that tree today, and while I was doing it I heard this fella laughing ... laughing with joy ... and I looked around and it was me. I love you, Nancy. Nancy, Shirley, alla you, I love you and I love my goddamn tree. Please, if your hand trembles, take mine. If you want love, take mine. If you want to love somebody, love me. (*After a moment*) Believe me, none of that was easy without a telephone. (*He touches her cheek.*) You're beautiful. Forget pretty. Beautiful ...

NANCY: (*Softly*) Arthur, it's all new, it's ...

ARTHUR: No, looks to me like you been beautiful a long, long time ...

NANCY: Arthur, at night my old nose comes back to haunt the bedroom ... (*He carefully pulls the hood of the Mackinaw back off her face.*) It sniffles and moans all night ... (*He holds her face in his hands.*) It's terrible, you'll hate it ... (*He kisses her tenderly. They lean back against the slope of the dune, their arms around each other, the palm tree arched gracefully over them in the moonlight. She talks softly into his shoulder.*) Arthur ... Arthur, you figure we got a chance?

ARTHUR: Lady, I learned five chords on the banjo today ... *any*thing is possible.
(*She laughs, she kisses him; holding on to him tightly. They are silent for a moment, lying against the dune, their arms around each other.*)

NANCY: Arthur, God help us, we love each other ...

ARTHUR: Right ...

NANCY: We love each other, of all people ... (*Silence. They hold each other. Only the sound of the surf.*) Arthur ... (*Silence.*) Arthur, if you're asleep, I'll kill ya ...

ARTHUR: Awake, I'm awake . . . (*He suddenly lifts her up in his arms, celebrating.*) Awake!

NANCY: Hey, what're ya doin' . . . ?

ARTHUR: Carrying you. I told you, I'm very big on carrying things . . .

MAX'S VOICE: Put that daughter down! One partner with a coronary is enough!
(*Arthur puts her down, but they continue to hold hands. Max enters on boardwalk, at left, wearing a red-and-white-striped blazer and a straw skimmer, his overcoat over his arm. He makes a small spin, fashion-show style, at the top of the stairs.*)

MAX: And *this* . . . this is why they call it a blazer! (*Starts daintily down the stairs, continuing the fashion parade.*) Yessir, and here's Max again . . . this time in smart and tasty opening-night apparel, he—

NANCY: Max, put your goddamn *coat* on, it's—

MAX: Well . . . (*Takes note of them holding hands.*) Looks to me like goodbye Eddie, huh?

NANCY: Pop, I—

MAX: Listen, you want turtle soup, you gotta hurt a couple turtles, right? (*Coming down the stairs.*) Because while we're on the subject of people breaking up . . . there's certain other news . . .

NANCY: My God, not Mike and Sandra . . .

MAX: No; not Mike and Sandra . . . (*Picks up crowbar, returning to work at front of store.*) Max and Rosie.

NANCY: Who?

MAX: Me and your mother, Max and Rosie; in three and a half

weeks we're getting a divorce. (*Shouting to Arthur.*) What's with my sign? The organization is getting loose here! (*Hands the stunned Nancy a crowbar.*) Come, the boards. Three days! We gotta move here!

NANCY: Max, you—

MAX: (*As Arthur takes paint cans from carton.*) Get ready with the reds, get ready with the yellows; and I'll give you a tip, gold . . . (*Begins prying loose one of the boards covering the front of the store.*) Nancy, the boards . . .

NANCY: Pop, I don't believe it . . .

MAX: Believe it, and then help me with the boards.

NANCY: (*Holding his arm.*) Pop, you've been married now for— what is it—forty-three *years*—

MAX: What can I do, the marriage isn't working out.

NANCY: Pop, forty-three *years*, *five* children—

MAX: Well, you can't say we didn't try, right? (*Shouting to Arthur who works on the sign downstage, near the pier.*) Silver! Use also silver! For Silverman!

NANCY: (*Draping the overcoat on his shoulders.*) Max, *why* . . . after all these years, why *now?*

MAX: Because the woman looks funny at me . . . (*Turns to her.*) Shirley, the woman looks funny at me. Since I come from the hospital, she looks at me like she misses me . . . and I *didn't leave* yet! (*Whacks the first board; it falls to the sand. Begins prying second board.*) These ladies, one little heart attack, they start right away learning to live without you. Trouble is, they learn a little too good and a little too early and all of a sudden you wake up one morning in the same bed with your own widow! (*Shouting to Arthur, who has turned from his work to listen to Max.*) The sign! What's with the sign? You wanna be known only for your trees?

NANCY: (*Gently*) Pop . . . Pop, maybe if you talk to her . . .

MAX: *Talk* to her? Shirley, every morning I come in for break-fast, the woman is reading the obituaries. I say, "Good morn-ing, Rosie!" She says, "Guess who died." I say, "Who died?" She says, "Bing-bing. One minute he was here and then, bing-bing, he was gone." I say, "*Who, Rosie, who?* Who is Mr. Bing-bing today?" And then she tells me . . . And, Shirley, I swear to God, *I never heard of him!* (*Another whack, the sec-ond board falls to the sand.*) For Rosie, anybody who died is automatically a buddy! (*Puts crowbar down, grips Nancy's arm tensely.*) Shirley, Shirley . . . in my neighborhood they're gonna put up soon a lotta new apartment buildings . . . they paint these big *X*'s on the windows of the old houses they're gonna rip down . . . (*He is frightened.*) Last week we're watching the T.V.; I'm sittin' there in front of the set like a fish they took all the bones outa, fillet of person . . . and I catch Rosie lookin' at me . . . Shirley, she's lookin' at me like she sees *X*'s on my eyes . . . like she sees 'em painted right on there, like she hears the wrecking crew coming from blocks away. (*Shouting to them both.*) Maybe I'm gonna die, but I guarantee you it's not gonna be in the middle of the Late Show! Maybe it's the truth what she sees—but if that's the truth, I don't wanna hang around with it! (*Turns sharply to Arthur.*) Gimme that sign! (*Crosses quickly down to Arthur, throwing his overcoat off on the way.*) The coat! The coat covers my outfit!

(*He grabs the sign from Arthur, lifts it easily onto his shoul-der, starts up the boardwalk steps with it. The sign is about five feet by four and does not face the audience at this point.*)

ARTHUR: Max, let me help you with—

NANCY: Pop, damn it, you shouldn't be—
    (*Max, ignoring them both, moves briskly to the top of the*

stairway and then a few steps along the boardwalk until he is directly over the store; he lifts the new sign up over the railing, intending to hook it in place over the old one—he suddenly stops, staggers . . . He turns away from them and us, grips the railing for support. Nancy and Arthur stand paralyzed for a moment, terrified . . .)

NANCY: (*Whispering.*) Oh, my God—

ARTHUR: Max—
(*They both rush forward to the stairs—Max suddenly turns to them, quite calmly, smiling.*)

MAX: Don't make funeral arrangements. I just stopped to take a breath . . . (*He looks at them both; then looks at Nancy for a long moment. Her back is to us; he sees something in her face that we cannot see. He shakes his head.*) Shirley . . . son-of-a-gun . . . you're lookin' funny at me . . . (*Quietly, to them both*) Oh, my sweet children; won't you be shocked . . . my darling children with your frightened eyes, won't you be surprised when I live forever . . . (*He turns the new sign around, hooks it onto the railing over the old one. The gold and silver letters against a deep-red background are not completely painted in, but still clearly annouce: "Max's New Original Hawaiian Ecstasies." Max moves to the side, takes a few steps down the stairs to view the bright new sign above the old store.*) Twenty-two years, every day, somebody asks me, "What's new?" I say, "Nothing's new." Next week they'll ask; I'll say . . . "Me." (*Shouting.*) The sign is up, the sign is up and then the business starts again . . . look, look, my darling babies . . . soon it begins again . . .
(*His arms raised, shouting, as . . .*
There is a Blackout.
Immediately in the darkness, we hear the Dixieland Devils, an eight-piece Dixieland marching band—trumpet, trombone, clarinet, tuba, snare, cymbals, field drum, and

marching drum—they go into a strong and strutting intro-
duction to "Over the Waves."

To the beat of this music, light bulbs start to pop on, one
at a time, along the perimeter of the pier. In the light of
these first few bulbs we begin to see more clearly that it is
Max who is putting these bulbs in, taking red, yellow, and
orange bulbs from his shopping bag and placing them along
the pier; they light up in time with the music.

Toward the end of the intro, there are three downbeats to
the march itself; on the first downbeat, colored footlights go
on across the stage. On the second, the pier lights pulse on
brighter; and on the third, Max marches from the pier to the
beach as . . .

A sunrise begins in the blackout; a four- or five-minute
blossoming of light; from gray to pink, from pink to vivid
red, and from red finally to a golden orange . . . In this
gradual revelation of light we will see the old stand being
transformed into the new one, all of it done by Max, Nancy,
and Arthur working in unison. All of their work should be
completed when the sunrise reaches its peak and then—the
sky goes night-black, the entire stage brightly illuminated,
amid the dark, deserted beach around it.

It is three days later, early evening; all three people are
just completing the last of the tasks we have watched them
perform through the changes of light and time; and there,
beautiful and ugly and glorious, is the New Original Max's
Hawaiian Ecstasies. The motif is, of course, Hawaiian; the
stand appears brightly repainted and it is hung with grass
matting, native-hut style; long blades of plastic grass engulf
the store, they glisten and rustle in the February wind. The
store is framed on either side by two palm trees now, the
trunks running up the sides of the building and bursting
with enormous palm fronds that dovetail across the roof of
the stand; two smaller trees frame the sign above. The
counter, hung with fronds and grass, polished and shining,
has been outfitted with two new grills, a bubbling tank of

coconut drink, and other bright new counter fixtures. The interior of the stand has been decorated with imitation jungle birds, tropical vines, and Tahitian tribal masks. On the sand in front of the store are two round, wicker beach tables surrounded by wicker chairs; umbrellas rise up from the tables, the poles painted like palm bark and the umbrella tops covered with plastic palm fronds. There are colored lights everywhere, the most outstanding light display being a neon frankfurter that forms an archway between the two lampposts on either side of the top of the stairway; each time the frankfurter blinks on and off, it grows smaller, as though bites are being taken out of it—three huge bites; on the fourth bite the frankfurter is gone, and then it reappears whole again. The Dixieland music is coming from a record player on the counter, the record spinning, the music continuing through part of this next scene.

As the lights shift from sunrise to the early evening of this scene, each one of the three people is completing a final task, the music building to a peak . . .

Arthur turns on a glowing red light at the center of a small plaster volcano that he has just placed on the roof of the store.

*Nancy staples a final large palm frond on the second palm tree. Max takes a furled banner from inside the store and, half marching, half strutting, carries it to the end of the pier, hooking it onto the tallest of the pier ties, then lets it unroll facing the ocean and the audience; it has silver letters against a blue background and a silver arrow at the bottom; it says: "*TO ALL BOATS. STOP HERE FOR MAX'S.*" At the same moment that the banner unfurls, Arthur turns on his volcano light and Nancy staples the palm frond, their three tasks completed simultaneously.*

Max turns from his banner now as the Dixieland music builds to a finish; he looks at the store, at Arthur and Nancy. He takes his hat off to it, to them, and to himself. Then, as if by mutual signal, all three leave their separate positions and rush forward to the center of the beach, where they join in a huge three-person hug.)

MAX: (*Kissing them both; then squeezing one face with each hand.*) I love everything here, each item . . . everything and everyone here . . . until further notice. (*Crossing to coconut drink on counter.*) Now the toasts . . . (*Pours out three drinks in coconut-shell goblets.*) I understand '79 is a very good year for coconut drink . . .

NANCY: Silverman, I'd appreciate it if you'd put on your coat, it's—

MAX: (*Raising his goblet.*) To what we did here . . . (*They all raise their goblets, gathering around one of the wicker tables.*) To three days that have changed the face of the North Atlantic coastline . . . to Shirley's palm leaves, each a beauty . . . to Arthur's volcano, which I am considering at this moment for a loan-out to the Metropolitan . . . also to Arthur's frankfurter sign, which if I wasn't talking right now would leave me speechless . . . and to Benny Kalsheim . . .

ARTHUR: Benny Kalsheim?

MAX: He come over with me on the boat from Russia, I include him in all toasts. (*Raising his goblet higher.*) And to Mr. Marcus Soloway, who comes tonight . . .

ARTHUR: You spoke to him—

MAX: Spoke? Spoke? Sang! We *sang* to each other! A duet! Twin cantors on the telephone!

NANCY: Did he say he'd—

MAX: Soloway don't do business on the phone. He is a person, in person, with a face and no lawyers. He comes to argue, to holler, to hustle; business! I wouldn't miss a minute!

ARTHUR: Yes, but did he say he'd—

MAX: (*Gesturing about with goblet.*) The truth, partner: do you see a "no" here anywhere? Even a "maybe"? (*Raising his goblet.*) To all those present, relatives and associates, lovers and partners . . . and to all Hawaiians everywhere! (*They clunk glasses and drink. Sips thoughfully.*) Another dash rum, more shreds coconut, we got here easy a dollar-fifty item . . .

ARTHUR: I have a toast . . . (*They raise their goblets again.*) To the Silvermans, both of them; and to the sun rising tomorrow on our land . . . the land of Silverman, Soloway, and Korman . . . the blessings of a new day . . . to Coney, island of dreams, island of—

MAX: Wrap it up; we got work here. (*They clunk goblets and drink.*) Now you, Shirley, a toast . . .

NANCY: (*She turns to them, raises her goblet.*) To the store, to the Ecstasies . . . and to the men I love most.

MAX: The best one. She did the best one. (*They clunk goblets and drink.*) O.K., party's over! (*Crossing to phone booth.*) To-morrow we open, Soloway comes soon.

ARTHUR: O.K. (*Clapping his hands.*) Nancy, Lafayette Electric closes at eight. I've arranged for ten heaters at eighteen-fifty a unit; tell them we'll take a dozen if they come down a dollar each— |

NANCY: (*Stacking goblets on counter.*) A dozen if they come down a dollar, right—

ARTHUR: Velásquez is parked on Stillwell, he'll help you carry them. (*To Max, who is in booth, dialing*) Max, when Soloway comes, seat him at Table 2, it's the best view of the area . . .

MAX: Yessir.

ARTHUR: (*Gathering stack of posters and tape.*) O.K., thirty left, that makes about four hundred posters spread around the—

MAX: Velásquez, he put 'em in the high schools? (*Arthur nods.*)

Good. For the young people, out here will be the in place.
Moonlight and coconuts— (*Into phone*) Hello, Abrams? Then
get me Abrams . . . (*To Arthur*) The posters, Arthur—Stillwell, Tenth, and don't forget the boardwalk. Soloway should
see them whichever way he comes—

ARTHUR: Max, we'll surround him.

> (*Arthur starts upstairs with posters, Nancy heads under
> boardwalk to street.*)

MAX: (*Shaking the phone.*) What's with Abrams? I gotta tell
him where the parade starts . . .

NANCY: (*About to exit.*) Parade . . . ?

MAX: Yessir; comes down the avenue at dawn, a fine organization, the Dixieland Devils, to advertise the opening . . .
(*Stands in booth.*) Rampart Street on Coney Island Avenue!
From the land of Dixie, led by Irwin Abrams, what a sound,
clean and perfect, everybody struttin' along . . . What, you
don't recall those devils? That's them on the record, Shirley;
same group when I opened thirty years ago, you marched with
me in the parade, you and Michael . . .

NANCY: (*Remembers, smiling.*) Jesus; they must be very—

MAX: O.K., a tuba died since; also a clarinet; but tomorrow Irwin
himself leads, still spunky, a trumpet takes your heart away
. . . (*Gestures with receiver.*) Takes a little while to get to the
phone, otherwise perfect. (*Nancy and Arthur enjoying the ro-
mance of it as Max rhapsodizes.*) The selection, naturally, is
"Over the Waves"; what could be better? Tomorrow at dawn,
windows go up, doors open, everybody looks: "What's that?"
A band, eight pieces, a float with a sign "Come to the Ecstasies! On the Beach at Tenth Street!" (*Nancy blows a kiss to
Arthur and they exit to their tasks. Max speaks into the
phone.*) Hello, Abrams? Silverman! I said *Silverman* . . .
That's right, I'm still alive. Yeah, still since yesterday . . . *Yes-*

terday, Abrams; I spoke to you yesterday! (*Shouting into phone.*) *Batteries*, Abrams; get new batteries for your machine! *Spend* a dollar . . . Good, it's coming back to you; good, Silverman's parade; you remember. Between the memory and the ears, you're charging too much; how about you come down fifty dollars? . . . Oh, *that* you heard, you heard that one! Abrams, I love you! (*There is the burst of a match flame on the boardwalk, at left. The flame lingers on the face of Marcus Soloway; lighting his cigar, slowly, elaborately. He is an old man wearing a very new fur-collared ski coat. He blows out the match, steps forward into the light of Arthur's frankfurter sign at the top of the stairs. He looks up at it, thoughtfully. All this as Max continues on the phone.*) Abrams, you and the boys, you'll rendezvous with the float at Surf and Stillwell. Then you'll start down the avenue; you got that? Good, good. And, Abrams, *loud;* you'll play loud! Loud, goodbye! (*Hangs up; shakes his head.*) *Old* people . . .

MARCUS: (*Shouting.*) Silverman! Soloway is here!

MAX: Soloway! (*Leaves booth.*) Soloway! (*Steps forward to bottom of stairs.*) Soloway, look at you!

MARCUS: Silverman, look at you! Oh boy, *old!*

MAX: Look at *you! Older!*

MARCUS: (*Coming down steps.*) I heard you was sick.

MAX: They put me in a new ventricle.

MARCUS: Oh boy.

MAX: Dacron.

MARCUS: Oh boy.

MAX: Plastic. Can you believe it?

MARCUS: I believe it. They put me in a pacemaker.

MAX: Oh boy.

MARCUS: Makes me a pace.

MAX: The coat. I like the coat. Sporty.

MARCUS: Thank you. Your coat I don't like. Coats, you never knew. (*Sits at a table, looking around at store, nodding.*) Coconuts, you know. But not coats. (*Pointing at boardwalk.*) I seen a poster on the boardwalk.

MAX: Good.

MARCUS: A fella is standing next to it; pointing and smiling.

MAX: My partner.

MARCUS: A partner. A pointer and a smiler.

MAX: (*After a moment, indicating the store.*) Well . . . ?

MARCUS: (*Nods.*) Nice. (*Looks about at the lights, the tables; nods.*) Nice.

MAX: (*Pouring him goblet of coconut drink.*) Here. Taste.

MARCUS: (*He sips the drink. Reflects on it a moment; then nods.*) Nice.

MAX: Well . . . ?

MARCUS: Close it up. Max, take the money and close it up.

MAX: You! From the devil! You're taking money from the devil!

MARCUS: Why not? I never heard from him before. Twelve thousand dollars; when it comes, I'll take it. At my age, that's a good salary; could be a thousand dollars an hour. You gather me, Max? You gather my meaning? (*Leans forward at table.*) I come to tell you personally: take the money and close it up.

MAX: Marcus, you won't take the money, you'll join me here . . . I got an instinct and a feeling, it's our turn again . . .

MARCUS: Max, when it was our turn even, it wasn't our turn.

(*Rising from table.*) Twenty years ago we was flops in July; how come we'll be such winners in February? Take the instinct, take the feeling, take the money, and close it up. (*Crossing to water's edge.*) You know what you got here? *Wintertime.* Coldness, Max. And I'm not talkin' in the soul; I'm talkin' in the toes, the nose, and the elbows. Who'll come to shiver with a frankfurter? (*Turns to him.*) Even alone, Max; what's the hurry? You can't wait for sunshine?

MAX: A Dacron ventricle don't wait for sunshine.

MARCUS: (*Nods.*) This is a point.

MAX: (*Comes toward him.*) You'll come back— (*Shouting.*) What's wrong with you? The season is by the doorstep! Every day it gets warmer!

MARCUS: Listen to you! Max, I don't see you now a long time because you make me nervous! Always excited and you holler too much! Three years ago, the hurricane; I come around here the next day, I'm hoping this place would blow away. The sea should come and get it, it wouldn't aggravate me any more. You gather me? But it didn't blow away and neither do you! You're still around hollering and you make me nervous, Silverman . . . (*Crosses to Max.*) Take my advice, I come to tell you personally: be an old man, you'll live longer . . . (*Takes his arm.*) Max, listen to me . . . this year I started doing old-man things. I tell stories for a second time, just like an old man. Sometimes for a third time. It's coming out of my mouth about how I got a good buy on my new car, the third time I'm telling it to my daughter and her husband. I *know* it's the third time, but I go right on, it doesn't bother me; just like an old man. I fall asleep in front of people like it's my right and my privilege, just like an old man. I can remember what I did, what clothes I wore, names of people from when I was eighteen, and if you told me I was in Hong Kong yesterday, I would believe you, because I don't remember; just like an old

man. So, I finally figured it out. The reason I'm behaving like
an old man . . . is because I'm an *old man*. A *revelation* to me,
Silverman; and for the first time in *years* I'm not annoyed with
myself. Silverman, I was not a top businessman. I was good,
but not first-class. I was an O.K. husband; and as a father, not
a knockout. But, Max . . . I'm a *great old man*. I do that the
best. I was born for it. I'm seventy-two, Max, and it fits me like
a glove. You, you're a crazy. I wish you well with the business; but I can't join you . . . (*He smiles.*) See . . . I'm too
old for it. (*He crosses under the boardwalk at right to leave;
turns, points to one of the tables.*) The tables. How much you
paid?

MAX: Thirty-eight fifty; Colby's on Fourth Street.

MARCUS: Dumb! Coulda got from Harold's for twenty-five, on
Canal Street. You coulda made— (*He stops himself, turns.*)
Now I'm leaving. Best good wishes to you and yours . . .
(*Crossing into the shadows under the boardwalk at right.*)
Notice how I don't take the stairs. Regard me, how I take the
easy way under the boardwalk. I'm seventy-two, Max, and I
got one interest in life: seventy-three. You gather me, Silver-
man . . . ?

   (*He exits. Max looks around at the store for a moment, then
   shouts in the direction of Marcus's exit.*)

MAX: The hell with you! A gold mine like this; who needs you
anyway? The coat; I lied to you about the coat. I didn't like
it! (*He nods to himself, satisfied with his outburst. He looks
up at the boardwalk, sees an unlit bulb on the string along
the railing.*) A red bulb is out. Leaves a dark spot . . . (*Rummaging among bulbs in box on the table.*) Must be no dark
spots . . .) (*Finds a red bulb, starts up the stairs with it. He
stops about halfway up.*) How come yesterday twenty-two
steps . . . today a thousand?
   (*He sits on the top step.*)

ARTHUR'S VOICE: Beautiful . . .
(*He walks into the light of his frankfurter sign at the top of the stairs, carrying the roll of tape, the posters apparently distributed.*)

ARTHUR: Max, you can see this whole place glowin' half a mile away.

MAX: That was the intention.

ARTHUR: (*Coming down the steps.*) Everything dark, the whole beach, and just this place glowin' like a jewel, Max . . .

MAX: Like a jewel was the intention.

ARTHUR: Neighborhood's covered with those posters, nobody'll be able to walk down a street without—

MAX: Arthur, listen; Soloway was here . . .

ARTHUR: Well . . . ?

MAX: Good news, Arthur. He's selling his share.

ARTHUR: (*Sitting next to him on steps.*) Doesn't sound like good news, Max . . .

MAX: You gotta have an ear for it . . . (*Turns to Arthur, smiling.*) Arthur, we're rid of him! The man was unfortunately an invalid. A liability to the organization. (*Taps his chest.*) A pacemaker in waltz time. (*Snaps his fingers.*) Suddenly old.

ARTHUR: Max: . . . that means Mister Hot Dog is our partner . . .

MAX: Why not? We open *our* store, we give *them* a percentage, and we don't have an old man hanging around. All we gotta do is show profits by June . . . (*Holds Arthur's arm, happily*) The good news, partner . . . the good news is honor. Honorable battle with Mister Hot Dog. Arthur, if we do good here by June, if we stop *them, that* is a number one victory! A world is covered with plastic and we make a dent! Mister Hot Dog, the nation's number one killer—we're not just keeping a *store* open, it's a public service! (*He stands.*) A whistle is blown in the face of the junk parade! Everywhere Mister Hot Dog, but not *here*, Arthur, never *here*.

ARTHUR: (*Rises, goes a few steps down the stairs, looking about at his work.*) It's really . . . it's so beautiful . . . we've got three months, we've got a chance . . .

MAX: When I pick a partner, I pick a partner! (*Sits back down on the steps.*) Poor old Marcus, he lost the eye for paradise . . .

ARTHUR: (*Touching the palm next to the stairs.*) Gotta say so myself, I did a terrific job on these trees . . . It's the angle of them that does it, I think . . .

MAX: (*Handing him the red bulb.*) Here, there's a light out on the railing . . . (*Arthur takes bulb, going quickly up steps to boardwalk railing.*) Look for the dark spot . . .

ARTHUR: (*As he puts the bulb in*) Listen, did anybody happen to . . . has anybody said anything to you about my trees?

MAX: References were made.

ARTHUR: Yeah, it's mostly the angle of them that does it. The shape and the angle; I mean, you *know* it's a palm tree . . .

MAX: Velásquez brings the tables yesterday, I give you verbatim, he says, "Look what you got here, *palm* trees."

ARTHUR: Tell ya what we need, Max. (*Crossing left, on boardwalk.*) One more tree, right here . . . right up here . . . something you can see from the street. Whaddya think? (*No reply*) Thing is, I'm gonna have to work out some kinda weatherproof glaze for the plaster; it's—

MAX: Now I can't talk. I'm busy.

ARTHUR: O.K., later; but it's—

MAX: Not later either. I'm busy having a heart attack.

ARTHUR: What . . . ?

MAX: A regular heart attack . . .

ARTHUR: Max—
   (*He races across the boardwalk to the steps.*)

MAX: I'll tell you what I'm doing. I'm dying.

ARTHUR: (*Running down the steps, about to go past Max to the phone.*) I'll call your doctor—an ambulance—

MAX: (*Grabbing Arthur's hand.*) No-sir. No time. No-sir.

ARTHUR: Max, the phone, I'll be a second—

MAX: No-sir—

ARTHUR: (*Kneels next to him on step.*) Max, what should I do, I—

MAX: I don't know. I never died before.

ARTHUR: (*His arm around Max.*) Oh, my God . . .

MAX: Look at you. If I don't hurry, you'll beat me to it . . .

ARTHUR: Max, can I . . . can I . . . how do you feel?

MAX: Not in the pink. (*He stands.*) Too busy! Who needs this? It's stupid! So stupid! (*Staggers down the few steps to the sand.*) I got business. There's business . . . (*Arthur moves down in front of him, trying to hold him.*) I got business. I got business . . . (*He is spent; he falls into Arthur's arms. Arthur holds him, kneels with him on the sand. There are a few short bursts from a car horn offstage.*) Arthur . . .

ARTHUR: Yes, Max . . .

MAX: Tell Rosie, say to her . . . (*He suddenly laughs; a whispered, desperate, delighted laugh.*) Say to Rosie . . . guess who died. (*His head falls against Arthur's chest. He is dead. Arthur holds him. There is a gust of wind; Arthur automatically puts Max's coat collar up to protect him. Nancy enters at the top of the steps.*)

NANCY: The heaters are in the car; you'll have to help . . . (*She sees immediately what has happened. She stands quite still. Arthur looks up at her. She begins to nod; slowly, quietly*) Sure . . . sure . . . (*She comes down the steps, stands near Arthur and Max; she continues to nod, almost hypnotically, whispering.*) Sure . . . sure . . .
   (*The carnival lights go off; leaving only dim moonlight for a moment, and then there is a . . .*
   Blackout
   Immediately in the darkness we hear Nancy's voice.)

NANCY'S VOICE: To all boats. Stop here for Max's . . .
   (*During this next speech we will see a gradual change of light lasting the several minutes of her dialogue, the darkened beach turning slowly to bright dawn.*
   In the first beginnings of light we discover Nancy sitting at the edge of the pier next to the silver and blue banner on the pier tie that reads "TO ALL BOATS . . ." Max is gone, but Arthur remains seated at the bottom of the steps where we last saw him. The effect is such that Nancy has been seated at the edge of the pier all night, speaking through the night till dawn. There are no tears left.)

NANCY: (*As the dawn lights begin to dim up; she touches the banner.*) Sure. The *Queen Mary* was gonna stop here, right? Frankfurters at the captain's table . . . You wanna know who was gonna show up here? (*Imitating Max's accent.*) I'll tell you who. Nobody. (*Arthur comes to the end of the pier,*

stands behind her. She continues, angrily.) How dare you, Silverman. How dare you go and die. I paint forty-eight palm
leaves and then you . . . Sneaky, sneaky, crazy old man, how
dare you die. You hustled me, Silverman; you said you were
gonna live forever, and you didn't. So all bets are off, Max. No
more crying. I did that last night. That's all you get . . . Am I
talking to myself, Max; or am I talking to you? Well, I couldn't
tell the difference when you were alive, either. (*Arthur sits
next to her; the sunrise grows brighter.*) This crazy place. He
conned us, Arthur. Alive and hollering, he made it look possible: palm trees in February, lovers on sand dunes. But now
you are dead, and where are the customers, Max? (*She closes
her eyes, whispering.*) Listen to the ocean, Arthur; the noise it
makes; it roars. If it had an accent I'd think it was him . . .
What do I do now? I don't know . . . (*A blank, wide-eyed
stare.*) Here's me, not knowing. It's my best number . . .

(*The phone rings.*)

ARTHUR: (*Rises, going to phone.*) That'll be Gallino's; I better
cancel the bread order. And Glickman's Meats, gotta call them
also . . . (*Picks up phone.*) Hello . . . (*Quietly; awkwardly*)
Bill; how are ya? . . . Jesus, has it been three days? Sorry
about that, I . . . The beach project? Well, it didn't work out
very well, no . . . Bill, it's not really funny. Not funny at all
. . . (*There is the sudden sound of an eight-piece Dixieland
marching band hitting a loud downbeat, offstage.*) Jesus . . .
(*The band hits a second downbeat; he turns to Nancy.*) Jesus,
the Dixieland Devils; I forgot to cancel the parade . . . (*Into
phone*) Hang on a second, Bill; be right back . . . (*He races
up the stairway; as he reaches the top of the stairs the band
hits a third downbeat and swings into a strutting, blasting arrangement of "Over the Waves." The offstage music grows
gradually louder as the band marches up the unseen avenue
parallel to the boardwalk. Arthur, at the top of the stairs, cups
his hands around his mouth and shouts in the direction of the*

music.) Mr. Abrams! Mr. Abrams! Stop! Hey! Mr. Abrams—
(*Arthur's hands drop to his sides; he begins to smile.*) Jesus
Christ, that's the oldest bunch of musicians I ever saw . . .
(*The music grows louder; Nancy crosses anxiously to the foot
of the stairs.*)

NANCY: Arthur, you better go down there and tell them . . .

ARTHUR: Jesus, look at 'em go.

NANCY: Arthur . . .

ARTHUR: They've got this sign . . . it says "Come to the Ecstasies" . . . all that noise . . . people'll see the sign . . .
maybe they'll . . .

NANCY: Arthur, listen to me . . .

ARTHUR: And there's posters everywhere . . .

NANCY: Arthur, Arthur . . . nobody's gonna come . . .

ARTHUR: Every day it's getting warmer . . .

NANCY: (*Shouting above the music.*) Arthur . . . you're not
gonna open the store, it's crazy . . .

ARTHUR: (*Shouting down to the open phone.*) Hey, Bill! Ya
hear that, Bill? That's a parade! Hey, Bill; got a great idea for
our Easter display! How about a bunny nailed to a cross? By
the ears! Ya like that one, Bill? Are ya laughing, Bill? Just keep
laughing, Bill! Goodbye, Bill! Goodbye! Merry Christmas to
all, and to all a good night! (*Shouting to Nancy.*) Hang up the
phone!

NANCY: Arthur—

ARTHUR: Hang up the phone, Shirley! (*She hangs up the phone;
he turns to look at the parade again, bouncing with the
rhythm.*) Boy oh boy, what a class operation . . . Come look,
come on . . .

M49

NANCY: (*Shouting.*) Arthur! Listen to me! This place, it's hopeless! It's a monument to hopelessness!
(*The music reaches a strutting, blasting, swinging peak.*)

ARTHUR: (*Turning to her, smiling.*) I told you, lady . . . I'm crazy about monuments . . . (*Shouting above the music.*) Come on . . . just come and look . . . come see the parade . . . come on . . . come on . . .
(*Holding his hand down to her, shouting, as . . .*)

Curtain